Timeless Truth
in the Hands of History

Princeton Theological Monograph Series

K. C. Hanson, Charles M. Collier, D. Christopher Spinks,
and Robin Parry, Series Editors

Recent volumes in the series:

Paul G. Doerksen
*The Church Made Strange for the Nations:
Essays in Ecclesiology and Political Theology*

Lisa M. Hess
Learning in a Musical Key: Insight for Theology in Performative Mode

Jack Barentsen
*Emerging Leadership in the Pauline Mission: A Social Identity Perspective
on Local Leadership Development in Corinth and Ephesus*

Matthew D. Kirkpatrick
*Attacks on Christendom in a World Come of Age: Kierkegaard,
Bonhoeffer, and the Question of "Religionless Christianity"*

Michael A. Salmeier
*Restoring the Kingdom: The Role of God as the "Ordainer of Times
and Seasons" in the Acts of the Apostles*

Gerald W. King
*Disfellowshiped: Pentecostal Responses to Fundamentalism
in the United States, 1906–1943*

Timothy Hessel-Robinson
*Spirit and Nature: The Study of Christian Spirituality
in a Time of Ecological Urgency*

Paul W. Chilcote
*Making Disciples in a World Parish:
Global Perspectives on Mission & Evangelism*

Timeless Truth
in the Hands of History

A Short History of System in Theology

Gale Heide

PICKWICK *Publications* · Eugene, Oregon

TIMELESS TRUTH IN THE HANDS OF HISTORY
A Short History of System in Theology

Princeton Theological Monograph Series 178

Pickwick Publications
An Imprint of Wipf and Stock Publishers
199 W. 8th Ave., Suite 3
Eugene, OR 97401

www.wipfandstock.com

ISBN 13: 978-1-55635-497-7

Cataloguing-in-Publication data:

Heide, Gale.

Timeless truth in the hands of history : a short history of system in theology / Gale Heide.

x + 220 pp. ; 23 cm. Includes bibliographical references.

Princeton Theological Monograph Series 178

ISBN 13: 978-1-55635-497-7

1. Theology, Doctrinal — History. I. Title. II. Series.

CALL NUMBER 2012

Manufactured in the U.S.A.

To my wonderful teachers
who taught me to love the wisdom discovered in history
and allowed me to follow after them
in the well-worn path of discipleship.
In your teaching and your lives, I have seen Jesus.
Thank you for making education the best kind of friendship!

". . . I have called you friends, for all things that I have heard from My Father I have made known to you." —John 15:15

Contents

Preface

HISTORY IS ALWAYS A MATTER OF CONTEXT. AS SUCH, IT IS ALMOST impossible to grasp a complete or accurate picture or interpretation of events and thoughts, especially when dealing with the separation of centuries and cultures. In the pages that follow, I am certain that I have not *captured* the events in an exhaustive manner. Nor have I understood with the eyes of divine providence. I am only giving a glimpse of the thoughts and intentions of men who wrote for the church and communities they loved. I hope it is an accurate portrayal (hope is here a word of labor). Further, I expect to be proved wrong or inaccurate. I welcome the fact that someone takes my work seriously enough to disagree with it. Such a conversation is perhaps the best compliment an author can receive.

I have written this work as a theologian. I say that to confess I am not a historian, at least not in the modern sense. I find I cannot write objectively, that is, without taking a view. I do my best to present the evidence on every side in a manner conducive to taking the alternative view. However, I find my work incomplete if it has no conclusion. I ask historians to bear with such a pre-occupation with finality. I also ask theologians to remain open to conclusions that could be changed. It is a wonderful testament to the history of humans that it always bears further study.

My regard for history is due to many who have read it and conveyed it to me in a way that grants justice to its importance. I have valued the insights of men and women who are far superior in their sensitivity to circumstance and movement in events. I know of no way to tell them of their value to my work other than to invite them to be a part of the conversation. Many have already begun the conversation with me over the years. Professors Ken Hagen, Michel Barnes, David Steinmetz, George Marsden, Stanley Hauerwas, Brad Hinze, Holly Wilson, Fr. Philip Rossi, Geoffrey Wainwright, and Bruce Ware all deserve credit for meaningful insight and exception from the blunders, which I have made on my own. The staff and board of directors at Montana Bible College have also borne the load of writing this with me as they have given their time and energies to afford me the opportunity to spend hours and weeks tied to desks and books. Thank you all for your generous endurance. Grace is perhaps best understood in the patience of friends.

The greatest friendships that shape any project I engage has always been my family. Having two girls, Trina and Alethia, is a testimony to hope—hope that the Lord will not be slow to develop their character and hope that our training as parents has been a gift and not a weight. The value of having children is not primarily in their growing up and becoming something. Their value is in their existence as children. They remind us that we are all children, dependent and in need. The lessons I teach I am still learning. I have and always will find my greatest achievement in walking beside these young lives as they teach me to be a better expression of the divine gift of humanity. May I never grow tired of the satisfaction found in knowing I too am a child.

Mary is a constant in all my work. I say thank you, knowing that gratitude implies independence, which is a mistake. Anything I do is a part of our life together. You are such a part of me that I cannot think any longer of life distinct from you, which is your misfortune but my gain! I cannot give the equal of your goodness to me, but I give you my love in the hope it will outweigh the burden of my life as a teacher. Teaching means always being distracted, but then again, distractions are the glory of loving. Jesus must find our human lives a constant burden of distractions, but it is a burden He Himself carried joyfully. The burden and joy of expected perfection is a distraction with which I can live for a lifetime, especially when it can be shared with you!

Introduction

A FEW SHORT DECADES AGO, IT WAS COMMONPLACE TO HEAR THEOlogians describe the Scriptures as systematic, or at least as filled with facts that could be arranged into a system. While true of both liberal and conservative scholars, references to the facts contained in Scripture seemed to predominate conservative Protestant thought. Scripture was portrayed as something like a gold mine of material waiting to be uncovered or discovered. Each nugget fit as a piece to the whole treasure of theology. A brief examination of the theological prolegomena of an influential theologian demonstrates the type of rationalism that lent itself to such a course of study.

The American Presbyterian Charles Hodge (1797–1878) spent almost his entire theological life as a student and professor at Princeton Seminary. His convictions concerning Scripture are well known, largely due to his widely regarded *Systematic Theology* (1872–1873). It is in the early pages of this work that he describes the method by which the theologian constructs a system.

> [I]n theology as in natural science, principles are derived from facts, and not impressed upon them. The properties of matter, the laws of motion, of magnetism, of light, etc., are not framed by the mind. They are not laws of thought. They are deductions from facts. The investigator sees, or ascertains by observation, what are the laws which determine material phenomena; he does not invent those laws. His speculations on matters of science unless sustained by facts are worthless. It is no less unscientific for the theologian to assume a theory as to the nature of virtue, of sin, of liberty, of moral obligation, and then explain the facts of Scripture in accordance with his theories. His only proper course is to derive his theory of virtue, of sin, of liberty, of obligation, from the facts of the Bible. He should remember that his business is not to set forth his system of truth (that is of no account), but to ascertain and exhibit what is God's system, which is a matter of the greatest moment. If he cannot believe what the facts of the

1

Bible assume to be true, let him say so. Let the sacred writers have
their doctrine, while he has his own.[1]

Here Hodge explains his belief that the Bible contains facts that are discoverable through observation and can be organized into an appropriate
(i.e., universal or systematic) understanding of the knowledge of God
revealed in Scripture. While this may not be the same thing as saying
that we can have a comprehensive knowledge of God by ordering the
facts of Scripture, it does mean that if the facts are placed into an appropriate arrangement, they will constitute some reasonable grasp on
the knowledge God wishes for us to have about Himself.[2] The inductive
method provides Hodge with the knowledge necessary to complete the
system as given by God and recorded by the authors of Scripture.[3] As is
evident from the quote above, the belief in Divine inspiration has made
it possible for Hodge to presume that all the pieces are a part of the same
puzzle, rather than pieces to several different puzzles.

In a bit less sophisticated manner, some have gone so far as to say
that the authors of Scripture themselves were systematic.[4] Perhaps the
most common reference to a Scriptural author as "systematic" is in relation to Paul's authorship of the epistle to the Romans. Melanchthon's
commentary on Romans (1532) represents an early form of the traditional interpretation of the letter as a "timeless compendium of dogmatic
theology."[5] This interpretation understands Romans to be primarily a
treatise rather than a letter written for a specific occasion.

With the decline of rationalism, these views have fallen from favor
in most scholarly circles. No longer is it defensible to think of Scripture
as a storehouse of facts waiting to be arranged. While still affirming a
sense of Divine inspiration, many contemporary scholars are poignantly
aware of the individual authorship of works and the situations their writings were meant to address. And even though some would still wish to

1. Hodge, *Systematic Theology*, 13.

2. Ibid., 15–17.

3. Ibid., 17.

4. Though one would likely not find many contemporary scholars defending such a
position, this is a position often cited in less scholarly or pre-critical works. This position
was the traditional position with regard to Paul's letter to the Romans (see Guthrie, *New
Testament Introduction*, 398).

5. Brevard Childs recounts the history of the interpretation of Paul's entire corpus in
his *The New Testament as Canon*, 243–427. For his comments regarding the history of
interpreting Romans, see 247ff.

affirm that Scripture is primarily a propositional document, even they recognize that it is also filled with much more than simple statements of fact regarding God, and that at times their propositions need to be teased out from amidst a very intricate narrative.[6]

Scripture, however, has not been the central issue in the debate over the use of system, at least not in recent years. The focus of the discussion has centered more on the question of whether a systematic method is a modern convention, and as such, if it is a good thing for the church. The first part of this discussion is the focus of the chapters below.[7] How has theology been constructed and conceived over the centuries of living with and under the authority of a text and community of faith?

Underlying this debate over when system began is the question of what is system. On the historical front, the question regarding a definition typically centers on the existence of philosophical intentions in the texts of various historical figures. As Wolfhart Pannenberg has asserted regarding even the earliest of theologians,

> Greek philosophy was in search of the true nature of the divine, which led to the conclusion that there can be only one God. The one God of the people of Israel, however, who was also the God of Jesus and the early Christians, was viewed by the Greeks as an alien deity of an alien people and so could not command their allegiance. It was therefore *necessary* to make the argument that the God of Israel is, in fact, the one God conceived by the philosophers . . . The affirmation that the God of Israel and the God of the philosophers is the one and same God—an affirmation that entails the reception by Christian theology of the philosophical argument for the one true God—is a *constitutive* and *permanent* feature of Christian faith.[8]

Neither side in the debate has trouble with the notion that theologians have always used logic and such principles as non-contradiction (this may be considered a rather general definition of system). Where the two separate is on the subject of philosophical intentions. Was the theologian attempting to be comprehensive and integrated in his/her approach to every doctrine of Christian theology? Was there a purported universality

6. See Carl Henry's discussion of the propositional nature of revelation in his *God, Revelation and Authority*, 455–81.

7. For a discussion of system's appropriateness for the church, see my *System and Story*.

8. Pannenberg, "God of the Philosophers," 31. Emphasis mine.

to the theology, or was it engendered and delimited by some historical/ pastoral circumstance? Philosophical grounding (e.g., foundationalism) and an affirmation of the universal import of doctrinal claims (e.g., a referential or representative theory of language) seem to mark a more rigid definition of what constitutes system. Two brief examples from the chapters below illustrate ways in which pre-modern theologians have been construed as systematic.[9]

The first example is found in Origen's work *De Principiis*. Origen sets a rather bold course for himself when he states at the conclusion of his Preface:

> Everyone therefore who is desirous of constructing out of the foregoing [outline of doctrines to be studied] a connected body of doctrine must use points like these as elementary and foundational principles, in accordance with the commandment which says, "Enlighten yourselves with the light of knowledge" (Hosea 10:12, Sept.). Thus by clear and cogent arguments he will discover the truth about each particular point and so will produce, as we have said, a single body of doctrine, with the aid of such illustrations and declarations as he shall find in the holy scriptures and of such conclusions as he shall ascertain to follow logically from them when rightly understood.[10]

This statement of intention, along with other statements regarding methodology in Origen's work, have been understood by some to indicate that Origen was engaging in a work meant to be systematic, in that it is Origen's attempt to outline his own philosophical understanding of Christian doctrine.[11] Others believe that Origen was a man of the church, a mystic whose main concern was to substantiate the authoritative witness of Christian doctrine according to the Tradition and to enable believers better to understand and live their faith.[12] In the latter case, his

---

9. As the resolution of this debate would take this study well beyond its scope, I will merely illustrate briefly the historical debate here without offering any conclusions or critique.

10. Origen, *On First Principles*, Preface, 10.

11. Berner, *Origenes*, provides a summary of the viewpoints, including a list of representatives from every side of the debate. Those who would hold to the view that Origen is a systematician include: F. C. Bauer, Bigg, von Harnack, Loofs, de Faye, Miura-Stange, Koch, Karpp, Nygren, Lietzmann, Jonas, Hanson, and Kettler.

12. Berner's (ibid.) compilation of figures who take this position include: Bardy, Völker, Lieske, de Lubac, and Crouzel. A mediating position is attempted by Cardiou, Daniélou, Kerr, Harl, and Wickert. Runia also adds Chadwick to the mediating group (see Runia, *Philo in Early Christian Literature*, 169).

was an apologetic concern premised on the historical occasion of the early church. His intentions, then, were more pastoral, and not systematic. Within this, both sides may agree that Origen was systematic in the sense that his intentions were to be orderly and logical, even attempting to summarize certain recurring themes in the Bible. However, those who would affirm him as systematic in a more philosophically rigorous sense are seen as anachronistic by others who would argue such philosophical intentions as foundationalism, providing a justification for propositional language, or constructing a summary based in human reason were not within the purview of theologians until the Enlightenment.

Another historical figure attracting attention in this regard as well is John Calvin. Though much has been written regarding Calvin's methodology, and a general consensus reached regarding his overarching concern for method, challenges have arisen recently regarding Calvin's intentions and underlying reasoning throughout the *Institutes*.[13] Writing with regard to the purpose of his *Institutes*, specifically as it relates to the primary document of the church, the Scriptures, Calvin states: "For I believe I have so embraced the sum of religion in all its parts, and have arranged it in such an order, that if anyone rightly grasps it, it will not be difficult for him to determine what he ought especially to seek in Scripture, and to what end he ought to relate its contents."[14] Commenting on his intentions, Francois Wendel argues that Calvin, by 1560, "[P]aid no great attention to form, although this remains very fine. What mattered to him above all in his last editions was to give strict precision and as logical a structure as possible to his thought . . . The principle changes are due to the new arrangement of the material, according to a more systematic plan and a stricter internal logic."[15] Wendel believes that Calvin's efforts in the later editions may constitute, at least, something akin to the systematic effort along the lines of modern theology. On the other hand, William Bowsma has argued strongly in favor of the notion that Calvin was a humanist engaged primarily in rhetoric, and as such could not have been a systematician, at least not according to Bowsma's

---

13. Though Calvin may not rightly be considered a Calvinist, some epistemological tendencies do seem apparent in his theology. Cf. Dowey, "Book Review, 'John Calvin: A Sixteenth Century Portrait,'" 847; and Leith, "Calvin's Theological Method and the Ambiguity in His Theology," 107–8.

14. Calvin, *Institutes of the Christian Religion*, I, Preface (1559) 4.

15. Wendel, Calvin, 119–20.

definition of systematics.[16] Again, Bowsma believes attributing the term systematic to Calvin is both misguided with regard to his intentions and anachronistic.

These brief forays into the historical debate may sound familiar, since many have discussed the purported intentions of both these theologians. However, these two are merely beginning of the conversation. The theological method of several figures in the theological history of the church has come under scrutiny. Is the assumption of systematicity dating to early church theologians due simply to the presuppositions of the modern historian/theologian? Or does something in the pre-modern theologians' work indicate the existence of universal attention to philosophical concerns, meaning such concerns are not limited to only the modern period? For the sake of discussion, Origen and Calvin focus the debate quite well, given their stated intentions, but what of other theologians in history? What of Thomas Aquinas and the authors of the creeds?

In regard to this last question, this study will attempt to draw out the methodological intentions of several historical figures and periods, evaluating the relationship of ancient to modern through the lens of what constitutes system and how order played a role in works written by various theologians. Irenaeus, Origen, and Constantine help focus the issues of method in relation to the community of faith in the early church. In each, we will see that though method may have been a concern, it was hardly foremost in their minds. Pastoral and political convictions played a far more important role, but does this constitute a systematic dependence upon external philosophical beliefs? Wycliffe, Thomas Aquinas, and Calvin serve to illustrate how the philosophical presuppositions of modern historians can skew the perspective of how pre-modern theology is read and understood. Each of these theologians has, at one point in modern historical study, been accused of being systematic. However, their systematicity is questionable when seen in light of their historical circumstance and apologetic/pedagogical concerns. Finally, examples of how the Enlightenment affected method in philosophy and theology are seen in the developments of Descartes, Kant, and Hegel. Though no one

---

16. See Bowsma, *John Calvin*. Though Bowsma is reticent to define what elements he would deem systematic in theology, he does give some indication that they include transhistorical knowledge, non-pedagogical intentions (philosophy?), and finally, he believes systematics is necessarily tied to the rise of modernity (see pp. 5, 160, esp. notes 100 and 191).

figure, or even a group of figures, can be seen as "responsible" for how system came to used in post-Enlightenment epistemology, these specific Enlightenment figures represent, or illustrate, tendencies in method coming under widespread criticism by post-liberal theologians. It is with such critiques in mind that the final chapter outlines Kierkegaard's critique of Hegel and the influence of Kierkegaard on Barth and subsequent post-liberal/postmodern theologians. Some correction of the standard reading of Kierkegaard's critique of Hegel seems in order; however, the thrust of his emphasis on writing theology that is once again directed toward the faith of the church is a needed reminder of theology's scope and purpose. Further, the link to primary influences on contemporary theological method is finally made.

One distinct limitation of this study is that it only evaluates the written work of specific theologians. We will not attempt to incorporate oral interaction or even evaluate the importance of the written word in relation to the spoken. Literacy may already have assumed a certain level of academia in the intended audience of these theologians. Thus, a certain amount of presumption exists in this study's consideration of the relationship of theology to the church. However, such a focus on the written seems warranted, since the written word has endured and had by far the greater direct impact.

The larger question for this study is how theology is best used in and by the church. Each pre-modern theologian discussed below illustrates the varying ways in which the modern pre-occupation with method has forgotten historical circumstance. One can almost imagine each theologian puzzling over the question of method. Each had a pastor's heart and a grave concern for the health of their specific community. Such concerns come through in their writing, but are often forgotten in the face of pre-conceived paradigms by the contemporary reader. Though our study will still focus primarily on method, we will attempt to set such concerns in the appropriate historical context. Pre-modern theologians were, often, marked by a grave concern for the church, raising the mantle for what has passed as theology since the turn to modernism and postmodernism. These chapters are intended to serve as a reminder that theology written for an audience outside the context of the community of faith (i.e., any rational or "enlightened" mind) would not be recognizable as theology in much of the historical context of the church.

Theological Induction in the Canon and Irenaeus' "Rule-of-Faith"

The Orderliness of Apologetics

THE HISTORY OF THEOLOGY CERTAINLY HAS SEVERAL BEGINNING points. It would be, put simply, ignorant to speak of one beginning point for theology. Certainly Jesus' life, death and resurrection represent the grounding for the history of Christian theology. However, even within this, several historical points arise. The move from historical events to Scripture is also a journey fraught with questions related to the epistemological value of various types of literature and the way such literature was esteemed by specific communities. The process of relating the story of one piece to the stories of other pieces of literature certainly implies a means of evaluating each piece. Short of discovering a list of criteria for what was to be regarded as divinely inspired, we are unable to ascertain with certainty the ways in which certain books were included and excluded in Scripture. Certainly, specific instances of heresy in some works stand out due to their condemnation. However, for books included in the Bible, we are only privy to glimpses of the process through which they gained authority. It is key that we recognize this as a process, because as such, it includes many variables beyond the mere evaluation of statements within the text. As will be seen, one of these variables was an awareness of theological verification within the community of faith discovered in both textual comparison and in the performance of the texts in the life of the community. Though not discussed in this chapter, martyrdom played a major role in authenticating the belief of the community. Of course, the focus of most debates typically remained on the text of Scripture. At times, the issue became a debate over which

Scripture was to be regarded as authentic, but the more intense question was typically interpretations of texts upon which both sides agreed were authoritative. As will be seen below, such wrangling about interpretations is not far removed from even some of the more modest theological investigation of today.

The process of canonization may be described as both an internal and external process, in that both internal considerations of the substance of the literature and external considerations of its authenticity and value for the community were used to determine a text's authoritative position in the canon. As will be discussed below, the process was not a matter of simply applying a template to the texts to arrive at a determination. It was a drawn out consideration based primarily in the use of a text in various communities of faith. This process clearly involved the methodological discovery and application of certain criteria to a text as its authority came to be recognized. However, it is a further question as to whether the existence of a method for evaluation of texts external to the texts themselves constitutes a systematic theology. In order to understand how theology related to the text of Scripture in the early church, let us turn to a more detailed discussion of canonization and the theologians who helped shape the determination of orthodoxy.

The Canonization of Scripture

Canon and Intention

Of course the theological reflection of today is often marked by an assumption of objectivity equivalent to that of a science. As seen in the Introduction above, immodesty has led some to depict Scripture as a mine filled with facts simply waiting to be unearthed. This seems to be over-reaching, not on the basis of the nature of revelation, but in the way Scripture is denuded of its literary character. On the other hand, to say that Scripture is not simply a collection of facts does not mean that it is just a few old documents thrown together without any regard for the content or scope of the documents. The canonization of New Testament Scripture took hundreds of years and a great deal of debate regarding the inclusion of certain works. It is becoming more apparent today that the process was hardly one of establishing standards and subsequently evaluating the works according to those standards. The church did not establish the canon; rather, the canon came about through an intricate dialectic between the documents witnessing to the life of Christ and the early church, and the communities using those documents in their worship and life.[1]

One can already see the process of canonization beginning in the New Testament documents themselves (e.g., 2 Peter 3:15–16; Colossians 4:16). Brevard Childs and S. Pedersen both outline several passages reflecting a pursuit of ordering and selecting certain writings as authoritative.[2] Childs makes it clear that the church was being shaped by the canon even as it was helping to give shape to the canon: "Far from being objective conduits of received tradition, the tradents, authors, and redactors of the New Testament effected a massive construal of the material by the very process of selecting, shaping and transmitting it. At the heart of the process lay a dialectical move in which the tradents of the developing New Testament were themselves being shaped by the content of the material which they in turn were transmitting, selecting, and forming into a scriptural norm."[3] One of the primary concerns for early Christians was of course that later generations would have the opportunity to hear of Jesus in a manner relevant to their situation. The gospel narratives, as well as the epistolary witnesses to the gospel, served as a means to tell the story of Christ in a way that could bridge the historical distance. Far from being purely historical documents that were collected for the sake of posterity, the gathering of these works was intended to witness to the power of the gospel that had already helped shape the existing Christian community.[4] As Childs states, "Central to the canonical process was the concern to render the occasional form in which the gospel was first received into a medium which allowed it faithfully and truthfully to render its witness for successive generations of believers who had not directly experienced Christ's incarnation and resurrection."[5] It seems evident from Childs' study that the early Christian community was exercising intention and purpose as they attempted to provide both living and written

1. The view of canon developing as a result of this dialectic has been most carefully examined by Brevard Childs in his works *The New Testament as Canon* and *Biblical Theology of the Old and New Testaments*.

2. Childs, *New Testament as Canon*, 22.

3. Ibid.

4. James Barr has pointed to the canon as a formal, even accidental, event (see Barr, *Holy Scripture*, 67). This seems to miss the significance of the hermeneutical process for the community of faith.

5. Childs, *New Testament as Canon*, 22.

witness to the significance of Christ's life, death, and resurrection. They
were not simply saving the documents for the sake of remembrance.
They wished for the documents to have a continuing impact on future
generations of the church. Thus, they included several Gospel stories and
epistles with varying attractions and insights, though a unified story and
theological perspective. They recognized, perhaps only dimly, that these
documents had helped to shape their own community. In order to maintain some sense of continuity and to secure the "orthodoxy" of their own
and future generations, the early church sought to provide their children
and grandchildren with the same testimony that had shaped their own
belief.[6]

It is also important to note that such considerations were not simply
directed toward the testimonies gathered after the resurrection of Christ.
The early church also had to come to grips with their relationship to
the Scripture of the Jews. As is evident from both the inclusion of the
Jewish Scriptures as the Old Testament and the discussions in the New
Testament devoted to how to handle the Jewish Scriptures in light of
the revealed Messiah, much attention was given to how to fit the church
into the Old Testament. The early church was in a dialectical relationship
with both Old and New Testaments. Though the Old Testament canon
had already taken its basic shape, it was nevertheless incumbent upon
Christians to evaluate their relationship to it.

Canon and the Whole

The theological significance of this dialectical relationship is found in the
fact that the early church was beginning to shape criteria upon which to
evaluate the testimonies of witnesses. These criteria included such external considerations as authorship, date, etc., but internal considerations
also played a major role. As mentioned above, the church did not have
categories already formed by which they could evaluate the veracity
of the documents. Instead, the value of a document was established in
and through usage by the communities. (Thus, the rise of heated debate
between communities using varying texts and arriving at differing con-

---

6. Childs (ibid., 25) again makes this clear with reference to the dialectical process:
"The canonical process which established a special relationship between Scripture and
people reflected both the influence of the historical communities on the shaping of the
literature and conversely the influence of the sacred writings on the self-understanding
of the community."

clusions.) The theological significance of the documents came not as a later addition by clerics or because of ecclesiastical function.[7] Instead, theological significance developed as the canon was beginning to take shape. It was as the pieces began either to fit together or rub each other too roughly that the whole canon began to take its final form. Childs believes that while this formation was not without continuous conflict, it did develop over time into the canon of the New Testament. "Canon consciousness thus arose at the inception of the Christian church and lies deep within the New Testament literature itself. There is an organic continuity in the historical process of the development of an established canon of sacred writings from the earliest stages of the New Testament to the final canonical stabilization of its scope."[8] This continuity is developed as the pieces of the canon begin to take a more permanent place within the canon. The dialectic then expands its textual pole so that an interplay amongst the texts is allowed to help evaluate the appropriateness of a specific text. However, it would be inappropriate to portray the interplay as only a dialogue between text and text. Other factors were beginning to gain a voice in the conversation. Even after the canon was relatively fixed, it did not function as the final formulation of the gospel. "The canon therefore provided a context for the gospel, but did not attempt a final formulation of its message. It marked the arena in which each new generation of believers stood and sought to understand afresh the nature of the faith. It did not establish one doctrinal position, but often balanced several or fixed the limits within which Christians might rightly disagree."[9] Other extra-Scriptural factors were coming into the dialogue, such as early credal assertions, already traditional uses of the texts in worship and in understanding the faith, and the effects of certain teachings on the community of faith. The "rule-of-faith" began to establish parameters within which the church could appropriate the teachings of certain documents, including them as part of their working canon. Describing the intentions of his canonical work in contrast to critical methodology, Childs notes:

> [T]he canonical approach to the New Testament begins with those historical communities who received and heard the gospel in ways congruent with portions of the New Testament canon.

7. Childs, *New Testament as Canon*, 21.

8. Ibid.

9. Ibid., 29.

> They found their identity in these particular apostolic constru-
> als which served finally to overcome earlier historical diversities
> within early Christianity. In spite of the constant emphasis on the
> diversity within the New Testament by modern scholars, histori-
> cally by the end of the second century, if not before, the gospels
> were being read holistically as a unity within the circumference
> proscribed by a *rule-of-faith*.[10]

The canon began to function as somewhat of a whole unit early
in its life, even before the church was compelled to recognize it as a
fixed unit. The process of inclusion or exclusion involved a great deal
more than simply deciding the authorship or date of a particular text.
It also included fitting the text into the whole of the canon so that the
works might function as a unit in their witness to the gospel. While this
is something quite different from putting together a whole/complete
system of doctrines in the modern (i.e., Hegelian) sense, it nevertheless
demonstrates a concern for orderliness and consistency in the testimony.
There is a sense in which the whole had an effect on the parts and played
an important role in securing the final form of the canon. This is one element of systematicity that seems present even in the earliest of Christian
communities: an awareness of doctrinal comprehensiveness and consistency. Obviously, it does not make the authors of Scripture or the early
theologians systematic in the modern sense, since the comprehensiveness is related to the text of Scripture and not a corpus of knowledge
external to Scripture. However, it does make them concerned for an
appropriate understanding of the witness to the gospel, and this witness
seems bound in part to an appropriate rendering of the significance of
the texts in Scripture. An interplay between the whole of Scripture and
its various parts is crucial. Perhaps this can be best illustrated by an explanation of the early usage of the rule-of-faith.

Irenaeus' Apologetics and the Rule-of-Faith

During the years Eleutherus was bishop of Rome (AD 182–188),
Irenaeus composed a lengthy work meant to combat the many facets of
Gnosticism facing the Christian church.[11] As bishop of Lyons and previ-

---

10. Ibid., 42–43. Emphasis mine.

11. Despite Irenaeus' comments regarding an addressee ("friend"), it seems unlikely
that *Against Heresies* was a commissioned work. See Vallée, "Theological and Non-
Theological Motives in Irenaeus's Refutation of the Gnostics," 174.

ously as an emissary to the bishop of Rome, he had great concern for not only his own local flock, but also for the whole of the growing church. His intentions in the work *Against Heresies* was to attempt to distinguish the teachings of Christianity from Gnostic "heresy," and to attempt to stamp out the heretical teachings that had already crept into the church.[12]

The important point for our discussion from this work comes as Irenaeus attempts to describe the manner in which the Gnostics produced their heresies. By means of philosophical, theological, and Scriptural refutation, Irenaeus set out to disprove the Gnostic heresies. The philosophical arguments were first because they were the weakest. Irenaeus had little regard for philosophy, though he was relatively conversant in it.[13] He later turned to Scriptural arguments since they were the more weighty and important considerations in the debate. The Gnostics certainly attempted to use Scriptural passages as authoritative witnesses to the gospel they were preaching. Irenaeus' concern was that they mishandled the Scripture, particularly in regard to how the Scriptures fit together into a unified view of the truth (i.e., the gospel of Christ). While the canon was beginning to become somewhat fixed by this time, the inter-relatedness of the various texts within the canon to one another was creating problems. Not only were the heretics bringing external ideas to the Scriptures, they also used the Scriptures in an inappropriate manner to support their teachings.

> [The Valentinian heretics] gather their views from other sources than the Scriptures [literally "reading from things unwritten"]; and to use a common proverb, they strive to weave ropes of sand, while they endeavor to adapt with an air of probability to their own peculiar assertions the parables of the Lord, the sayings of the prophets, and the words of the apostles, in order that their scheme may not seem altogether without support. In doing so, however, they disregard the order and connection of the Scriptures, and so far as in them lies, dismember and destroy the

12. Indeed, it seems apparent that Irenaeus' work serves to establish more securely the previously vague lines of distinction between "orthodox" and "heretical." See Vallée, "Theological and Non-Theological Motives in Irenaeus's Refutation of the Gnostics," 174–75. For a more complete discussion on the sociological impact and reasons for defining heresy and orthodoxy in both the pre- and post-Constantinian eras, see Gager, *Kingdom and Community*, 76–92.

13. Irenaeus only makes one positive reference to a philosopher in *Against Heresies*, and that is simply to say that Plato is superior to Marcion (III.25.5). This is not a tremendous compliment in Irenaeus' eyes.

truth. By transferring passages, and dressing them up anew, and making one thing out of another, they succeed in deluding many through their wicked art in adapting the oracles of the Lord to their opinions. Their manner of acting is just as if one, when a beautiful image of a king has been constructed by some skillful artist out of precious jewels, should then take this likeness of the man all to pieces, should rearrange the gems, and so fit them together as to make them into the form of a dog or of a fox, and even that but poorly executed; and should then maintain and declare that *this* was the beautiful image of the king which the skillful artist constructed, pointing to the jewels which had been admirably fitted together by the first artist to form the image of the king, but have been with bad effect transferred by the latter one to the shape of a dog, and by thus exhibiting the jewels, should deceive the ignorant who had no conception what a king's form was like, and persuade them that that miserable likeness of the fox was, in fact, the beautiful image of the king. In like manner do these persons patch together old wives' fables, and then endeavor, by violently drawing away from their proper connection, words, expressions, and parables whenever found, to adapt the oracles of God to their baseless fictions.[14]

Irenaeus' debate was not about which Scriptures to use, although he does suggest the heretics are proposing external teachings to be proved by the Scriptures, which could be looked upon as "another gospel." Instead, the primary focus of his debate was on how to use the Scriptures appropriately when teaching or explaining the truth. The heretics had been taking Scriptures out of context to use them to support teachings learned elsewhere. Irenaeus believed that it was inappropriate both to rearrange the Scriptures into a pattern that deviates from the original and to use such a rearrangement to support teachings that do not agree with the original teachings. However, he recognized that both he and the heretics were using Scripture. The question then became, "How is one to know who is using it appropriately?" To answer this question, Irenaeus turned to the "ruleof-truth" or the "rule-of-faith" (*regula fidei*). Comparing the work of the heretics to a haphazard gathering of Homeric verses, Irenaeus made it clear that both the original context of the verses and the accepted tradition as to whom they refer and in what way are crucial for appropriately understanding each one of them.

14. Irenaeus, *Against Heresies* I.8.1.

Now, what simple-minded man, I ask, would not be led away by such verses as these to think that Homer actually framed them so with reference to the subject indicated? But he who is acquainted with the Homeric writings will recognize the verses indeed, but not the subject to which they are applied, as knowing that some of them were spoken of Ulysses, others of Hercules himself, others still of Priam, and others again of Menelaus and Agamemnon. But if he takes them and restores each of them to its proper position, he at once destroys the narrative in question. In like manner he who retains unchangeable [literally "immovable in himself"] in his heart the rule of the truth which he received by means of baptism, will doubtless recognize the names, the expressions, and the parables taken from the Scriptures, but will by no means acknowledge the blasphemous use which these men make of them. For, though he will acknowledge the gems, he will certainly not receive the fox instead of the likeness of the king. But when he has restored every one of the expressions quoted to its proper position, and has fitted it to the body of the truth, he will lay bare, and prove to be without any foundation, the figment of these heretics.[15]

Irenaeus continues by illustrating the inconsistency of the various heretics, demonstrating that only the truth of the Christian church represents the gospel and the Christ who is at its center.[16] The rule-of-faith is a guide to correct understanding of the Scripture, placing passages into their appropriate context. The obvious question at this point seems to be "What is it that constitutes the rule-of-faith? Is it simple ordering of Scriptural texts, or is a doctrinal awareness of the texts also in view?"

The rule-of-faith to which Irenaeus appealed is not something altogether new. Though he and Tertullian are the first to call it such, the rule-of-faith may be traced back at least to the Muratorian Fragment (c. 180), and even back to the authors of the New Testament. With respect to the problem of including four gospel accounts in the canon, the Muratorian Fragment concludes: "And therefore, though various ideas are taught in the several books of the gospels, yet it makes no difference to the faith of believers, since by one sovereign Spirit all things are declared in all of them concerning the nativity, the passion, the resurrection, the conversation with his disciples and his two comings, the first in lowliness and contempt, which has come to pass, the second glorious and with royal

15. Ibid., I.9.4.
16. Ibid., I.9.5—I.31.4.

power, which is to come."[17] Joseph Lienhard traces the rule-of-faith back to the authors of the New Testament themselves by understanding early credal formulations found in the New Testament to be forerunners of the rule-of-faith and baptismal confessions.[18] This seems appropriate given the various descriptions of the rule-of-faith offered later by Irenaeus and Tertullian.[19]

Whatever the date of origin for the rule-of-faith, its function was to limit the boundaries of truth within the Christian community as it attested to the gospel of Jesus Christ. It was not the same as Scripture, but it functioned alongside Scripture, both as a hermeneutical guide and a substantive tool for evaluation, to see that Scripture was appropriately understood. Lienhard believes that the rule-of-faith was quite encompassing in its scope:

> The "rule-of-faith" means both the norm that guides the Christian's faith and the Christian's belief as normative. It is equivalent to the whole teaching of the Church as that teaching was proclaimed by the apostles and the prophets and recorded in the Scriptures. The term "rule-of-faith" always refers to what is original, to what is established in and preserved by the Church as true—in other words, the truth itself that was proclaimed by the Lord and the apostles. The rule-of-faith has no fixed form; each writer adapted it to his immediate goals and intent. It is not identical with the creeds, nor with Scripture, although it cannot contradict Scripture. The rule-of-faith is tradition in the original sense of the word, that is, the faith that has been handed on from the beginning.[20]

Childs basically agrees with this description, though his Protestant background may give him a bit more pause in equating the rule-of-faith with tradition in any general sense of the term:

> The rule-of-faith by which Irenaeus sought to establish a framework of interpretation was once thought by scholars to be a bap-

17. Cited by Lienhard, *Bible, the Church, and Authority*, 95.

18. Ibid., 96–98.

19. Ibid., 98–100. Lienhard surveys the many references by Irenaeus and Tertullian to the rule-of-faith. All seem to resemble a creed-like affirmation or explanation, including at times the three names of the Father, Son, and Holy Spirit.

20. Ibid., 99–100. Lienhard is here relying on the description given in Hägglund's, "Die Bedeutung der 'regula fidei' als Grundlage theologischer Aussagen," 1–44.

tismal confession, but more recent research has confirmed that the rule is a *summary* of the truth which comprises the faith of the church. It refers to the totality of the faith as the criterion of correct interpretation. It is the content of scripture, but not identical with the Bible; rather, it is that to which scripture points. It is contained in the proclamation of church tradition, but it is not as if the written Bible required an additional oral formulation. Its content is decisive for faith and is reflected in a unified teaching in both its oral and written form.[21]

To call the rule-of-faith a summary puts it on a par with modest attempts at systematic theology, particularly as both are concerned with coherence amongst doctrinal or Scriptural assertions. Though the focus is still upon Scripture as the primary authority, Childs makes it clear that Irenaeus did not simply regard the rule-of-faith as a hermeneutic for Scripture. Indeed, it was much more than a method of Scriptural interpretation.

> Irenaeus did not see the rule-of-faith as the church's 'construal' of the Bible, but rather as the objective truth of the Apostolic Faith, which has been publicly revealed and not concealed in a secret gnosis. There is a succession of true witnesses ([*Against Heresies*], IV.26.2). Its truth is unambiguous (III.2.1) and can be demonstrated in the actual history of the past (III.5.1). Yet this truth is not a static deposit from the past, but the 'living voice' (*viva vox*) of truth. Irenaeus speaks of the symphony of scripture, of its harmonious proportion (III.11.9). It provides the church with the normative criterion against which critically to measure the Gnostic distortions.[22]

What is most interesting about Childs' description of the rule-of-faith is both the fact that it is not equivocal with simply an explanation of Scripture and the idea that it is used as a summary of the truth. The rule-of-faith is not simply an abridgment of the message found in the Scriptures, though it is at times described by Irenaeus in credal terms or formulae (e.g., *Against Heresies*, I.22.1). Nevertheless, it is apparent that the rule-of-faith is bound to a conception of the truth that includes an appropriate understanding of Scripture, or at least the message of the Scripture. Speaking of the fox or dog being constructed from the jewels used to form the image of the king, Childs states: "[The Gnostics]

21. Childs, *Biblical Theology of the Old and New Testaments*, 31–32. Emphasis mine.
22. Ibid., 32.

operated from the wrong context. They had no concept of the whole. [Irenaeus] therefore appealed to the church's rule-of-faith, the *regula fidei*. This comprised a holistic reading of the gospel which included the sum of tradition constituting the true revelation on which the faith was grounded and to which Scripture testified."[23] Thus, the Scripture and an appropriate understanding of its message are the keys to grasping the truth of the gospel message. However, as seen above, the Scriptures must be appropriated in a manner consistent with the teaching of the apostles and prophets. As Childs mentions, this coincides with the formation of the canon. But more than just the process of canonization is at work in Irenaeus' apologetics. He is also beginning to formulate conceptions of doctrinal truth, which though derived from Scripture are not identical with Scripture. For example,

> The rule of truth which we hold is, that there is one God Almighty, who made all things by His Word, and fashioned and formed, out of that which had no existence, all things which exist. Thus saith the Scripture to that effect: "By the Word of the Lord were the heavens established, and all the might of them by the spirit of His mouth." [Psalm 33:6] And again, "All things were made by Him, and without Him was nothing made." [John 1:3] . . . Holding, therefore, this rule, we shall easily show, notwithstanding the great variety and multitude of their opinions, that these men have deviated from the truth; for almost all the different sects of heretics admit that there is one God; but then, by their pernicious doctrines they change [this truth into error], even as the Gentiles do through idolatry,—thus proving themselves ungrateful to Him that created them.[24]

Irenaeus has already formulated a conception of God as creator that is congruent with Scripture, but is not simply the repetition of Scriptural passages. Irenaeus is here going beyond mere commentary on a text to actually attempting to harmonize the pertinent texts on a specific doctrinal subject. It would seem that Childs is correct in understanding this as a theological activity, a summarizing of the message of Scripture. Armed with a brief statement of what is true belief, Irenaeus is prepared to set about the task of disproving the heretical claims of other teachers.[25] Childs and Lienhard also seem correct in describing Irenaeus' un-

---

23. Childs, *New Testament as Canon*, 28. See also 32.

24. Irenaeus, *Against Heresies* I.22.1.

25. Irenaeus dedicates the remainder of Book I (chapters 23–31) to outlining the

derstanding of the rule-of-faith as an appeal to the whole of Scriptural teaching as it is represented in the words of Scripture and in tradition.[26] Since Irenaeus is dedicated to refuting *all* the teachings of the heretics he has encountered in various forms, it is important that he bring the full scope of the Scriptures to bear. This includes not only the words of Scripture, which he uses abundantly, but also the traditional teachings (dare we call them doctrines) he has inherited from the faithful teachers of the church. As Irenaeus states,

> True gnosis is [that which consists in] the doctrine of the apos-
> tles, and the ancient constitution of the Church throughout all
> the world, and the distinctive manifestation of the body of Christ
> according to the successions of the bishops, by which they have
> handed down that Church which exists in every place, and has
> come even unto us, being guarded and preserved, without any
> forging of Scriptures, by a very complete system of doctrine, and
> neither receiving addition nor [suffering] curtailment [in the
> truths which she believes]; and [it consists in] reading [the word
> of God] without falsification, and a lawful and diligent exposition
> in harmony with the Scriptures, both without danger and with-
> out blasphemy; and [above all, it consists in] the pre-eminent gift
> of love, which is more precious than knowledge, more glorious
> than prophecy, and which excels all the other gifts [of God].[27]

The question that remains for our discussion is, "Does this some-how constitute a systematization of the Scripture, or of the truths gar-nered from Scripture?" If one means by this that Irenaeus was putting together a system of doctrines that he believed represented the truth for all time in his one historical representation, then the answer must be negative. Irenaeus did not believe he was fixing for all time *the* appropri-ate understanding of Scripture. He believed that what he represented was a living truth; a truth that moved and shaped each subsequent Christian community by the teachings of the apostles and prophets and through the power of the Holy Spirit. The rule-of-faith set the boundaries for appropriate Christian belief. It did not necessarily establish the beliefs themselves.[28]

---

claims of the heretics and disproving them, although the latter effort is the explicit sub-ject of Book II.

26. Childs, *The New Testament as Canon*, 28.

27. Irenaeus, *Against Heresies* IV.33.8.

28. This may sound remarkably similar to the cultural-linguistic model of George Lindbeck in his *The Nature of Doctrine*. However, Lindbeck's work stills seems to har-

On the other hand, if one attempts to answer this question according to a more modest formulation of system, Irenaeus' apologetics seems to have led him to exercise great concern over coherence and a sense of comprehensiveness of the Scriptures.[29] If our definition of system includes simply considerations, or even an expectation, of orderliness and consistency, these would seem to parallel the definition of the rule-of-faith given by Irenaeus. Indeed, some would say that such concerns are best left as an anthropological question rather than an epistemological question since all humans are concerned for orderliness and a sense of appropriate structure. Speaking with reference to a holistic rendering of Scripture, Scalise claims: "The discovery of patterns—the ways in which different parts come together to make a whole—is a basic element in the process by which we as humans perceive and claim to know meaning in the world. Canonical hermeneutics maintains that the process of recognizing and describing the patterns we find in the Bible is at the heart of understanding the Bible's authority in a deeper way than that afforded by the historical reconstruction of critical scholarship."[30] While this perhaps seems to claim too much and may simply be the product of an Enlightenment anthropological/epistemological heritage, we cannot simply ignore the concerns for order demonstrated by Irenaeus. Mathematics has by this time become fairly fixed in its representations. Certainly, Irenaeus and others in his culture were keenly aware of the relationship of parts to the whole. But Irenaeus is not a post-Enlighten-

bor much of the modern enterprise given his concerns to use the model he proposes for specifically ecumenical reasons. While ecumenism does not necessarily make his work modernistic, he still seems to be under modernism's spell by treating the need for ecumenism as a self-evident propositional truth. Further, though Lindbeck is relying on narrative theologians to fill in the blanks as to what kind of community lives up to his cultural-linguistic ideal, it does not appear as though the "dialectic" between community and doctrine in his model relies on the same criteria as Irenaeus' rule-of-faith. Lindbeck may be attempting to make room for the Spirit in his living community, but more reasonable, or even rationalistic, concerns seem to have filled the space.

29. This appears to be the reasoning behind Frances Young's (Young, *Making of the Creeds*, 22–23) claim that Irenaeus created the first "systematic theology" with his theory of recapitulation, although Young may also be equating systematics with the use of an *a priori* theory in theological investigations. Taken in a somewhat broad fashion, this may be accurate, since Irenaeus did have heretical ideas for disproof in mind when he wrote much of his own original substantive work. On the other hand, if Young intends to say that Irenaeus had a theory regarding the whole of doctrine already in mind when he wrote, this may be presuming too much.

30. Scalise, *From Scripture to Theology*, 86–87.

ment figure. His concerns for the relationship of the parts to the whole are still set within a context of communal identification and purification, and more importantly, Scriptural interpretation. He is not simply talking about numbers or equations nor is he merely enamored with coherence. Rather, he is addressing people and communities who claim to be a part of the Christian church, which reads and attempts to live the Scriptures. His intentions are focused on purification, not construction of a set of doctrines that are coherent simply for the sake of internal consistency or to adhere to the law of non-contradiction. However, we cannot deny his concerns for order and consistency, even in spite of the lack of a clear *statement* of belief or the like. While it is true that the rule-of-faith was not a written document or a formal formulation of doctrine, it does appear to contain the seeds of doctrinal formulation and certainly serves in a manner similar to the later doctrinal formulations (e.g., the creeds) used to demarcate heresy.

Some have attempted to display more clearly what is deemed authoritative about Irenaeus' teaching and have come to the conclusion that it is his systematic method, or "hypothesis." As P. Hefner explains, "[T]he one highest authority [that stands out in Irenaeus' work] is the system, framework, or 'hypothesis' of the Faith whose substance is comprised in God's redemptive dispensation on man's behalf."[31] For Hefner, this means that the hypothesis is "the authority which holds together all others and to which all others are subordinated: scripture, tradition, church, bishop, creed and revelation."[32] D. B. Reynders has likewise identified the highest authority for Irenaeus as the "synthese doctrinale" which is "le corps de vérité."[33] The hypothesis, or system, is equivalent to the rule-of-faith.[34] Irenaeus rests his attention finally on how the Gnostics treat the truth. Gérard Vallée believes Irenaeus equated their disregard of the inter-relationship of the facts with blasphemy. "Gnostics freely subtract from and add to the hypothesis of truth. This arbitrariness is not only opposed to Irenaeus's temperament and his positivist emphasis on the clear

31. Hefner, "Theological Methodology and St. Irenaeus," 295.

32. Vallée, "Theological and Non-Theological Motives in Irenaeus's Refutation of the Gnostics," 256 n. 17.

33. Reynders, "La polémique de saint Irénée. Méthode et principes," 16–17.

34. N. Brox (*Offenbarung, Gnosis und gnostischer Mythos bei Irenäus von Lyon*, 113) describes the rule as "Inbegriff dessen, was er (Irenäus) für heilsnotwendig, für tatsächlich geschehen, von Gott geoffenbart und darum für unüberbietbar hält."

and real facts of the economy, it is also blasphemy."[35] Such renderings of Irenaeus seem a bit anachronistic in the way they attribute a modern persona to the intentions of Irenaeus. What appears as a concern for objective clarification of the facts may, in actuality, be a desire for Scriptural unity. Irenaeus' concerns are likely pastoral, not philosophical.

Wisse believes that Irenaeus has misunderstood the Gnostics by expecting their works to be primarily doctrinal, rather than regarding them according to their intention, which was as mystical poetry.[36] Wisse goes even further to claim that Irenaeus apparently assumed that doctrinal unity was the only type of unity that mattered, thereby making the Gnostics look like doctrinal heretics when in fact they were not attempting to be doctrinal: "By taking the differences in mythological detail as doctrinal differences, Gnosticism came to look like an absurdly fragmented movement."[37] While Wisse's comments may grant too broad a scope for the intentions of the Gnostics, such statements as these make it appear as though Irenaeus had a fairly clear picture of doctrine in mind when he addressed the Gnostics. His analysis of their shortcomings was based upon their lack of "fit" with his own system. He evaluated them according to their differences from each other and from his own conception of doctrine, which he regarded as Scriptural.

Of course, though Scriptural/theological concerns may have been of primary importance to Irenaeus, that doesn't mean that other factors were not coming into play in his evaluation of Gnosticism. He had already addressed the issues briefly from a philosophical perspective. It is also likely that social concerns were driving him to find the differences represented by the Gnostics and root them out.[38] Finally, it seems unlikely that Irenaeus was so fixed in his conception of the truth. Granted,

35. Vallée, "Theological and Non-Theological Motives in Irenaeus's Refutation of the Gnostics," p. 178. Vallée is here relying on the work of W. C. van Unnik ("De la regle Mhte prosqeinai mhte afelein dans l'histoire du canon," to make it clear that the idea of adding to or subtracting from a received tradition was widely regarded as blasphemous in antiquity.

36. Wisse, "The Nag Hammadi Library and the Heresiologists," 222.

37. Ibid., 221.

38. Vallée believes that social concerns loomed large in Irenaeus' mind. He was quite disturbed by the way in which the Gnostics were disrupting the social fabric of the church and the society. His desire to quash them derived from his desire to maintain order within the culture as much as it did from a desire to see truth vindicated in the church. (See Vallée, "Theological and Non-Theological Motives in Irenaeus's Refutation of the Gnostics," 181–85.)

he did seem to have fairly distinct ideas about the rule-of-faith. But he does not spell it out in so many words as though it could be ahistorically fixed in one form. He uses it as an evaluative tool, but he does not presume to have arrived at as strong a position as indicated by some above.

Conclusion

Irenaeus seems systematic in the sense that he is concerned for order and does function as though the whole is related to and is as important as the parts making up the whole. He is not systematic according to some notion of finality or universal knowledge placed outside of historical circumstances or derived from any sources besides Scripture. All of his doctrinal or doctrine-like assertions are an attempt to harmonize the teachings of various passages in Scripture. His primary concerns revolved around the purity of the church. It was only with this goal in mind that he set about the task of identifying heresy in her midst. He was not engaging in theological investigations for their own sake or even for the sake of knowledge. He was primarily concerned with the community that identified itself as the body of Christ, and wished to provide a pure witness to His life in her members. This is apologetics first and foremost, but it is apologetics being done with careful attention to how best to refute the arguments of the opponent. (Perhaps one could call this a communal, or even ecclesiological defining of orthodoxy.) This not only implies a methodology; it also makes such a methodology quite apparent. Then again, method is not the same thing as a system.

2

Is Origen the Archetypal Systematician?

Introduction

WHILE IT SEEMS APPARENT IRENAEUS MAINTAINED CERTAIN METHOD-ological concerns in his application of the "rule of faith," particularly when set against the backdrop of canonical formation, he did so without stating a specific agenda or procedure for his method. In other words, he did not spell out his prolegomenal concerns prior to engaging a method in his response to and evaluation of the Gnostic heretics with whom he debated. As seen above, this did not mean he was without methodological intentions in the way he constructed his response to the Gnostics. He simply did not feel compelled to justify the grounding of his argument prior to making it. This was seen especially in the way he used Scripture. Both Irenaeus and the Gnostics assumed an authority of Scripture that bounded their argument and helped to establish a guiding method for constructive development of specific themes without ever explaining why it was authoritative. Irenaeus certainly took the Gnostics to task for misinterpreting Scripture, but he did so on the constant assumption that they shared a common regard for the authority of Scripture. As discussed above, all of this indicated a certain amount of systematic intentions in the work of Irenaeus, not in the modern sense of providing prolegomenal warrant for truth claims. Rather, Irenaeus represents a modest sense of system through his concern for coherence and integration of doctrinal truth indicative of an awareness of the whole of theology and the necessity for consistency throughout. Though he never felt compelled to justify his knowledge on epistemological grounds and never stated his methodological intentions, he maintained a concern for order throughout his work.

If one desires a methodological intention that is spelled out prior to an engagement in theological investigation and construction, one need not look far for an early theologian who devised a specific plan for his theology, even laying out that plan as a part of the introduction to his work. Origen's (185–254) study *De Principiis* makes a clear attempt to be ordered according to a preconceived plan. Further, as will be seen, his plan is derived from intentions not specifically related to any one Biblical passage or book. He allows his apologetic purposes to set the stage for how his theology was constructed. While this again does not constitute a modern turn to prolegomena, Origen's orderedness and coherence are indicative of the way in which modestly systematic intentions could be combined with other intentions, or were perhaps even inherent in intentions such as apologetics.

Origen scholarship has engendered a great deal of interest in the last several decades, particularly with regard to his method as a theologian. Admittedly, the question of method continues to be a more specifically modern concern. However, implicit methodological concerns within early Christian writings have afforded modern scholars the opportunity to examine these writings according to their structural tendencies and pedagogical purposes. The question, as it has come to be applied to Origen's work by modern historians, is whether it is fair to depict it as systematic.

As will be seen in the discussion that follows, one of the primary reasons Origen is of interest in this respect is because of explicit statements he makes regarding methodology. Unlike Irenaeus in the previous chapter, Origen makes explicit claims regarding his method in *De Principiis*. Whether he lives up to those claims and whether he intended them to be understood as a methodological outline are questions that need to be resolved. Whatever the answers, Origen's statements have led historians down a difficult path regarding analysis of an early theologian's method. One must always keep in mind that even asking the question of method may be tantamount to committing an anachronism of tremendous proportion. Nevertheless, the question of method does not seem to be problematic for historians *prima facae*. The more important question for them seems to be what kind of method is in question and what use Origen makes of method.

Representative figures will be used to outline the various ways in which this question has been considered by historians recently. Primary focus will be given to Origen's *De Principiis* since this work is at the center of the debate. The working thesis of this study is that Origen does display a methodology in this work that qualifies it as a modestly systematic effort. This does not necessarily negate other pursuits, in fact it may actually reinforce his apologetical intent. In the final analysis, it appears that Origen considered his particular method in *De Principiis* the best medium for his pastoral concerns. This strikes at the heart of the debate of recent years. As will be seen, most Origen scholars fall on one side or the other regarding whether Origen qualifies as a systematic theologian. The underlying assumption is that he must be either systematic or something else. This study intends to demonstrate that a theologian can employ methodological principles resembling a system and, at the same time, intend his/her theology to be used for purposes beyond the interests of mere construction. In other words, though Origen may use some systematic elements in putting together his argument, he does not make use of system for its own sake. The focus on theological prolegomena may be of recent origin, but the use of methodology and certain inherently systematic concerns is not.

Surrounding the question of Origen's systematicity is of course a host of other questions that establish some of the presuppositions for a study such as this. Such questions as: Again, what are the criteria that need to be met in order for something to qualify as a system, i.e., what is system? Is system an explicit or implicit methodological consideration? Can system be used to further other methodological or ecclesiological purposes, e.g., apologetical, polemical, or pedagogical intentions? The answers to these questions will ultimately dictate how one answers the overarching question of depicting Origen, or any other theologian, as a systematician. But before we begin an analysis of how our perception of method influences the characterization of Origen's theology, let us briefly examine Origen's own depiction of the method followed in *De Principiis*. The best place to begin is with the background of the text itself.

The Text of De Principiis

Date

Origen's *De Principiis* was most likely written between the years AD 219–230. Scholars have posited such a dating due to several factors.[1]

---

1. Most commentators on Origen agree with this approximate date for *De Principiis*. I am here relying on the dating evidence provided by G. W. Butterworth in the

The text was written prior to Origen's departure from Alexandria in 231. Evidence from within the text indicates that it was written subsequent to certain portions of his commentaries, but prior to other portions. This places it within the time he was writing commentaries, more specifically within the time he was writing his commentary on Genesis, but after he had written his commentary on John, which he calls "the first fruits of my labors in Alexandria."[2] Judging from the statements of the commentaries quoted in *De Principiis*, one may conjecture that it was written at a point when the commentaries were in their early stages. This may put the date somewhere prior to 225.[3] However, this is only conjecture. Eusebius' account of Origen's commentaries implies they were begun after his visit with Mammæa, the aunt of the Emperor Elagabalus, which most likely took place around 218. This places the writing of *De Principiis* somewhere between 219–230.

Preservation

The text of *De Principiis* we have today is the Latin translation of the work by Rufinus, a supporter of Origen's thought throughout the controversies engendered largely by Jerome's opposition to some of Origen's teachings. In places, we do have a few Greek passages quoted by other authors, particularly Jerome. However, for most of the text, we are dependent upon the translation by Rufinus.[4] Two precautionary measures must be mentioned with regard to this translation. First, as a supporter of Origen, Rufinus was quite determined to present Origen in the best light possible. This has led to the suspicion that he altered some texts

---

"Introduction" to his translation of Koetschau's text of *De Principiis*. See *Origen: On First Principles*, xxviiiff.

2. Origen, *Commentary on St. John,* I. 2.

3. This is Butterworth's opinion relying mainly on evidence from the commentaries on Genesis and Psalms. See Butterworth, "Introduction," xxix–xxx. This is certainly possible; however, we must remember that Origen could just as easily have been simply quoting the passages of Scripture in *De Principiis* he felt were most relevant, rather than only passages on which he had taken the time to comment. I am engaging in speculation here, as is Butterworth, since a date more certainly fixed is impossible with the evidence at hand.

4. The primary reason for Rufinus' work being all that remains is the later (553) condemnation of Origen as a heretic. Subsequent to such a proclamation, an author's works would be regarded as worthless, or perhaps even dangerous, giving rise to systematic destruction of his/her writings.

to make them less discordant to the late third-early fourth century ear. Second, our suspicions are confirmed when comparison of controversial passages is made with the quotations of those passages by the opposition, or in some cases, even by other supporters. Though not ruling out the idea that perhaps the opposition would be apt to misquote Origen's work, most scholars agree that Rufinus has in fact altered the original text. Some passages make this plain, while in others it is difficult to know for certain. The result is that we cannot completely trust the translation of Rufinus on controversial issues.[5] Since this is the only text available at this point, any substantive study must attempt to work through the text, giving careful attention to the pertinent issues causing the debates surrounding Origen's doctrine. However, our primary concern is with his method, necessitating that we give only scant attention to the substance of specific portions of his work.

Organization

Several statements made by Origen concerning his purpose and the structure he intended to follow in De Principiis have given rise to the debate over the systematicity of this work. The primary statements to be considered are found in the Preface to the work in which Origen outlines the plan of the book and provides some insight into why he would wish to follow such a plan. Other statements that serve as transition statements or reminders of the plan can be found in later divisions of the book; however, these are generally consistent with the outline he gives at the beginning.[6] Since these statements of purpose and structure would have given little cause for alarm in the first several centuries of Christianity, it is unlikely they have been altered in any significant way. Therefore, we will accept Rufinus' translation as an accurate portrayal of Origen's original statements of purpose and transition. With these preliminary remarks in mind, let us turn our attention to the text itself with some brief explanation of Origen's purpose. The use of these texts in the debate over Origen's systematicity will be the subject of our next section.[7]

---

5. For a summary of the reliability of the Rufinus text, see Butterworth, "Introduction," xlvi–lii.

6. More will be said later with regard to how the plan of the book given in the Preface unfolds in the rest of the work.

7. What follows is a general outline of De Principiis relying partially upon the thought of Kannengiesser (cf. Kannengiesser, "Origen, Systematician in De Principiis,"

In paragraph 2 of the Preface, Origen begins to identify the plan he will follow in the rest of the book as he offers his account of what is the true doctrine of the church.

> Many of those, however, who profess to believe in Christ, hold conflicting opinions not only on small and trivial questions but also on some that are great and important; on the nature, for instance, of God or of the Lord Jesus Christ or of the Holy Spirit, and in addition on the nature of those created beings, the dominions and the holy powers. In view of this it seems necessary first to lay down a definite line and unmistakable rule in regard to each of these, and to postpone the inquiry into other matters until afterwards.[8]

In this passage we may observe three crucial points with regard to Origen's plan and purpose. First, it seems quite evident that Origen's purpose for writing this work is to enter into debate with those who hold the "conflicting opinions." Origen's primary purpose for composing this work is as an internal apology. He is writing for those who are truly believers but who might be swayed by the opinions of the opposition. Alongside this, or even parallel to it, he also had polemical interests in mind, i.e., to refute the opposition by critically examining their teaching in the light of what he understood as the teaching of the apostles and Christ.[9]

Second, Origen has outlined the plan he will follow in examining the "conflicting opinions" and offering his own explication of what he believes is the "teaching of the church."[10] He will begin with the nature of "God, the Lord Jesus Christ, and the Holy Spirit"; then he will examine the nature of the "created beings, the dominions and the holy powers." Origen is already establishing a Trinitarian format in his opening paragraph as a paramount structural consideration. Further, he has outlined the order in which he will consider all the teachings of Christian doc-

---

397ff). However, as I will make clear below, Kannengiesser's thesis as to what constitutes the bifurcation and where the division is to be placed differ quite obviously from what I have outlined in this study.

8. Origen, *De Principiis*, Preface, 2; all quotations of Origen in the text of this study are taken from Butterworth's translation of *Origen: On First Principles*. Reference will also be given in subsequent citations to the critical edition of *Origène: Traité des Principes*. The quote above is found in vol. I, 78.

9. Origen, *De Principiis*, Preface, 2; *Origène: Traité des Principes*, vol. I, 78.

10. The teaching of the Church is the main subject of the first section (I.1–II.3).

trine. An important point to note in this respect is that this order does not appear to be dictated by the opposition but is the fashion in which Origen believes the doctrines should be considered.[11]

Third, Origen has indicated a bifurcation in the body of his study. He wishes to begin by first moving to "lay down a definite line and unmistakable rule in regard to each of these [doctrines]."[12] Consequently, he will "postpone the inquiry into other matters until afterwards."[13] He is not here setting out a proposal for considering other subjects in a subsequent work on a different topic. He is proposing first to lay down what is clearly understood, or what he believes is plain to all. Once this has been done, then other considerations *of the same subjects* may be taken into account and explored. The third paragraph of the Preface makes this clear.

> But the following fact should be understood. The holy apostles, when preaching the faith of Christ, took certain doctrines, those namely which they believed to be necessary ones, and delivered them in the plainest terms to all believers . . . The grounds of their statements they left to be investigated by such as should merit the higher gifts of the Spirit . . . There were other doctrines, however, about which the apostles simply said that things were so, keeping silence as to the how or why; their intention undoubtedly being to supply the more diligent of those who came after them, such as should prove to be lovers of wisdom, with an exercise on which to display the fruit of their ability.[14]

Origen believes he is one who could display his ability and intends to do so as soon as he has outlined what is the plain teaching of the apostles, which he equates with the traditional teaching of the Church.[15]

11. One of the questions raised by this second point is whether Origen is doing something new in structuring his argument this way. As will be discussed below, some authors believe he was simply engaging in a commonly used pedagogical pattern. Unfortunately, there is little evidence with which to substantiate that Origen is following an accepted pattern. However, this does not warrant positing that he was in fact engaging in a novel project. Since our study is not greatly affected by how one answers this question, it will not consume our attention here.

12. Origen, *De Principiis*, Preface, 2; *Origène: Traité des Principes*, vol. I, 78.

13. Ibid.

14. Ibid., Preface, 3; *Origène: Traité des Principes*, vol. I, 78, 80.

15. Origen does appear to make some more speculative statements while he is yet establishing the first definite line he wishes to lay down. This is the way in which I am interpreting the statement of transition at the beginning of Book I, chapter 6. More will be said on this below.

As one continues through the Preface, Origen begins to give shape to the plan he briefly mentioned in the first three paragraphs. The remaining paragraphs each deal with specific doctrines of the Church. Origen is careful to state what is clearly the teaching of the apostles or what he also calls accepted Church teaching.[16] He further gives some indication as to where his speculations may offer further reflections upon the doctrines of the Church. Some doctrines not mentioned in the early paragraphs, but placed in the sequence of later doctrines, are those of Scripture and its interpretation, whether God is incorporeal, the work of powers in salvation, and the life of the sun, moon and stars.[17] These do fit in the Church tradition and Origen explains what is official teaching and what is his own speculation. However, they are not a part of his first section, since they do not appear to be included as doctrines plainly taught by the apostles.

Origen's arrangement of subjects and his discussion of the plain teachings begins in Book I chapter 1, and is completed at the end of Book II, chapter 3. He considers each doctrine in order. He then wishes to begin once again with further attention given to the relevance of each doctrine for his contemporary audience, offering his own speculation into questions not plainly taught by the apostles or in the Church tradition. Book II, chapter 4 begins: "Now that we have, to the best of our ability, discussed these matters briefly in order, it follows from the plan which we adopted at the beginning that we proceed to refute those who think that the Father of our Lord Jesus Christ is a different God from him who gave Moses the sayings of the Law and sent the prophets, and who is the God of the fathers Abraham, Isaac and Jacob.[18] This is the beginning of the second section which continues until Book IV, chapter 3, at which point Origen turns his attention to a summary of what he has said on the doctrines mentioned in the previous section.[19]

16. E. g., Origen, *De Principiis*, Preface, 5, 6, 7, 10.

17. Origen, *De Principiis*, Preface, 8, 9, 10; *Origène: Traité des Principes*, vol. I, 84–88. Though these doctrines are placed later in the sequence, they are by no means peripheral. Origen sees each as a part of the path to follow for those who love wisdom. Perhaps they may not be plainly taught or easy to grasp, they may not even be meant for everyone. Nonetheless, they are still essential for anyone who wishes to discover the 'connected body of doctrine' that we shall discuss further below.

18. Origen, *De Principiis*, II, 4, 1; *Origène: Traité des Principes*, vol. I, 276. Origen is here attacking the view propounded by the Marcionites.

19. Kannengiesser ("Origen, Systematician in *De Principiis*," 397ff) believes that the eight chapters of Book I and the first three chapters of Book II of *De Principiis* con-

stitutes the original *De Principiis*, or *De Principiis* proper. He divides this section into three parts. The first part, chapters 1–5, constitutes the definite line of Church teaching. The second part, chapters 6–8, constitutes some of the postponed speculative matters on which Origen said he would expound. The third part, chapters 1-3 of Book II, are a sort of annex to the other two sections. The summary of Book IV. 4 is a recapitulation attached to the end of the original work. Kannengiesser grounds this division on the statement made by Origen at the beginning of chapter 6: "We have previously pointed out what are the subjects on which clear doctrinal statements must be made, and such statements we made, I think to the best of our ability, when speaking on the Trinity. Now, however, we are dealing, as well as we can, with subjects that call for discussion rather than for definition." Relying on this dividing statement and the statements of Origen in the Preface as to his purpose to expound the clear teachings first and postpone speculation until afterward, Kannengiesser makes this the dividing point for the two main sections of *De Principiis* proper. Here is where Origen completed the work he originally outlined in the Preface, with the polemical intent being primarily anti-Valentinian.

The remainder of *De Principiis*, II.4–IV.3, was a later editorial addition, according to Kannengiesser. Origen, focusing more explicitly on an anti-Marcionite polemic, expanded slightly the preface of the work and wrote these many later chapters following once again the original plan. What we have then in the final form of *De Principiis* is two polemical manuscripts written under the same Preface according to the same structural plan. Each work deals with a different problem, but attempts to use the same format and apologetic strategy.

By characterizing Origen's work as two texts belonging to two distinct periods, Kannengiesser is able to find a precise systematically coherent thesis in the original *De Principiis*, thereby demonstrating the systematic capabilities of Origen. Though the later addition is more imprecise and rather clumsily argued, the general outline remains and points again to the logical tendencies of the author. Different concerns called for differing expositions. What we have then in the first exposition is Origen the pure systematician.

My own response to Kannengiesser's thesis is first to question whether his search for the systematic Origen warrants positing such a division of the work, even to the point of denying portions of the text, which are not as cogent and lucid, a place in *De Principiis* "proper." However, such a response is only a criticism of Kannengiesser's historical method and not the subject matter of his thesis. To respond to his thesis in detail would take much more room than is available here. Nonetheless, allow me to make two observations with regard to the text of *De Principiis*. First, Kannengiesser does not seem to pay close enough attention to Origen's statements regarding the clear Church teaching on subjects which he treats subsequent to the Trinity in Book I. The clear line Origen wishes to set down includes the teachings on the nature of "created beings, the dominions and the holy powers"; subjects not treated until what Kannengiesser calls the speculative section. Second, Kannengiesser further does not consider seriously enough the statement of Origen regarding the way the apostolic tradition has come down to his day. I would agree, it seems to fit the statement at the beginning of Book I chapter 6 if we allow chapters 1–5 to be the doctrines delivered in the plainest terms. In other words, the apostles spelled everything out with regard to the Trinity, leaving Origen simply to lay down "fixed and certain conclusions." Book I chapters 6–8 and Book II chapters 1–3 would then constitute doctrines that were simply stated by the apostles as the way things were and in need of explication by those who were "lovers of wisdom." The "discuss-

One final statement must be examined since it is at the center of the debate concerning Origen's systematicity. This statement is the final paragraph of Origen's Preface in which he appears to be restating the plan and purpose of *De Principiis*. He has given the outline of his program of doctrinal explication in the previous paragraphs of the Preface. He now gives us insight into his own method.

> Everyone therefore who is desirous of constructing out of the foregoing [outline of doctrines to be studied] a connected body of doctrine must use points like these as elementary and foundation principles, in accordance with the commandment which says, "Enlighten yourselves with the light of knowledge" (Hosea 10:12, Sept.). Thus by clear and cogent arguments he will discover the truth about each particular point and so will produce, as we have said, a single body of doctrine, with the aid of such illustrations and declarations as he shall find in the holy scriptures and of such conclusions as he shall ascertain to follow logically from them when rightly understood.[20]

Origen has outlined his plan of doctrines he wishes to consider. But as he considers them, he will attempt to do so according to the method he describes here. Whether or not his work measures up to this standard and whether this qualifies his work as systematic are the subject of the next section.

---

ing and investigating" which took place in I.6–8 and II.1–3 is Origen's attempt toward some explanation for these doctrines. However, this is not the end. All of this explication constitutes laying down the clear line of teaching. The further reflection on these initial principles remains for the remainder of Origen's work. I believe Kannengiesser has mistakenly referenced Origen's dividing statement of I. 6 back to the original plan of the entire thesis as it is stated in paragraph 2 of the Preface rather than to the need for some speculative explanation, *even in the initial statements of doctrine* prior to the further reflection, as discussed in paragraph 3. All this is to say that what Kannengiesser takes to be a major division is merely an insertion of Origen's "wisdom" into the overall scheme of the work. He is not making a break, but merely offering reflection and subsequently returning to the original plan.

20. Origen, *De Principiis*, Preface, 10; *Origène: Traité des Principes*, vol. I, 88. It may be possible for one to argue that Origen's work does not seem to fit this exact format in every instance. However, he does certainly try to follow this plan. Though his work may not read as a precise or logical manual of interconnected doctrines, he believes this is the method that characterizes his work.

Origen as Systematician

As mentioned above, the question of systematic method is a relatively modern concern. However, this does not necessitate that such a depiction might not serve a useful purpose when applied to ancient theologians. At the center of the debate over Origen's systematicity is his own characterization of his method. Two schools of interpretation have taken opposing positions in the debate, one decidedly against calling Origen a systematician, the other considers his logical tendencies to be an early form of systematic theology. A third group of interpreters has attempted to take a mediating position between the two schools. The arguments used in support of the theses of the two opposing schools are many and varied. I will attempt to briefly consider some of the main tenets of the arguments below. Let us begin by further examining each of the schools and what exactly their position entails.

Ulrich Berner has capably outlined the two schools of thought and the mediating position with regard to Origen's theological method.[21] One group holds that Origen is indeed a systematic thinker who is attempting to outline his own philosophical understanding of Christian doctrine. The other group believes that Origen is a man of the Church, a mystic whose main concern is to substantiate the authoritative witness of Christian doctrine according to the Tradition and to enable believers

---

21. Berner, *Origenes*. Runia also provides a cogent summary of each position as Berner has classified it; see Runia, *Philo in Early Christian Literature*, 169. Runia's project in identifying the two schools is to discover how each has understood the Philonic influence on Origen, particularly in the area of Origen's exegesis. Much of the debate up to this point in historical studies has centered on the philosophical influence in pedagogical implementation of technical language and methods by Origen. Obviously the two are inter-related, and perhaps the best way to discover philosophical influence is by determining the level of dependence upon a specific "school" of interpretation. Of course, then one would have to determine whether the exegesis was influencing the philosophy, or if the philosophy was influencing the exegesis. Runia rightly points out that this avenue has not yet been developed sufficiently in the debate (170–71). Unfortunately, the analysis below does not contribute to the discussion of exegetical method or to the inter-relationship. The scope of this study is limited more specifically to the idea of a philosophical method or genre having an impact on Origen, if in fact such a genre existed. I am presupposing by this, somewhat hazardously perhaps, that Origen's understanding of philosophy is prior to, or at least foundational for, his exegetical examinations of Christian doctrines. My warrant for this is found in Origen's own desire to set out a method, albeit one he may believe is thoroughly Christian, for his own theological project. He is doing something in *De Principiis* that is very distinct from his commentaries, and he wants his audience to recognize this.

better to understand and live their faith.[22] Two points of contention are consistently held up as focal points for each group in this classification. First, a substantial difference exists in how each group, or individuals within each group, define what is a system and how it is predicated of Origen. Second, each group weighs the significance of *De Principiis* differently. Each of these differences will be examined further below.

What Is a System for Origen?

Once again, it is not hard to understand why a definition of system is perhaps the most important point in the debate. Depending upon how one defines system, it could broadly apply to almost every theologian who has ever written or spoken about God, or it could only apply to the narrowest of methods, which perhaps includes only a few theologians who attempted to do theology as a post-Enlightenment scientific discipline. Neither school can agree upon what definition of systematic is to be applied to Origen. Indeed, one must wonder which depiction is actually coming first, the characterization of Origen or the definition of system. Both schools seem to have a definition they subsequently apply to the theologian in question. However, it appears as though perhaps a prior understanding of Origen has helped to shape each definition. In other words, it appears as though both schools have perhaps formulated their definition of systematic to fit their prior characterization of Origen, i.e., as either logically systematic or pastorally minded. Nevertheless, we will make an attempt to outline the definition of system offered by each school with a view to finding points of convergence and displaying opposing lines of argument.

Origen's System as Philosophy

The definition of system offered by those who consider Origen systematic is founded on the conception of *De Principiis* as primarily a philosophical work written in a manner congruous with the philosophical treatises

---

22. Berner's list of representatives of the first group includes: F. C. Bauer, Bigg, von Harnack, Loofs, de Faye, Miura-Stange, Koch, Karpp, Nygren, Lietzmann, Jonas, Hanson, and Kettler. The second group includes: Bardy, Völker, Lieske, de Lubac, and Crouzel. A mediating position is attempted by Cardiou, Daniélou, Kerr, Harl, and Wickert. Runia also adds Chadwick to the mediating group (see Runia, *Philo in Early Christian Literature*, 169).

being written during his time or perhaps prior to his time.[23] As such, it can be analyzed according to its various philosophical arguments and examined according to how Origen wishes to fit those arguments together, specifically how he wishes to construct a unified whole of Christian doctrine grounded in a philosophical scheme. Historians compare the method of Origen's *De Principiis* with the method of works they consider more specifically philosophical. A crucial marker for Origen's work in this respect is found in the statement of method he makes at the end of his Preface, which we quoted above.[24] This logical construction, when viewed as a parallel of earlier and contemporaneous systematic works of philosophy (followed implicitly or explicitly by Origen), constitutes an ordered whole, which could subsequently also be labeled a system.

This thesis of philosophical parallelism began at least as early as 1932 with Hal Koch's essay, "Pronoia und Paideusis: Studien über Origenes und sein Verhältnis zum Platonismus," though certainly earlier authors had also posited the resemblance.[25] Basilius Steidle picked up on the implications of Koch's thesis and in 1941 was prepared to report "surprising parallels between *Peri Archon* and the contemporary teaching of philosophy."[26] Steidle believed the philosophers of that day followed a pedagogical cycle in their considerations of certain subjects. Origen was following this pattern and presenting his own thought according to the logic of this cyclical method. Based upon this outline of secular thought, and its comparison with Origen's *De Principiis*, Steidle discovered the three divisions of the work to which we alluded above (I.1—II.3; II.4—IV.3; and IV.4).

Two contemporary thinkers have sought to build upon the thought of Steidle. Marguerite Harl added to Steidle's thesis by labeling these divi-

---

23. Kannengiesser outlines the history of this interpretation of Origen's *De Principiis* with particular attention to Basilius Steidle's work. See Kannengiesser, "Origen, Systematician in *De Principiis*," 395ff. Berner traces this interpretation of Origen's project as parallel with philosophy back through several historians in the last two centuries, beginning with the works of Thomasius and Schnitzer in the mid 1830's. See Berner, *Origenes*, 9ff.

24. See n. 20 above.

25. See Berner, *Origenes*, 9ff. One can easily trace the idea of Origen as a systematician back to von Harnack and the editions of his *Dogmengeschichte* from 1885 through 1909 (see the 1909 edition, esp. 662–63, no. 2).

26. Steidle, "Neue Untersuchungen zu Origenes," 240.

sions according to their rhetorical purposes. Gilles Dorival attempted to discover the philosophical evidence that would provide warrant for Steidle's divisions.[27] However, Harl and Dorival still search in vain for any physical evidence of the philosophical parallels that would constitute the classification of Origen's work as belonging to a specific genre of philosophy.

In an interesting twist on the bipartite division of *De Principiis'* main body, Josep Rius-Camps has granted primacy to the second part of Origen's work, even going so far as to call it the "first exposition."[28] He does this largely because he considers the second part to be the more complete, and presumably more valuable, exposition of the doctrines. This seems to be an extreme position and even other authors who advocate the systematicity of Origen's work recognize the inappropriate stress being given to one part of the division over the other.[29]

The only comparative analysis that perhaps demonstrates awareness and use of philosophical categories, which is something different from dependence, is P. M. O'Cleirigh's study "The Meaning of Dogma in Origen."[30] Building on the claims of F. H. Kettler regarding Origen's systematicity, he attempts to demonstrate the historical development of the concept of *dogma* in philosophical systems and Christian thinkers prior to Origen.[31] The use of dogma by the Stoics and the reception of various points of the concept of interconnected ideas by Clement leads O'Cleirigh to believe that Origen was at least aware of such a usage. O'Cleirigh then proceeds to demonstrate from Origen's use of the word dogma in *De Principiis* and in his commentaries that a sense of logical order and interconnectedness still prevailed in Origen's thought.[32] O'Cleirigh is careful

27. Both presented papers on these subjects at the 1973 Colloquia Origeniana. See Harl, "Structure et cohérence de *Peri Archon*," 11–32; and Dorival, "Remarques sur la forme du *Peri Archon*," 33–45.

28. Rius-Camps, *El Peri Archon d'Origenes.*

29. Kannengiesser, "Origen, Systematician in *De Principiis*," 401ff. Kannengiesser is quite uneasy about this parallel between Origen and secular works of philosophy. However, he does see Origen as fitting into the heritage of other authors who have divided their work according to a twofold schema, e.g., Paul, Philo, Justin, Irenaeus, and Clement.

30. O'Cleirigh, "The Meaning of Dogma in Origen," 201–16.

31. See Kettler, *Der ursprüngliche Sinn der Dogmatik des Origenes.*

32. O'Cleirigh, "The Meaning of Dogma in Origen," 210–12. O'Cleirigh is here drawing on Origen's comments with regard to the relationship of the OT to the NT in his argument against Celsus. O'Cleirigh also draws attention to Origen's comparison in his

to distinguish the Christian distinctives of Origen's work. While he may still be employing a category inherited from the philosophical schools of his day, Origen was not simply uncritically adopting their thought or method. He was careful to use Scripture as his overarching authority, and was highly critical of the way in which the philosophers glorified the works of their minds.[33]

Origen's System as Coherence

Another avenue taken in attempting to discover what constitutes systematicity in Origen is to examine his text from the standpoint of internal consistency, rather than comparing it with external examples of other works considered systematic.[34] Of course implicit within such an examination is the definition of system according to criteria such as internal consistency and logical or hierarchical order in presentation. When such a definition is applied to Origen, his remarks on method in the Preface seem to fit quite nicely into the systematic mold this definition creates. As he fleshes out his outline, his considerations of order and his continued reference back to the plan for *De Principiis* give some credence to the claim that he is working systematically.

Attempting to work from a decidedly internal perspective, Kannengiesser pieces together what he believes is a doctrinal patterning of the first section (Book I, chapter 1—Book II, chapter 3) and final Recapitulation (Book IV, chapter 4) of *De Principiis*.[35] He observes that the desires of Origen's teacher, Clement of Alexandria, for a work outlining an apologetic for the true first principles as opposed to those of the middle-Platonic philosophers were finally carried out by Origen.[36] However, Origen further believed his task was to demonstrate the supe-

---

Commentary on Matthew of the Scriptures to "a single musical instrument of which the seemingly different parts all contribute to one saving song" (213).

33. O'Cleirigh, "Meaning of Dogma in Origen," 210–16. Interestingly, O'Cleirigh suggests that Origen's subordination of the Son may have been precisely because he sensed this to be the teaching of Scripture, rather than because he simply adopted the philosophical principle that the effect is less than the cause. Though the principle may have provided the impetus for his thinking, Origen may not have found it contradictory to his understanding of Scripture (215).

34. This appears to be Kannengiesser's primary criterion for evaluating Origen. Cf. Kannengiesser, "Origen, Systematician in *De Principiis*," 397ff.

35. Kannengiesser, "Divine Trinity and the Structure of *Peri Archon*," 231–49.

36. Ibid., 237.

riority of the Triune God of Christianity. As Kannengiesser states, "[I]t is Origen's epoch making initiative as a Christian theologian to have integrated the middle-Platonic traditions on divine principles (αρχαι) into his notion of a Triune Godhead."[37] Kannengiesser goes on to explain how the Trinity is fleshed out in Origen's study, establishing it as the structural motif for the first part and Recapitulation of *De Principiis*, if not for the entire work.[38]

One final point needs to be noted in regard to a way in which the question of Origen's systematicity may be answered. Like Irenaeus in the last chapter, Origen is concerned with harmonizing the teachings of Scripture. As such, he engages in a method quite distinct from his commentaries. He attempts to discuss all the pertinent passages regarding a specific subject. While this may be more technically associated with what, in modern terms, is called Biblical theology, it bears some similarities to systematics in that it is constructed according to an outline not derived from Scripture. The clear line of doctrines laid out by Origen is a grouping of subjects selected with respect to issues Origen wished to address; and they are laid out in a hierarchical fashion for the sake of argument. As will be demonstrated below, this clearly constitutes an apologetic strategy, perhaps even to the point of saying his apologetics were more primary in his organization than a consideration of the hierarchy of doctrines. Nevertheless, his apologetics still follows a pattern external to any Scriptural book or text, giving further credence to the notion that even apologetics is somewhat inherently systematic, or at least arranged on the basis of non-Biblical considerations. Of course, this only addresses the issue of order, which is but one part of the modern definition of system.

---

37. Ibid., 237–38.

38. Ibid., 242-46. Kannengiesser makes it clear that though the second part of *De Principiis* is not structured according to a Trinitarian pattern, it nonetheless depended on the outline given in the first part. As he explains, "[Origen] wanted to have the numerous questions debated in the second exposition framed by a substantial dogmatic statement on divine Trinity, a Trinity considered in itself and in view of a universal salvation" (246).

THE UNSYSTEMATIC NATURE OF ORIGEN'S WORK

In contrast to our discussion of systematicity thus far, as was stated above, another school of thought has developed with regard to whether Origen is systematic. We have outlined the first school and must now turn our attention to the second. In opposition to the characterization of Origen as a systematician, two complementary arguments are offered. The first is a negative criticism of systematicity. The second is a positive alternative understanding of Origen offered as a truer representation of his intentions and his methodical considerations. First, it is argued, Origen cannot be described according to a definition of systematic that has contemporary overtones. Even if we are to grant that Origen had logical tendencies in his thought, this does not constitute a primacy of subscription to a philosophical program, especially if that program is defined by terminology which is loaded with contemporary baggage. Henri Crouzel summarizes this criticism well.

> If reference is made to the definition [of system] in the *Larousse Encyclopedia* (1964, X, 123), "a gathering of principles co-ordinated in such a way as to form a scientific whole or a body of doctrine," it has to be admitted that Origen is not at all systematic. His research theology, the antithetical tensions that he does not bother to balance on the spot, his statements made in inconclusive form, would constitute too many cracks in such an edifice. Anyhow, can a theologian be systematic? How could you confine God in a rational principle and draw logical conclusions from Him, when in his absolute simplicity. He is far beyond the grasp of man, who can only glimpse Him in a multiplicity of ways, some antithetical to others. Let us not forget that Thaumaturgus (*RemOrig* XIV, 158–73) tells us how sharply Origen criticized the broad systems of the philosophers and also how he often accused them of idolatry because they worshiped the work of their minds. So Origen's expositions are rarely systematic even in the *Treatise on First Principles*.[39]

Crouzel's criticism of systematics involves two issues. First, he is concerned about anachronistically discovering a systematic tendency in Origen's method that is a modern development. The definition of system Crouzel wishes to guard Origen against is that which is represented by post-Enlightenment conceptions of what constitutes a system, particularly the rigors of logical consistency in every statement and the building

---

39. Crouzel, *Origen*, 167–68.

up of a wholly interconnected unit of thought.[40] Second, he questions the whole systematic enterprise as it seeks to confine the Infinite within the finite. He does not believe it possible to capture God within a conception encumbered by our finite language and our improbable grasp of God's ontology.

The second response offered by those who do not wish to characterize Origen as a systematician centers around the depiction of Origen as a pastor.[41] According to this position, Origen was primarily concerned with countering false doctrines of the heretics and with giving substance to the true Christian response. As a man of the church, he used philosophical categories and terminology, but only to be able to speak the language of the heretics. Further, he used philosophy in a rather eclectic manner, unlike someone concerned primarily with presenting a system. The quote from his preface should be understood as outlining a way to respond, not a way to build.[42]

Before moving on to discuss the importance of *De Principiis* in Origen's thought, we should first attempt to settle the matter of what definition is usefully applied to Origen. Certainly, we must agree with Crouzel that it would be inappropriate to apply a modern conception of system to a figure of late Antiquity. Likewise, we would not wish to characterize Origen according to a thoroughgoing rationalism when most

40. One cannot help but hear echoes of Kant's "Transcendental Dialectic" from his *Critique of Pure Reason* or Hegel's "Absolute knowledge" in Crouzel's criticism. It is also possible to perceive in this criticism an anti-scholastic preoccupation. This is made explicit in the commentary of *Origène: Traité des Principes*, vol. II, 10–11.

41. Henri de Lubac (De Lubac, "Introduction," to the Torchbook edition of *De Principiis*, x) illustrates this line of thought well when he states, "We must rid ourselves of the view, still far too common, which presents Origen as almost entirely an intellectual, esoteric and rationalizing, and see him as the man of the spirit, the apostle, the man of the Church which he was above all else."

42. Crouzel, *Origen*, 167–68. Crouzel certainly recognizes the philosophical heritage from which Origen draws much of his thought and in which he is couching his arguments (cf. Crouzel, *Origène et la Philosophie*, 214–15). The interpretive difference comes from how he believes Origen uses the teachings of the philosophers. Crouzel believes Origen pursues what the former calls a "research" theology (*Origen*, 163ff.). According to this plan, Origen's primary impetus for doing theology is the desire to search the depths of the wisdom discovered in Christian Scripture and doctrine. (Also cf. Crouzel's "Introduction" to *Origène: Traité des Principes*, vol. I, 46ff.) Interestingly, Crouzel does believe that the philosophers of Origen's day worked within "systems" of thought (*Origen*, 158ff.). Crouzel believes that Origen simply picked through these systems using what was salvageable for his own pastoral project.

commentators would agree that his primary interests were pastoral, even within the text of *De Principiis*. However, there is no reason to believe that these precautions are *necessarily* antithetical to the broader conception of a system outlined above as internally consistent and methodologically ordered. We may even fairly say Origen was aware of the relationship between the parts and the whole in Christian doctrine and sought to devise a scheme in which to display that relationship. What we must wrestle against here is the caricature of both the systematician and the third century pastor. To depict the systematician as a model builder who cannot recognize approximation in theological language and is never satisfied with anything but a complete and thorough classification of all reality is to define systematic so narrowly that it is impossible to conceive of anyone who would fit this definition. Likewise, to define pastoral concerns as somehow antithetical to or unconcerned with questions of logic and order is to miss one of the primary duties of a third century pastor for his listening, and reading, audience. A pastor in the early centuries of Christianity could hardly avoid responding to the movements that challenged the more traditional teachings of the Church, and most often these challenges, though couched in Christian rhetoric, were replete with philosophical doctrines, requiring just as philosophical a response. Indeed, it is a question as to whether one could tell the difference between philosophical presuppositions and Christian doctrine. As Henry Chadwick notes with regard to Origen,

> So sensitive is he to the charge of adulterating Christianity with Platonism that his attitude to Plato and the great philosophers becomes prickly and even aggressively rude. He wanted to be a Christian, not a Platonist. Yet Platonism was inside him, *malgré lui,* absorbed into the very axioms and presuppositions of his thinking. Moreover, this penetration of his thought by Platonism is no merely external veneer of apologetic. Platonic ways of thinking about God and the soul are necessary to him if he is to give an intelligible account of his Christian beliefs.[43]

Origen used philosophical categories and terminology, perhaps even philosophical method, whether he recognized it or not. Indeed, one must put the question back to Crouzel, can anyone escape using philosophy if he/she wishes to write theology, even pastoral theology. Certainly, Origen is attempting to give specifically Christian answers to the ques-

---

43. Chadwick, *Early Christian Thought and the Classical Tradition,* 122.

tions being considered by the philosophers and the Gnostic heretics, and he was doing this out of concern for those who might be ensnared from true Christian doctrine into their teaching. However, he does still appear to be using a method and order that are not specifically Christian, at least they are not dictated by Scripture.[44] Granted, the explicit evidence of a philosophical genre seems wanting, but this does not negate the fact that he has laid out a specific method that has philosophical foundations and he uses argumentation steeped in philosophical overtones. Daniélou captures this tendency well when he states

> There were certain problems which [Origen] shared in common with the philosophers of his time; we have noticed some of them in connection with the ideas of God, the world, demonology, the soul, and allegory. But within the framework of the common set of problems, Origen's mind pursued a course diametrically opposed to the one taken by the pagan philosophers. They were alike in that they asked the same questions, but the answers they gave were fundamentally different.[45]

If we take Origen's closing remarks in the Preface seriously, we must grant that he is attempting to explicate the doctrines of the Church in an orderly fashion consistent with the logic and reasoning used by theologians and philosophers alike in the early third century. This is most certainly not a systematic effort if one is defining system according to the modern notion of systematic, including, at least, inflated claims regarding human knowledge of God. However, if one defines system more broadly according to a method that is internally consistent and carefully ordered, Origen's *De Principiis* would most certainly fit within this classification. But can we regard *De Principiis* as the most representative work of Origen? That is the question of our next section.

---

44. Kannengiesser ("Divine Trinity," 238–47, esp. 246–47) claims that this method is simply an adaptation of the middle-Platonic theory of first principles. However, he is unwilling to go so far as Robert Berchman (Berchman, *From Philo to Origen*) who claims that Origen was "the consummation of Middle Platonic thought" (100), or that he "formally argued his first principles, and demonstrated a Middle Platonic theoretic and epistemology from the premises of this sacred scripture" (251).

45. Daniélou, *Origen*, 99.

The Place of De Principiis in Origen's Writings

Since the work of Origen in *De Principiis* is laid out according to a plan and has the explicit goal of providing a sort of unified whole of Christian doctrine, those who wish to find systematic tendencies in Origen focus primarily on this work. Those who do not understand Origen to be a systematician wish to place this work in the larger whole of Origen's written works and in the context of a person filled with pastoral concern.[46] What becomes clearer in the debate is not so much the question of what is the true Origenist thought, rather it is the bias of the historian influencing the interpretation of Origen's thought. As we have seen, one group considers him a systematician. Another group considers him a pastor. Each interpretation of Origen's personality seems to be the overarching concern when deciding which works are most representative of his thought.[47] This leads the systematic group to believe that *De Principiis* is perhaps his most developed and complete theological position. The pastoral group believes this work to be apologetic in nature and serving a more focused purpose. Accordingly, *De Principiis* was written with a temporal circumstance in mind, not intended to become an enduring work of theological prominence, as he perhaps intended his commentaries.

Once again it seems as though the purposes of each school may not be entirely antithetical to one another. It is certain that Origen would have deemed his work usable against any recurrence of the heresies he intended to refute. But on another level, it is extremely difficult to imagine that at the time he wrote this work he considered it a comprehensively "eternal" or "universal" document in the same sense as the theological works of eighteenth and nineteenth century rationalism. Perhaps he was optimistic about his explications of doctrine, hoping they would serve future generations, but he was quite ready to admit that other explanations may be found that would refute his speculations.[48] He was aware of

---

46. Crouzel, *Origen*, 168-69. Crouzel outlines the faulty history of the interpretation of the importance of *De Principiis* in isolation from Origen's larger context.

47. I am not here accusing either side of psycho-analyzing Origen. They are attempting to work from the texts. However, the picture of Origen as a vocationally specific person has not allowed some on both sides to consider the possibility that one person could be consistently fulfilling two strategic tasks at the same time.

48. Origen appears to be especially modest on several occasions, for example in his closing remarks on the nature of God (I.1, 9), the nature of Jesus Christ (I.2, 13), Scripture (IV.3, 15); plus his desire to proceed on certain subjects according to a course of discussion rather than definition (I.6, 1). One wonders if perhaps these statements of

his limitations, as all good theologians should be, and he wrote for the people of his time.

What all this means is that he did have explicitly apologetic intentions in mind when he wrote *De Principiis*. But that does not preclude his belief that he could structure his explications of doctrine so that they might serve future generations in their speculations and their consideration of the truths the "apostles" and the "Church" taught. He did not believe he was setting in stone the eternal truth once given for all ages. He was modest about his own task and the possibility of his understanding the wisdom he was exploring. Nevertheless, he could not give up pursuing each line of thought to its logical end, limited only by his own abilities and inabilities. In this sense, one might consider him a model systematic theologian, one from whom we could all learn a lesson in both method and modesty.

Conclusion

The study above has given us a brief glimpse at what constitutes a theological method of an ante-Nicene Church Father. But perhaps even more importantly, we have observed that this method was complementary to the pastoral tasks paramount in Origen's mind. He does represent a type of modestly systematic theologian, perhaps even the archetype of what a systematic theologian should be. However, the concerns of those who would wish to understand him in more pastoral terms must be noted. If systematicity means doing theology for the sake of simply developing a coherent structure that exists solely for its own sake or claims comprehensive, even final, knowledge regarding God, then certainly Origen was not a systematician. However, if system is defined, as we have above, in terms allowing for pastoral concerns to be met in the logical method of a coherent unity, then Origen seems to fit within this characterization. Origen used an orderly method to meet his overarching need of a pastoral response to the influence of heretical teachings. The result was a monumental work that continues to give us insight into the formation of the Tradition we call Christian.

---

modesty have been added by Rufinus to make Origen's work more palatable to his critics. However, Crouzel offers a fairly convincing defense of Origen's modest statements. See Crouzel, *Origen*, 164ff.

3

Theology Becomes Politics

Constantine and the Nicene Council

The Reign of Constantine in the Church

Toleration

THE FIRST FEW CENTURIES OF THE CHURCH WERE MARKED BY MANY different claims of Christian identity. However, none seemed to engender more disdain from those within the church than the accusation of one as a *traditore* (someone who gave up the Scriptures for burning, rather than suffer some form of torture, and perhaps even martyrdom) or as having *lapsed* (one who had rejected faith in Christ when threatened with physical harm or death). The pure church included only those who could faithfully claim they had not compromised their commitment to Christ under the threat of punishment. While the actual threat of martyrdom was fairly inconsistent during the earliest centuries of the church, its presence was always looming. Each generation had its own stories of those who had stood fast and those who had lapsed when threatened with physical harm or death. Though the actual number of martyrs is relatively small, their faith set the standard for the church. To be a Christian meant demonstrating a willingness to face any persecution as the apostles had once done, even to the point of giving one's life for the faith.

In the spring of AD 311, the fortunes of the Christian church were about to change. Galerius, the ruler of the eastern Roman Empire, issued an edict of toleration for the Christian practice of religion. In 312, Constantine, after having visions of a Christian cross and symbol that promised victory, conquered Maxentius at the Milvian bridge outside of Rome. This conquest made Constantine the sole ruler throughout the western Roman Empire. Early in 313, Constantine met with Licinius (eventual conqueror of Maximin Daia, Galerius' successor) at Milan. They came to terms in a letter to be issued regarding the practice of Christian religion. Since it was perceived as relatively harmless and could promote unity within the empire, Christianity was recognized as a legal faith within the Roman Empire. In what is known as the Edict of Milan, both Augusti agreed that

> [N]o one should be denied the opportunity of devoting himself either to the cult of the Christians or to whatever religion he himself felt most suitable for himself, so that the highest Divinity, whose religion we obey with free minds, can exhibit to us in all things his customary favor and benevolence . . . Since you see that this has been granted to the same by us, your Excellency understands that, for the sake of peace in our time, free and open liberty of religion or cult has been similarly granted to others, in order that every individual may have unrestrained opportunity to pursue what worship he chooses.[1]

Latter portions of the Edict proceeded to restore seized property and places of worship to the churches. Constantine's reasons for tolerating the Christian faith, and for going so far as to return their property, may have been manifold. However, two seem to be suggested most prominently by scholars. First, it is believed that Constantine was simply recognizing the strength and size of the Christian populace, and therefore his toleration is politically motivated to help substantiate and solidify support for his rule.[2] This may have especially been the case following his defeat of Maxentius, who had suppressed, tortured and killed the Christians at Rome. If Eusebius' account of Maxentius' behavior is ac-

---

1. Eusebius, *Ecclesiastical History*, X.5.5–8.

2. Smith, *Constantine the Great*, 145; Charles Cochrane (*Christianity and Classical Culture*, 214–15) also seems to attribute Constantine's favor of the Christian religion to political aspirations. For a brief discussion of the reasons for opposing the political interpretation and favoring a religious one for Constantine's favor of Christianity, see Keresztes, *Constantine A Great Christian Monarch and Apostle*, 41; Dörries, *Constantine the Great*, 43ff; and Alföldi, *The Conversion of Constantine and Pagan Rome*, 1–24.

It is likely that the Christian population at the beginning of Constantine's reign was only about one-tenth the total population of the Roman Empire. But within a century, due primarily to imperial favor of Christianity and the eventual legislation against paganism, Christians comprised the majority of the population. See Neusner, *Judaism and Christianity in the Age of Constantine*, 14–18.

curate, the Christians would have been ecstatic to receive Constantine as their deliverer:

> Having grabbed the Imperial city, [Maxentius] was most daring in his acts of impiety and wickedness . . . He would, for example, separate lawful wives from their husbands, and insulting them most shamefully he would send them back to their husbands. He practiced this drunken behavior not toward common and obscure men, but to those who held the first places in the Roman Senate. Although he shamefully dishonored a great number of free women, nevertheless he was unable to satisfy his intemperate and undisciplined spirit. But when he made attempts against Christian women, he was no longer able to contrive an easy way to adultery. For they would rather lose their lives than submit their bodies to him for corruption . . . And even though [all men] kept quiet and suffered the bitter slavery, there was still no deliverance from the bloody cruelty of the tyrant. Once, for example, on some trifling pretense, he let the people be slaughtered by his own body-guard, and countless multitudes of the Roman people were slain in the very middle of the city by the spears and weapons, not of the Scythians and barbarians, but of their own fellow-citizens. It is, besides, impossible to count how many senators were murdered with a view to the seizure of their own estates, for at times multitudes were put to death on various fabricated charges.
>
> The greatest of the tyrants crimes was that he had recourse to sorcery, when, for the purposes of magic, he, at times, ripped up women with child, but at other times he searched into the inward parts of new-born babies, and slew lions and was engaged in some abominable practices for evoking demons and averting the war. For he hoped that by these means he would gain victory.[3]

As is evident from this quote, Maxentius was indiscriminate in his oppression. He killed and tortured both Christians and non-Christians alike. Thus it is not surprising that both Christians and non-Christians celebrated Constantine's triumphal entry into Rome.[4]

The fortunes of Christians in the east would not be transformed as quickly as those of the Christians in the west. Licinius was slow to proclaim the Edict of Milan, and many of his supporters were old

---

3. Eusebius, *Life of Constantine*, I.33–36. The cited translation is from Keresztes, *Constantine*, 14–15.

4. Lactantius, *De Mortibus Persecutorum*, 44.

Roman, meaning they did not support the toleration of Christians.[5] If Constantine foresaw the delays and eventual open hostility of Licinius toward Christians, it would have been politically prudent for him to demonstrate open acceptance of Christianity. His half of the empire would have looked much more attractive than the oppression occurring in the east, making eventual conquest and rule of the eastern empire much easier.[6] Another reason to consider Constantine's toleration of Christians as politically motivated is that though he professed to be a Christian, he waited until just before his death to receive baptism.[7]

A second reason that is offered for Constantine's openness toward Christianity is that he professed Christianity as his own religion. The reasoning behind this claim begins with his Christian visions (conversion?) prior to and during the conquest of Maxentius at the Milvian bridge. This was followed by declarations of toleration for Christianity, presumably motivated from some type of devotion to the Christian God. Constantine eventually made it clear in various proclamations that he wished to be considered a Christian. He finally took part in and convened various councils, Nicea (325) being the most prominent. During this period, Constantine appears to believe himself to be a guardian of the church, in many respects, similar to the role of the bishops within the church, though he himself was responsible for both Christians and non-Christians in the Roman Empire.[8]

5. Keresztes, *Constantine*, 45ff.

6. Grant, *Augustus to Constantine*, 239. Relying primarily on Eusebian record of Constantine's correspondences and the activities surrounding them, Keresztes (*Constantine*, 102–11) records the oppressions by Licinius and his eventual defeat by Constantine. After Constantine defeated Licinius, he issued several edicts relieving the oppression of Christians in the east.

7. Keresztes (*Constantine*, 167ff.) devotes several paragraphs to a defense of Constantine's Christian profession, despite his delayed baptism. Keresztes' reasoning is dependent primarily on the statements of Constantine at his baptism and what Keresztes believes is by this time a common practice of delaying baptism until the end of life. This would provide for a "clean slate" just before death, meaning no sins would follow the soul into the afterlife.

8. Jones, *Constantine and the Conversion of Europe*, 169–81. The thrust of many works regarding the life of Constantine has been to demonstrate and defend his Christian belief. Such an interpretation was first given by Eusebius of Caesarea in both his *Ecclesiastical History* and *Life of Constantine*. However, contemporary authors are no less prone to extol the commitment of Constantine to the God of the Christians and the Christianizing of the Roman Empire (e.g., Keresztes, *Constantine*).

Answering the questions concerning Constantine's Christian commitment is of little import for this study. What is important is that he demonstrated obvious favor toward Christianity, even to the point of using his office to further goals and purposes of the church. It is at this point in history that the church takes a decidedly different turn in its relationship with the state. Theology had functioned as a marker for true belief. Further, public confessions of faith served to provide warrant for martyrdom. However, the church had always been outside the workings of the state. She had previously been either opposed or tolerated, but never invited in as a positive force in the rule of the state. With Constantine, all this changed. How this change took place is the focus of our next section.

Calls for Unity

One of the reasons it is difficult to measure the reasons for Constantine's initial toleration of Christianity is that his edicts were couched in calls for unity within the Empire. As quoted above in the Edict of Milan, Constantine's toleration was "for the sake of peace in our time."[9] Further examination of Constantine's letters/edicts during the early period of his reign demonstrates that he believed toleration would help sustain unity within the empire.[10] Whether he may also have a commitment to the Christian God is another issue. What is clear is that unity was of great importance to him for his continued rule.

The Donatists

It is not long after Constantine became sole ruler of the western half of the Empire that he learned of a schism within the church. He had previously assumed that the church was "one united body of Christians, distinguishable from adherents of other religious cults."[11] However, Constantine, now in control of Africa, soon learned that the church in that region was not at all unified. Constantine's concerns for unity, and perhaps his desire for the church to be a true witness to the love

9. Eusebius, *Ecclesiastical History*, X.5.5–8.

10. Though attributing Constantine's concern to his Christian commitment, Keresztes (*Constantine*, 38–57) recounts several letters displaying Constantine's concern for unity and peace within the western half of the Empire.

11. Grant, *Augustus to Constantine*, 236.

of Christ, led him to become involved in settling the dispute. Thus, Constantine began to direct a resolution to the Donatist schism. Though the origins of the schism may be traced back to 305, the situation in which Constantine intervened began in 311 when Majorinus was made rival bishop of Carthage. The existing bishop, Caecilian, was eventually declared the legitimate bishop by a court of church bishops on October 2, 313. Donatus of Casae Nigrae was excommunicated since he was the leader of the opposition. Not satisfied with the results of this court, the Donatists (owing their name to either this Donatus or the next schismatic bishop of Carthage) asked the emperor Constantine for a new trial, thus appealing to the state to intervene in the church. Constantine complied by providing public transportation for church bishops from various regions to the next meeting. The synod at Arles in August of 314 expanded its scope both in terms of the number of bishops and their representation of various regions and in the subject matter under consideration. While the Donatist schism was considered and finally condemned, several other issues both practical and theological were discussed.[12] A precedent was now established regarding the resolution of schism within the church. Though the Donatist schism was never completely resolved by the courts or synods, a similar pattern for resolution was used by Constantine and the church in the face of the next great debate.[13]

THE ARIANS

When Constantine conquered Licinius in 324, he hoped to find a unified church in the east—one that could help him restore the unity of the church in Africa. Instead, what he found was a church embroiled in controversy and suffering from its own schismatic problems. As Constantine explained in his letter to the two primary adversaries, Alexander and Arius,

12. Keresztes (*Constantine*, 62–68) records various correspondence regarding the convening and transactions of the Council.

13. Constantine himself recognized that the schism had not been squelched when on May 5, 321, he issued a rescript to the vicar of Africa, declaring that no further persecution of the Donatists should take place. About the same time he wrote a letter to the bishops of Africa expressing his regret that his work had not led to the promotion of peace and unity. God would finally judge the Donatist schism and bring it to an end Himself. See Grant, *Augustus to Constantine*, 238–39.

> . . . I had a twofold reason for undertaking that duty which I
> have now performed. My design was, first, to bring the diverse
> judgments formed by all nations respecting the Deity to a condi-
> tion, as it were, of settled uniformity; and, secondly, to restore
> to health the system of the world, then suffering under the ma-
> lignant power of a grievous distemper. Keeping these objects in
> view, I sought to accomplish the one by the secret eye of thought,
> while the other I tried to rectify by the power of military author-
> ity . . . Finding, then, that the whole of Africa was pervaded by
> an intolerable spirit of mad folly, through the influence of those
> who with heedless frivolity had presumed to rend the religion of
> the people into diverse sects; I was anxious to check this disor-
> der, and could discover no other remedy equal to the occasion,
> except in sending some of yourselves to aid in restoring mutual
> harmony among the disputants, after I had removed the com-
> mon enemy of mankind [Licinius] who had interposed his law-
> less sentence for the prohibition of your holy synods . . . But, O
> glorious Providence of God, how deep a wound did not my ears
> only, but my very heart receive in the report that divisions existed
> among yourselves more grievous still than those which contin-
> ued in that country; so that you, through whose aid I had hoped
> to procure a remedy for the errors of others, are in a state which
> needs healing even more than theirs.[14]

The church in the east was in the midst of a schismatic debate that, in
Constantine's opinion, was causing even worse division than the schism
in Africa. While the specifics of the debate are well known and not relevant for our study, we must pay specific attention to how Constantine
responds to this schism. Whereas previously he had provided the context
in which to resolve division, he now took it upon himself to personally
resolve the Arian debate. Continuing his letter to Alexander and Arius,
he writes:

> Feeling myself, therefore, compelled to address you in this letter,
> and to appeal at the same time to your unanimity and sagacity, I
> call on Divine Providence to assist me in the task, while I inter-
> rupt your dissension in the character of a minister of peace. And
> with reason: for if I might expect, with the help of a higher Power,
> to be able without difficulty, by a judicious appeal to the pious
> feelings of those who heard me, to recall them to a better spirit,
> even though the occasion of the disagreement were a greater one,
> how can I refrain from promising myself a far easier and more

14. Eusebius, *Life of Constantine*, II.64–68.

speedy adjustment of this difference, when the cause which hin-
ders general harmony of sentiment is intrinsically trifling and of
little moment?[15]

Constantine continued in the remainder of the letter to address the need
for unity. However, he did not seem to understand the depth and com-
plexity of the differences between Alexander and Arius at this point. He
appealed to them to set aside this "trifling" issue as though it were of little
import to the faith. As he continues,

> Let therefore both the unguarded question and the inconsiderate
> answer receive your mutual forgiveness. For the cause of your
> difference has not been any of the leading doctrines or precepts
> of the Divine law, nor has any new heresy respecting the worship
> of God arisen among you. You are in truth of one and the same
> judgment: you may therefore well join in communion and fel-
> lowship . . . But I will refresh your minds by a little illustration,
> as follows. You know that the philosophers, though they all ad-
> here to one system, are yet frequently at issue on certain points,
> and differ, perhaps, in their degree of knowledge: yet they are
> recalled to harmony of sentiment by the uniting power of their
> common doctrines. If this be true, is it not far more reasonable
> that you, who are the ministers of the supreme God, should be of
> one mind respecting the profession of the same religion?[16]

Constantine obviously did not have a firm grasp yet on what was the
difference between Alexander and Arius.[17] What is perhaps more interesting from this statement for our study is the way in which Constantine
conceived of the faith as similar to the beliefs of the philosophers. Whether
or not his comparison is accurate, it is still interesting that he depicts the
doctrines of the philosophers as something that can be considered as a
whole unit consisting of distinct parts (doctrines). Constantine's conception of resolution seems to reflect a belief that the faith of the Christians
can be defined as a whole in fairly clear terms, while still maintaining
some distinctions in the various doctrines. While he was still obviously
concerned for preserving orthodoxy, Constantine was willing to allow
for some flexibility in doctrines he did not consider crucial to the united

15. Ibid., II.68.
16. Ibid., II.70–71.
17. Keresztes, *Constantine*, 123.

front of Christianity. Certainly this was a fairly naive approach to the Arian problem by Constantine, but it seems likely that the Nicene creed was an attempt to fulfill these expectations for unity in system, with difference in particulars. Constantine appears to have believed relative unity in the theological system or summary represented by the creed would likewise bring about social unity in the Empire, at least amongst Christians.

After learning of the schisms of Colluthus and Melitius, Constantine decided to call a council to settle all the schismatic problems facing the church, in particular the Arian controversy. Originally to be held at Ancyra, it was later changed to Nicea, which was a much better location. This council was preceded by the Council of Antioch, which took upon itself not only to settle on a successor to Philogonius, bishop of Antioch, but also produced a decidedly anti-Arian creed. This set the stage for Constantine's council at Nicea to settle the questions regarding Arianism in the church. Hosius (or Ossius), Constantine's ecclesiastical adviser, had presided over the Council of Antioch. The great Council of Nicea was overseen by the Emperor himself. Eusebius records for us the opening ceremonies including the Emperor's entrance and opening address to the Council, calling them to peace and unity.[18] A detailed account of the proceedings at Nicea is not available to us. However, from what can be pieced together from the correspondence that surrounded the Council, it seems apparent that Constantine not only presided over the Council, but even participated by suggesting that "homoousios" be added to the creed to make it absolute in its opposition to the Arian interpretation of the second person of the Trinity.[19]

Unity and Unified Knowledge Enforced by the State

Shortly after the Council of Nicea concluded, Constantine addressed letters to the church and to certain groups of heretics. The letters to the churches simply explained the results of the Council and exhorted the churches to unify in their worship and belief. He also wrote a letter establishing a single date on which to celebrate Easter. The letter to the heretics was quite direct and specific about its import.

18. Eusebius, *Life of Constantine*, III.6–12.

19. Athanasius records the letter of Eusebius of Caesarea to his church, in which Eusebius indicated that Constantine had inserted the word "Consubstantial." See Athanasius, *Epistola Eusebii*, 4.

Constantine addressed this letter to the "Novatians, Valentinians, Marcionites, Paulians [of Samosata], and you who are called Phrygians [Montanists], and all you who devise and support heresies by means of your private assemblies."[20] Though not addressed specifically to the Arians or Donatists, since they had supposedly been dealt with or left to the judgment of God, certainly they are aware that this letter's contents could be directed toward them in the future, if they were not reconciled to the church.[21] The text of the letter and its directions for how to handle these heresies are of primary interest for our study.

> Forasmuch, then, as it is no longer possible to bear with your pernicious errors, we give warning by this present statute that none of you henceforth presume to assemble yourselves together. We have directed, accordingly, that you be deprived of all the houses in which you are accustomed to hold your assemblies: and our care in this respect extends so far as to forbid the holding of your superstitious and senseless meetings, not in public merely, but in any private house or place whatsoever. Let those of you, therefore, who are desirous of embracing the true and pure religion, take the far better course of entering the catholic Church, and uniting with it in holy fellowship, whereby you will be enabled to arrive at the knowledge of the truth . . . And in order that this remedy may be applied with effectual power, we have commanded, as before said, that you be positively deprived of every gathering point for your superstitious meetings, I mean all the houses of prayer, if such be worthy of the name, which belong to heretics, and that these be made over without delay to the catholic Church; that any other places be confiscated to the public service, and no facility whatever be left for any future gathering; in order that from this day forward none of your unlawful assemblies may presume to appear in any public or private place. Let this edict be made public.[22]

Though Constantine had previously intervened and even made proclamation regarding the Donatist schism, he is here taking his resolution a step further by confiscating the meeting places of the various heresies. These are smaller heresies than the Arian schism, but such an Imperial act serves as a warning to the followers of Arius. Arius had been excommunicated at the Council of Nicea, but Constantine was unwilling to al-

20. Eusebius, *Life of Constantine*, III.64.

21. Keresztes, *Constantine*, 137.

22. Eusebius, *Life of Constantine*, III.65.

low the Arian controversy to dispel itself or be handled by the bishops of the church. He became quite proactive on behalf of what he believed to be the orthodox position. In a letter to the catholic church of Nicomedia, he makes it clear he is exiling two bishops for their support of the excommunicated Arius. Regarding the prominent bishops Eusebius of Nicomedia and Theognius, he writes:

> But to pass over the rest of his depravity, please hear what he [Eusebius], a short while ago, carried through with Theognius, the accomplice of his madness. I had ordered some Alexandrians who had fallen away from our faith to be sent to this place, because, through their activity, the torch of dissent was blazing up. But these excellent bishops, whom the truth of the council once brought back to repentance, not only received them, but also consorted with them in their depraved ways. Therefore, I decided to do this concerning these ungrateful people: I ordered them to be seized and banished to a place that is as far away as possible. Now it is your duty that you look to God with that faith which is known to have always existed, and ought to exist, and that you conduct yourselves in such a way that we may rejoice in having holy, orthodox and dutiful bishops. If anybody dares, thoughtlessly, to go so far as to revive the memory of or praise those destructive persons, he will be immediately restrained in his boldness by the power of the servant of God, that is, mine.[23]

The people of the churches at Nicomedia and Nicea listened and elected new bishops. Eusebius and Theognius were eventually allowed to return to their sees, but not until they had submitted to Constantine and proven full acceptance of the Nicene creed, particularly the meaning of the term Consubstantial.[24] Constantine continued his mission of unifying the faith according to the creed by writing to Theodotus, a bishop who supported Arius and was previously excommunicated at the Council of Antioch. In the letter, Constantine simply reminded him of what happened to Eusebius and Theognius when they disagreed with the orthodox creed. Apparently, Theodotus heeded the warning and agreed to the creed.[25] Constantine then took up the task of bringing Arius himself back to the fold, inviting him in 326 to the palace to discuss the issues.[26]

23. Athanasius, *De Decretis*, 41; as cited by Keresztes, *Constantine*, 140.
24. Keresztes, *Constantine*, 140-41, esp. n. 48.
25. Ibid., 140–41.
26. Ibid., 141–42.

While we don't know if any such meeting took place, we do know that Arius attempted to regain his position by offering an alternative creed.[27] This creed was somewhat vague and didn't address the crucial issue of Consubstantiality. However, Constantine relented and wrote to bishop Alexander of Alexandria to re-admit Arius to the church. In his letter to Alexander, Constantine states that Arius was "professing that he has the same views concerning the Catholic faith as were defined and confirmed by you at the Council of Nicea."[28] It is unclear whether Constantine was willing to accept the alternative creed offered by Arius or if Arius had actually professed agreement with the Nicene creed. Whatever the case, Alexander did not believe Arius was truly in agreement. This was the beginning of a struggle over Arianism and unity in the church between Constantine and Alexander. Alexander's successor, Athanasius, was eventually dismissed as bishop of Alexandria, partly because of his un-willingness to re-admit Arius. Alexander and Athanasius did not believe that the former pro-Arian bishops or Arius himself had actually come to agree with the Nicene creed. Instead, they felt that Arius and his follow-ers had simply succumbed to the threats of Constantine and the pres-sures of being excluded from the church.[29]

As is evident from our discussion above, the creed became a tool in the hands of the state. Though perhaps Constantine's aggressive pursuit of unity was born from a heartfelt desire to see God's church prosper, the means by which he accomplished unity was state induced coercion. In other words, while the church may have been the primary concern in Constantine's mind, which remains questionable, he was using his posi-tion as Emperor to accomplish goals of the church.[30] The creed served

27. For Arius' letter to Constantine containing this creed, see Socrates, *Ecclesiastical History*, I.26, and Sozomen, *The Ecclesiastical History of Sozomen*, II.27.

28. Cited by Keresztes, *Constantine*, 143.

29. Ibid., 142–66. Keresztes records the various correspondence and edicts that re-sulted in what he believes is a deception of Constantine by the pro-Arian bishops and finally Athanasius' exile by Constantine.

30. When some of Arius' followers, the Meletians, were attempting to have Athan-asius exiled by Constantine for actions he had in fact not done, Constantine warns them with civil punishment. Writing to Athanaius, Constantine states, "And finally, I will add, I wish this letter to be read frequently by your wisdom in public, that it may thereby come to the knowledge of all men, and especially reach the ears of those who thus act, and thus raise disturbances . . . Wherefore . . . I have come to this determination, that if they excite any further commotion of this kind, I will myself in person take cognizance of the matter, and that not according to the ecclesiastical, but according to the civil laws,

as the standard by which the state could measure orthodoxy, not unlike the oaths of allegiance given by prior generations of faithful Romans to the Emperor. Christian theology had evolved from its position as the schismatic disease of the Empire into an integral part of the design of Imperial identity. Though one need not necessarily be a Christian to be a Roman citizen, the Emperor now considered Christian allegiance an important attribute for the Empire. He became the one who protected orthodoxy and sought unity in the church. Doctrinal considerations that were once only the concerns of theologians for the sake of Christian identity were now under the influence of the Emperor for the sake of ecclesiastical orthodoxy, dare we even say Imperial orthodoxy. Theology is now wed to politics. But what does this theology look like?

Creed as Theology and Apology

The earliest creeds likely derived from baptismal formulae in specific regions. They were not initially used to measure the standard of orthodoxy within each community. Instead, they were pedagogical tools to help instruct and indoctrinate novices into the church. As Frances Young makes clear, "Creeds did not originate, then, as 'tests of orthodoxy', but as summaries of faith taught to new Christians by their local bishop, summaries that were traditional to each local church and which in detail varied from place to place."[31] The earliest baptismal formulae were likely interrogatory creeds divided into three parts. In his *Apostolic Tradition*, Ps.-Hippolytus (170–236) records an early tripartite baptismal formula:

> Dost thou believe in God, the Father Almighty?

> Dost thou believe in Christ Jesus, the Son of God, who was born of the Holy Ghost of the Virgin Mary, and was crucified under Pontius Pilate, and was dead and buried, and rose again the third day, alive from the dead, and ascended into heaven, and sat at the right hand of the Father, and will come to judge the quick and the dead?

---

and so I will in future find them out, because they clearly are robbers, so to speak, not only against human kind, but against the divine doctrine itself" (Athanasius, *Defence against the Arians*, 68).

31. Young, *Making of the Creeds*, 3.

> Dost thou believe in the Holy Ghost, and the holy church, and the resurrection of the flesh?[32]

These three questions seem clearly patterned after the command to baptize in the name of the Father, Son, and Holy Spirit given to the disciples in the Gospel of Matthew (28:19). It is likely that the candidate was submerged after giving an appropriate response to each question, three times in all. While it remains uncertain how the interrogatory baptismal creeds evolved into the more declaratory creeds of the late third century, we do know that the practice of reciting a creed and answering creedal questions prior to baptism remained a practice even well after the development of declaratory creeds. It is also likely that the tripartite shape of later declaratory creeds derived from the baptismal formulae.[33]

Regarding the content of each creed, whether interrogatory or declaratory, no fixed formula was agreed upon by the entire church until the fourth century. Prior to that, each community had formulated its own creed with specific attention being given to each local context. However, some common language was used by the authors of these various creeds and the Father, Son, Holy Spirit pattern was a constant. Scripture provided a familiar language, as did the writings of later theologians. As was seen in the first chapter above, Irenaeus and Tertullian, among others, relied on the rule of faith. This rule was not a fixed statement of faith, but rather a context specific summary of the faith.[34] Within each community, creeds were designed to give converts a concise summary of the faith that is proclaimed in Scripture. This was necessary, as Cyril of Jerusalem (318–386) explained, "For since all cannot read the Scriptures, some being hindered as to the knowledge of them by want of learning, and others by a want of leisure, in order that the soul may not perish from ignorance, we comprise the whole doctrine of the Faith in a few lines."[35] This "summary" of the faith was to be committed to memory and treasured in the heart because "the articles of the Faith were not composed as seemed good to men; but the most important points collected out of all the Scripture make up one complete teaching of the Faith."[36]

32. Quoted by Young, *Making of the Creeds*, 6.

33. Ibid.

34. For further discussion on the relationship of creed to the rule of faith, see ibid., 23ff.

35. Cyril of Jerusalem, *Catechetical Lectures*, V.12.

36. Ibid.

These early creeds were also somewhat flexible in their form and content to allow specific communities to combat heresies arising within their midst. Devising a creed to indoctrinate candidates for baptism into the church was also a means to guard against heresy. Though the early forms of the creeds were not tests of orthodoxy, at least not in the sense they finally became tests in the fourth century, they were nevertheless a way to ensure that the tradition of true faith was handed down to future generations without error. In the midst of competing claims concerning God, Christ, and the Holy Spirit, it was important for the church to tell the story well. This is how the creed functioned apologetically in the pre-Constantinian centuries of the church—as a pedagogical tool, not as an exclusionary device.

When Constantine and the church leadership began to use the creed as a test of orthodoxy, this was something new to the faith. As Young explains, "Bishops had met in Council before to deal with members of their own number who failed to teach what their consensus demanded. Excommunication had been used before, and false teachers anathematized. The new elements [with Nicea] lay in using a creed to define orthodoxy, and in the availability of imperial power to enforce the decisions of the council and provide the bishops with greater effectiveness in exercising their authority on earth."[37] The creed formulated at the Council of Nicea served this function in evolving ways until it was finally "canonized" at the Council of Constantinople (381). The creeds, in particular the Nicene creed, became a fixed formula used to measure the orthodoxy of individuals and the communities who followed them. It was certainly not that the earlier church had been unconcerned with truth, since Christianity was committed to a singular notion of what (or should we say Who) was the truth. The innovation is that now truth could be measured by the church according to a written standard that is enforced by the state. The creed was no longer locally contextualized; it was true for all the Christian (i.e., Roman) world. In other words, its summary was regarded as enduring, even universal.

As mentioned earlier, these confessions of faith are in many ways similar to how the Romans had measured "orthodox" allegiance to their Ceasers prior to Constantine.[38] It was this criterion that had been used

37. Young, *Making of the Creeds*, 13.

38. Though the Romans used no particular creed to measure allegiance to themselves and the ancient Roman gods, their edicts requiring everyone to offer sacrifice to

against the church during her centuries of martyrdom. Now the church, under Roman Imperial compulsion, measured orthodoxy according to her statements of belief. Denials of allegiance could, and eventually would, have just as dire consequences as for those who denied allegiance to the Ceasers.

Ironically, the very tool being used for unity became a pry-bar that wedged the schismatic factions apart. While this is true of many of the early schismatic divisions (e.g., Arianism), the *filioque* statement that was included in the creed by various churches in the west also serves as a good illustration. Meant as a clarification of doctrine, and therefore, a means to bring the true church together in appropriate belief, it served instead to help pry the east and west apart. Certainly this does not mean that creeds are an obstacle to fellowship, nor does it mean that belief should be left so vague as to conceal differences for the sake of unity. It is simply a historical observation that the fixedness of doctrine in the creeds meant to provide unity of belief served also as the means for dissolution of the unity of fellowship.

The creeds functioned as a summary of the Scriptures, though perhaps not a complete summary since little is mentioned of the history of Israel.[39] It must be recognized that the creeds were not simply a list of "articles of belief," nor were they meant to be a systematic set of doctrines.[40] One will notice that even one of the crucial doctrines under discussion, the Trinity, is not mentioned by name, though certainly doctrinal language is being formulated and used regarding these various issues. Instead of a system, they are "'confessions' summarizing the Christian story, or affirmations of the three 'characters' in the story."[41] Once again we see that the definition of system, if narrowly construed, does not fit with the actual theology of historical communities. If broadly defined, perhaps the ideas of organization and unity, and even internal consistency, might fit as a description of the creeds. However, an even more

---

their gods amounted to a written rule requiring compliance. Those who did not comply were beaten and sometimes killed. Those Christians who complied were excommunicated. See Grant, *Augustus to Constantine*, 225–34; and Sordi, *Christians and the Roman Empire*, 171–79.

39. Ibid., 5.

40. Ibid., 12.

41. Ibid. However, Young does seem to be somewhat flexible in his definition of system. He declares that Irenaeus "created the first 'systematic theology', a comprehensive attempt to see Christian teaching as a coherent whole" (22).

glaring similarity does exist between the use of the creeds to measure orthodoxy and the modern notion of system. The fixedness of belief in a single statement of the faith is a parallel use of each. The creed is being used to establish one statement of belief for all the communities in the Roman Empire, presumably for all time. Systematic fixedness also relies on the notion that its statements are universally true and ahistorical.[42] While each type of rigidity may have arisen from differing concerns and certainly with different ends in mind, nevertheless, each claims a stability that denies any notion of the context specific nature of belief.

The Golden Age

An interesting twist on the use of the creed as a test of orthodoxy and the way it became a fixed standard of faith is observed in its fusion with certain eschatological beliefs. Robert Grant points out the various approaches to eschatology taken during the second through the fourth centuries.[43] What is most interesting is the view attributed to Eusebius of Caesarea. The idea of the "Golden Age" had already been developed by Clement of Alexandria. Grant believes that Eusebius equated the inauguration of the Golden Age with the rule of Constantine. As Grant states, "[F]or a court theologian like Eusebius of Caesarea (himself an admirer of Origen) the golden age had really been initiated by the reign of the Christian emperor Constantine. The victory of the church was clearly a close approximation to the coming of God's reign."[44] This seems a plausible assertion given some of Eusebius' comments comparing Constantine's reign to that of Moses.[45] Eusebius goes even further to explain that certain prophecies meant for the coming kingdom were fulfilled by the reign of Constantine:

> [T]he Roman empire, the cause of multiplied governments being thus removed, effected an easy conquest of those which yet remained; its object being to unite all nations in one harmonious whole . . . And surely this must appear a wondrous fact to those who will examine the question in the love of truth, and desire not to cavil at these blessings. The falsehood of demon superstition was convicted: the inveterate strife and mutual hatred of the

42. One is again reminded of modern efforts such as Hegel's "Absolute knowledge."
43. Grant, *Augustus to Constantine*, 283.
44. Ibid.
45. Eusebius, *Life of Constantine*, XII.

nations was removed: at the same time One God, and the knowledge of that God, were proclaimed to all: one universal empire prevailed; and the whole human race, subdued by the controlling power of peace and concord, receiving one another as brethren, and responded to the feelings of their common nature. Hence as children of one God and Father, and owing true religion as their common mother, they saluted and welcomed each other with words of peace. Thus the whole world appeared like one well-ordered and united family: each one might journey unhindered as far as and whithersoever he pleased: men might securely travel from West to East, and from East to West, as to their own native country: in short, the ancient oracles and predictions of the prophets were fulfilled, more numerous than we can at present cite, and those especially which speak as follows concerning the saving Word. "He shall have dominion from sea to sea, and from the river to the ends of the earth." And again, "In His days shall righteousness spring up; and abundance of peace." "And they shall beat their swords into plough-shares, and their spears into sickles: and nation shall not take up sword against nation, neither shall they learn to war any more." These words, predicted ages before in the Hebrew tongue, have received in our own day a visible fulfillment, by which the testimonies of the ancient oracles are clearly confirmed.[46]

Subsequently it is not a far stretch to assert that, for many, Constantine's rule marked the initiation, or perhaps consummation, of the reign of God on earth. This may be a fairly simple form of apocalypticism, or it may be a combination of Christian apocalypticism and triumphalism.[47] Though subsequent generations would have difficulty reconciling the inauguration of God's Kingdom to the actuality of life on earth, it seems to have been the predominant view of most orthodox theologians regard-

---

46. Eusebius, *The Oration of Eusebius*, XVI.7. Eusebius is here quoting Psalm 71:7–8 and Isaiah 2:4 (Septuagint). For further comments on the nature of Eusebius' sermon and its triumphalistic nature, see Baker, *Constantine the Great*, 295–320.

47. David Olster (Olster, *Roman Defeat, Christian Response, and the Literary Construction of the Jew*, 30–50) believes the triumphalist spirit typically associated with imperial conquest also became a part of Christian belief as the Emperor Constantine attributed his victories to the Christian God. This seems a fair judgment when one reads Eusebius depiction of the wars following the Milvian bridge. According to Olster, "As Christians conflated imperial wars and pagan persecutions, they began to measure God's power, and his believers' faith, through military, not martyrial victory. The civil wars of Constantine were recast so that love of Christ inspired Constantine; hatred of Christians, his enemies" (31).

ing the relationship between church and state, at least up to the time of the Reformation.[48]

Conclusion

The impact on theology by this union between church and state and the expectation that the state was the new kingdom of God was tremendous. No longer were theology and creed simply the design of a local community, which could at any moment be dispersed through persecution or martyrdom without causing theological difficulties. Now the kingdom of God was represented in the whole of the earthly kingdom ruled by Constantine and later his heirs. Disloyalty to the emperor was equivalent to disloyalty to God.[49] Theology had become fixed in the form of a creed and was also being fixed in the form of a governmental structure. Precedent had been established for how the church would deal with schism and controversy. Ultimately, final appeal could be made to the emperor since he was God's agent for seeing that the church flourish in unity.[50] Theology as reflection on Scripture and doctrine was relatively fixed, since to challenge any doctrine was a challenge to the creed and the kingdom of God, and subsequently, a challenge to the state. Orthodoxy was guarded by the state. Though this by no means meant that schism and division was done (Pelagianism was yet to rear its head), it does mean that issues were now dealt with according to a pattern—a hierarchical form of governmental control— even, a political system. The sovereign had the right, indeed, the duty, to assist the church in maintaining unity and ridding its membership of heresy. Debates still occurred and churches, in fact, drifted further

---

48. Problems, of course, began to arise during and after the fall of the Roman Empire. Augustine wrestles with the relationship of the church and state in his *City of God*. However, it is still quite apparent throughout the next several centuries that the state feels compelled to act on behalf of the church, albeit at times for suspect reasons (e.g., during the crusades). Though questioned on grounds of authenticity, the church during the Reformation does not wish to separate itself from the state completely, although obvious separations occur due to Protestant and Catholic allegiance. For a good discussion of these issues during the earlier centuries of "Christendom," see Greenslade, *Church and State from Constantine to Theodosius*. For further discussion of the problems encountered by the church in its relationship to the state up to the Middle Ages, see Herrin, *Formation of Christendom*.

49. Greenslade, *Church and State*, 11.

50. Ibid., 9–23.

apart, but the church had now entrenched its theology in the laws of nations.[51] Theological methodology is now a part of the political process. The creed had established the boundaries in which debate could occur. It also established the boundaries inside which the state would tolerate disagreement. Those who stepped outside the confessions of the church were enemies of the state.

Two innovations have now helped to solidify the way in which theology will be done for centuries. By becoming fixed in the form of the creed, theological reflection was now bound to a written document external to Scripture, which presumably summarized Scripture. By becoming wed to political structure and the triumphalism of the empire, theology now must be consistent with the political progress of the "kingdom." To question or challenge doctrines was not simply heretical, but also treasonous. Theology, and perhaps even the interpretation of Scripture used to support orthodox theology, were now (though perhaps somewhat ignorantly) subject to the state.

To see what this means for later theological method, we must devote our attention to two figures of the Middle Ages: Thomas Aquinas and John Wycliffe.

51. Constantine himself began to legislate according to what he believed was a Christian morality. See Greenslade, *Church and State*, 21.

4

Summary as System?

Thomas and the Scholastic Method

Introduction: The Synthesis of Thomas Aquinas

IT HAS BEEN QUITE COMMONPLACE THROUGHOUT THE TWENTIETH CEN-
tury to speak of Thomas Aquinas (1226–1274) as a "synthesizer" of
Aristotelian and Christian thought. Though the success of his synthesis
may be questioned on one point or another, his legacy is still coupled
with the revival of Aristotelian thought in the thirteenth and fourteenth
centuries.[1] During this revival of Aristotle's thought, the predominant
Augustinianism of the church and its various orders found itself being
challenged by a pagan philosophy that was slowly being Christianized.
As this process unfolded, a new, or at least unique, epistemology was
taking shape within theological studies. However, such a revolution in
thought hardly developed without resistance. The theological debate
about the sources and measure of truth became intertwined with the
political struggles surrounding the University of Paris. It is within this
historical context that Thomas studied, wrote, and exposed his audience
of novice theologians to a perspective and method that quickly became
the center of attention within the schools of theology.

---

1. Duhem, *Le Système du monde*, 567–68. Duhem believed that Thomas was unorigi-
nal in his thought and only exercised originality in his synthesis of ideas already espoused
by his predecessors. Being unable to finally harmonize their ideas, Thomas retreated
to one or the other authoritative figure as an escape from the contradiction. Duhem
believes Thomas finally died without ever harmonizing the philosophical thought of
those who influenced him most (e.g., Aristotle, Augustine, Avicenna). For a critique
of Duhem's definition of philosophy and his examination of how Thomas proceeded
to harmonize his predecessors, see Pegis, *St. Thomas and Philosophy*, esp. sections I–V.

To portray Thomas as a systematic theologian is tantamount to saying he engaged in what may be considered from a modern perspective as philosophical theology. Reflecting upon his use of Aristotle, and the way in which he attempted to synthesize Aristotelian thought into Christian theology has led some to speculate that Thomas was the first systematician, or at least was dedicated to a systematic method.[2] As such, he is considered one of the first to consciously take philosophical principles and mold them into doctrinal tools of theology. He was the first to knowingly adopt a lesser science, philosophy, in the demonstration of the greater science, theology. Although it seems apparent that Augustine and others had done something similar with the neo-Platonism of the fifth century and earlier, Augustine used Platonic terms and ideas that could be found in varying forms in Scripture. Augustine was also making his case in somewhat of a vacuum since no other school of philosophy was predominant within the church. Even the heretics were working from within the broad limits of Platonism. Thomas worked within a context of competing philosophical grammars or ideas. At the same time, perhaps Thomas would have found a friendlier audience within the church had the renewal of Aristotle's thought not arisen first in Arab circles. Within the context of Arab extermination during the crusade era, it would have been difficult to convince anyone within the church of the merits of Arab philosophy. Whatever the context, Thomas is often singled out as an originator of systematic tendencies due in large part to his foundational use of philosophy in theological investigation. More will be said on the extent of Thomas' adoption of philosophy later.

Another aspect of Thomas' theology that has caused some to ponder its systematicity is the structure of the *Summa Theologica*. The seemingly circular nature of the work makes it a unified study of theology. Grace extends (*exitus*) from God to creation (particularly humanity) and returns (*reditus*) back to God as the teleology of the creation and the grace extended to it are most fully discovered in their exaltation of (return to) God. This circular pattern is the format used for Thomas' theological discussion in the *Summa*, and serves as the template for coherence within his theology. On this template are hung the ideas and principles of many other thinkers who had discovered, albeit in the realm of feeble human reason, truths about God and His universe. Consequently, some believe that Thomas wished to draw all these truths together into one coherent

2. Harak, *Virtuous Passions*, 53–54.

system that could be pointed to as *the* truth. As Harak explains, "Thomas was trying to unify all systems of thought in the *Summa*. Thomas, however, was also pioneering a new form of theology, where every part of that theology relates to every other part, and all of those parts to the whole. That new kind of study is now called *systematics*, or *systematic theology*, and the *Summa* is just such a work."[3]

The twenty-first century debate about the relationship between theology and philosophy in contemporary circles is certainly a volatile one. Theology in contemporary circles is experiencing a revolution, of sorts, in epistemology. However, contemporary debates can hardly compare to Thomas' context. The debate has never been more intense than during the thirteenth and fourteenth centuries. So much seemed to depend on the outcome. Both Thomas and his contemporaries were deeply immersed in these debates. This study will attempt to uncover the way in which Thomas viewed the relationship of philosophy to theology, and how this affected his theological method. In order to establish the historical context, the thought of other figures must also be discussed and compared to Thomas as they all attempted to write and teach theology for the sake of instructing future students. Much of the discussion regarding philosophical dependence will derive from Thomas' first question of the Prima Pars. However, we must first deal with the structure of the entire *Summa* and whether Thomas relied on a circular pattern.

Peter Lombard's *Sentences* and the *Summa Theologica*

Peter Lombard's *Sentences* was considered the standard "textbook" within the university by the early thirteenth century. Roger Bacon proclaimed the English master Alexander of Hales to be the first to lecture publicly on the *Sentences*.[4] Bacon decried Alexander's use of the *Sentences* as the fourth fault in the teaching of theology, since it led theologians in the university to prefer the subtleties of the *Sentences* over the simplicity of the Bible.[5] Thus it was that "Alexander, still a secular master of theology, began the practice among theologians at the University of Paris of using the *Sentences* of Peter Lombard as the ordinary text for his lectures in theology."[6] The editors of Alexander's *Glossa in quatuor libros*

---

3. Ibid.

4. Bacon, *Opus Minus* (1267), 329.

5. Ibid.

6. Principe, *Theology of the Hypostatic Union in the Early Thirteenth Century*, II, 14.

Sententiarum Petri Lombardi date the work to sometime between 1223 and 1227. Others were quick to follow Alexander in this practice, including Roland of Cremona and Hugh of Saint-Cher as both undergraduates and as fully qualified masters, from 1229 to 1235. The definitive role of the bachelor was established at Paris after 1231, and the task of giving ordinary lectures on the *Sentences* was restricted to the bachelor soon after. Apart from the short tenure of Alexander of Hales and a few others who lectured on the *Sentences*, the master was given the task of lecturing primarily on the Bible.

By the time Thomas arrived in Paris in 1252, it was common practice for the bachelor to become an apprentice under a master, to lecture on the *Sentences* for two to four years, and to respond to various objections in theological disputes. Though the bachelor was likely under the direct guidance of a master in choosing the questions to debate after the reading of the *Sentences* in each day's studies, he was nonetheless the one finally responsible for responding to those questions. After a section of the *Sentences* had been read, the bachelor would proceed to give a brief point by point explanation of the passage, then he would raise certain questions that needed to be addressed. In their commentaries on the *Sentences*, Albert the Great, Bonaventure, and Thomas maintained a fairly close adherence to the subject matter of the *Sentences* in their questions raised for discussion. However, by the fourteenth century, most commentators paid little attention to the subject in their questions. They simply raised questions on unrelated subjects and expounded on the questions with little regard for the subject under scrutiny in the text of the *Sentences*.[7]

Lombard's *Sentences* was generally divided into two groups, following the statement of Augustine that "all doctrine is either of things or of signs."[8] The first three books form one group describing things, including discussion of the Trinity, creation, Christ, and the virtues. The fourth book discusses the sacraments, which are signs, or symbols. Following a suggestion of Alexander of Hales, Thomas divided the *Sentences* into

---

7. Weisheipl, *Friar Thomas D'Aquino*, 68–70.

8. Lombard, *Sentences*, I.1.1.1. Lombard is here quoting Augustine, *On Christian Doctrine*, I.2.2. It should be noted that Lombard himself did not divide his work into two parts. The division appears to be due to a schema proposed by Alexander of Hales, and likely also Thomas (see Weisheipl, *Friar Thomas D'Aquino*, 219).

two groups of two each.[9] The first two books deal with the *exitus* of all things from God, while the second pair of books deal with the *reditus* of all things to God. Alexander was not original in his suggestion. This ordering reflects the Dionysian and Plotinian cycle of emanation and return. Some have posited that Thomas later seems to have organized his *Summa Theologica* according to the same pattern.[10]

However, Thomas' ordering of the *Summa Theologica* was not a simple reproduction of the *Sentences*. Thomas was dissatisfied with the confusion felt by novices when they tried to approach sacred doctrine through the teachings of the *Sentences* or the other summas and compendia available. As he explains in his brief prologue to the *Prima Pars*,

> Because the Master of Catholic Truth ought not only to teach the proficient, but also to instruct beginners (according to the Apostle: As Unto Little Ones In Christ, I Gave You Milk to Drink, Not Meat—1 Cor. iii. 1, 2), we purpose in this book to treat of whatever belongs to the Christian Religion, in such a way as may tend to the instruction of beginners. We have considered that students in this Science have not seldom been hampered by what they have found written by other authors, partly on account of the multiplication of useless questions, articles, and arguments; partly also because those things that are needful for them to know are not taught according to the order of the subject matter, but according as the plan of the book might require, or the occasion of the argument offer; partly, too, because frequent repetition brought weariness and confusion to the minds of the readers.
>
> Endeavoring to avoid these and other like faults, we shall try, by God's help, to set forth whatever is included in this Sacred Science as briefly and clearly as the matter itself may allow.[11]

Though certainly Peter Lombard was not the only author Thomas had in mind, he was perhaps the primary one, given that Lombard's work was the standard text used for beginners. Thomas' answer to the confusion of the novices was not to turn to the Scriptures or the fathers, since these were precisely the works to be explained; nor was the solution to turn to some other more contemporary work that would serve

9. Alexander of Hales, *Glossa in Quatuor Libros Sententiarum Petri Lombardi*, I.Introitus.8.4.

10. Chenu, *Introduction a l'etude de S. Thomas d'Aquino*, esp. 255–76.

11. Thomas Aquinas, *Summa Theologica*, vol. I, Prologue to the *Prima Pars*.

as a text for beginners in theology. As Weisheipl makes clear, "In the mind of Thomas, current works of theology were unsuitable for beginners because (1) they were too verbose and detailed, (2) they were all unsystematic, and (3) they were too repetitious because they were unsystematic. Not only were the *Sentences* of Peter Lombard a prime example of these deficiencies, but the Scriptures themselves lack a logical order . . . the training of a theologian requires that beginners in the "science" be aided by a systematic view of the whole of "sacred doctrine."[12]

The theologians of the twelfth and thirteenth centuries had attempted to provide novices with a general introduction to theology by organizing their studies according to the pattern set by the Apostle's Creed. Peter Lombard was no different in following this pattern. However, other theologians were not always able to maintain the logical order that Thomas and some later thinkers seemed to have had in mind. For example, writing in the sixteenth century, Melchior Cano chided all who depended upon the disorderliness of the *Sentences*. "Besides the word 'distinctions', into which the books are divided, you will find almost nothing distinct, or correctly and orderly distributed. You could call it a congestion of testimonies rather than a disposition and order of discipline."[13] Melchior points out that the Trinity is treated (Book I) before the essential attributes of the One God (Book IV); the virtues are discussed in Book III, while some vices are left until Book IV. All this confusion leads him to conclude that "Consequently for scholastics who clung to its vestige, everything is confused and almost chaotic."[14]

Thomas was not as openly critical about the works of his contemporaries, nor was he ready to cast aside scholastic "entrapments." In fact, though Thomas was unwilling to be satisfied with his commentary on the

12. Weisheipl, *Friar Thomas D'Aquino*, 218–19.

13. Melchior Cano, *De Locis Theologicus*, vol. III, 12.2.4.

14. Ibid. One can perhaps hear in Melchior's sentiments the impending emphasis on coherence and the primacy of theism found especially in the Enlightenment. It is a question as to whether Thomas or other scholastics are rightly to blame for originating such emphases. Certainly, as will be seen in a later chapter, the scholastic humanism in the young Descartes' training bore the fruit of a system steeped in much that Thomas would have opposed (e.g., the autonomy of rationalism, and the necessity of a more pure philosophy of religion prior to, or perhaps even in place of, doctrinal or Biblical considerations). Though some relationship certainly exists between figures like Thomas and later scholastic humanists, Melchior's critique is perhaps an anachronistic look at the early scholastics, in that he expects more than is historically warranted of the method of early scholasticism.

Sentences, since he did find the *Sentences* too disjointed for beginners, he nevertheless appeared to maintain some of the structure found in the *Sentences*. As was mentioned earlier, Chenu believes Thomas envisioned his own work as cyclical. The *exitus-reditus* pattern that was suggested by Alexander of Hales as a description of the *Sentences* also seems to have served Thomas with the substantial pattern for his *Summa Theologica*. As will be discussed below, Thomas easily coupled this with Aristotle's science in treating the cause before the effects. Following Airstotle, Thomas believed he must treat God first as He is in Himself, then move to His activities in creation to avoid reducing God to *merely* His effects. As Thomas states in his prologue to the second question of the *Prima Pars*, "Because the chief aim of sacred doctrine is to teach the knowledge of God, not only as He is in Himself, but also as He is the beginning of things and their last end, and especially of rational creatures, as is clear from what has already been said, therefore, in our endeavor to expound this science, we shall treat: (1) Of God; (2) Of the rational creature's advance toward God; (3) Of Christ, who as man, is our way to God."[15] In broad outline, Thomas appears to have followed the general pattern of the *Sentences*. Again Weisheipl is helpful in understanding the order.

> Removing the discussion of sins from Book II and the analysis of virtues from Book III, one can readily see that the plan of the *prima pars* and the *tertia pars* falls in line with the distribution of subjects treated by Lombard. The first part of the *Summa* corresponds to Peter Lombard's *Sentences* on the Trinity (Bk. I), creation, the angels, man, and first parents (Bk. II, dist. 2–20). The third part harmonizes with Peter's discussion of Christ the Incarnate Word (Bk. III, dist. 1–22), the sacraments (which Thomas calls "the relics of Christ's passion"), and the four last things (Bk. IV).[16]

It is the second section that sets Thomas' work most apart from the *Sentences*. It is here that Thomas "completely revised Lombard's discussion of moral questions, synthesizing man's return to God through the virtues (*secunda pars*) in much the same manner as Aristotle treats man's

---

15. Thomas Aquinas, *Summa Theologica*, I.2.Prologue. Later in the Prologue, Thomas explains that treating "Of God" includes "Whatever concerns the procession of creatures from Him."

16. Weisheipl, *Friar Thomas D'Aquino*, 219–20.

search for happiness in the *Nicomachean Ethics*."[17] On the subject of sanctification, it seems clear that Thomas wished to use what he found valuable in Aristotle's thought to right the problems faced by novices who were directed to use the *Sentences*. Thomas' work eventually served as somewhat of a replacement of the *Sentences*, but more quickly became a companion of sorts if no other resourses were available. His work came under severe scrutiny toward the end of his life due to his adoption of Aristotelian themes. It was only at the urging of Albert the Great, Thomas' mentor, that his work finally avoided being declared heretical. What is most interesting for our discussion at this point, however, is his use of Aristotle's guidance in re-ordering the novices' text for theology. Thomas brought the philosophical rules of Aristotle's *Posterior Analytics* to bear on the whole of his thought, making the orderliness of his own work more logical and scientific. He thus provided students of theology with an orderly presentation of the whole of sacred doctrine. But does this constitute an attempt to be systematic in this endeavor?

As intimated throughout our discussion of the *exitus–reditus* progression as a format for the whole of Thomas' *Summa*, not all have agreed that this is the best understanding of Thomas' scheme for his text. While a pattern exists in his work that indicates a cyclical approach, this pattern is disrupted in places and, further, is occasionally at variance with Lombard's *Sentences*.[18] The disruption seems significant enough to warrant another look at the method Thomas may have used. Stepping back from the simple proposition of total dependence on Lombard, debate exists over whether such a cyclical format followed a pattern set out, in Thomas' thinking, by revelation, logic, or history. M. D. Chenu, though perhaps not original, posited in the early twentieth century the *exitus-reditus* progression of Thomas' work according to a chronological progression.[19] "Such is the plan of the *Summa Theologique*, and the movement that it treats. *Prima Pars:* the emanation, God as principle; *Secunda Pars:* the return, God as end; and because, in fact, this return is made possible by Christ, the God-man according to the free and wholly gracious design of God, a *Tertia Pars* will study the 'Christian' conditions

17. Ibid.

18. Weisheipl (*Friar Thomas D'Aquino*, 219–20) qualifies Thomas' dependence on the *Sentences*.

19. Chenu, "Le plan de la Somme theologique de S. Thomas," 93–107. He later revised this article and reprinted it in his *Introduction a l'etude de S. Thomas d'Aquinas*.

of this return."[20] However, as Timothy Smith points out, such a depiction remains largely superficial as it leaves details unaddressed.

> Chenu failed to make clear, however, whether he was defining the development within the text or the nature of the structure; that is, whether he was pointing to the process itself within the text by which things proceed from and return to God. The question of motion then becomes important for defining the division. If the scheme is read according to temporal motion, the *reditus* does not begin until the Incarnation, the *Tertia pars*. If, on the other hand, the structure is conceived of as ontological only, then the *reditus* can be said to begin with Thomas' account of the moral life in the *Secunda pars*. Much of the debate focusing on Chenu's terms can be understood as a disagreement over the kind of motion within the system. Those who read it as a chronological structure find the text distasteful and poorly organized due to the implications of such temporal motion both in the three divine Persons following from the one divine essence and in the return of creatures to God "prior to" or "without" Christ. The idea of a movement of creatures back to God without Christ seems rather non-Christian or a-Christian. Take away the concept of temporal motion and the problems begin to disappear, for the movement of rational creatures to God is not prior to Christ in time but simply abstracted from the Incarnation for the purposes of systematic discussion . . . The majority of interpreters would agree with Chenu's basic thesis but also are generally reticent to say much more.[21]

Smith's point here is simply to illustrate that Chenu's conception has substantial difficulties, if left as simply proposed: the *Summa* follows a chronology of salvation history. Chenu's approach, while bearing some merit, based as it is in the progression of revelation in Scripture, leaves many questions and concerns unaddressed. Further, Chenu's proposal seems rooted in the neo-Platonic notion of emanation and return. This becomes especially clear as Chenu describes the movement from part two to part three of the *Summa*. "The transition from the *Secunda Pars* to the *Tertia Pars* represented the passage from the necessary order to

20. Chenu, *Introduction*, 98. I am here relying on the translation of Timothy Smith, "Thomas Aquinas' *De Deo*: Setting the Record Straight on His Theological Method," 127.

21. Smith, "Thomas Aquinas' *De Deo*," 127–28. A more detailed presentation of Thomas' theological method is found in Smith's more recent *Thomas Aquinas' Trinitarian Theology: A Study in Theological Method*. However, we will here use his "*De Deo*," article, since they appear to agree, and this will allow for a bit more brevity.

its historical realizations, from the domain of the structures to the concrete history of the gifts of God."[22] If such an adoption of a neo-Platonic scheme is an accurate assessment of Thomas' method, it could place his work directly in the line of a scientific method typically associated with modern systematics: philosophical foundations ground, or establish, the scheme and coherence of theological method and doctrinal assertions. However, Thomas is hardly neo-Platonic.

Max Seckler advanced Chenu's thesis by denying the neo-Platonic notion of emanation and replacing it with a more thoroughgoing Aristotelian sense of realism.

> According to God's plan and work of salvation, all things go out from the hand of God and return to Him who is the Alpha and Omega. Thus, the theologian also treats reality according to its relation to God in so far as He is the source and goal of all things. Surprisingly, we find here a narrow correspondence in the source and goal of history, the source and fulfillment of being, the first and last ground of understanding such that theology can become not only ordered to the science of salvation history, but salvation history bears within itself the fundamental design of theology. The theologian does not bring order to the chaos of salutary events, but the order of salvation structures theology.[23]

Seckler believes Thomas has taken a distinct turn from any previous neo-Platonic influence on theology. He identifies Thomas' structure as Christological throughout, due to Thomas' own view of the unity of God's historical relations to His creatures. "Thomas has a unified conception of the works of salvation; angels and humans are from the beginning created for salvation and grace. Creation is already grounded in an historical relation of God to creatures; therefore creation is also a contingent event. Hence, the *Summa* is throughout christologically structured."[24] In Thomas, the Christological grace of God expressed in salvation is not different from the grace expressed in creation, since the entirety of God's relations to His creation is an expression of His unified grace. Smith demonstrates that Chenu's neo-Platonic context for the *Summa* seems to imply a multifaceted emanation of grace from God. For Chenu, God's

---

22. Chenu, *Introduction*, 270.
23. Seckler, *Das Heil in der Geschichte*, 35.
24. Ibid., 39.

grace is expressed in creation and then later again in the incarnation and movement of God in salvation. However, as Smith makes clear,

> It is a false assumption on the part of Chenu that there is, in the *Summa*, a grace separated from Christ. The discussion of Christ in part III is not the entrance of a new radical contingency and a new form of grace. Chenu was confusing the chronology of revelation with the *ordo rerum* thereby making the interpretation of the *Summa's* structure a problem of theological knowledge. Hence, what Seckler sees as a crucial addition to Chenu's thesis is the assertion that Christ is only the way of salvation, not the goal, in as much as Christ is the revealer of the Father. Christ provides insight into the order of being, the *ordo rerum*. The content of this insight is the right understanding of creation and the way of salvation, not a new kind of *reditus*. There is then no "unhistorical" material or structure in the *Summa* wherein Thomas treats the truth of God "abstractly" over against the "concrete history" of God in Christ. The *Summa* is throughout a concrete history of salvation.[25]

Through his advance on Chenu's thesis, Seckler appears to have rightly observed that Thomas grounds his method in Christology. Seckler is able to maintain the cyclical pattern described by Chenu as an *exitus–reditus*. However, Seckler's own shortfall is his reduction of the incarnation to *merely* revelatory status. "Seckler's interpretation . . . lacks an appreciation of the soteriological dimension of the incarnation. It is not merely revelatory but also effective of salvation."[26] Smith, following Otto Pesch, sees the necessity to maintain the centrality of Christology; however, not at the expense of the Christological mission to fulfill the Father's will.[27] Thus, while salvation history and being are united by Thomas in his theological structure, the salvific acts of Christ are abstracted for the sake of preserving the centrality of God in theology. Trinitarian knowledge, which can only be gained through Christ, is post-poned in Thomas not because of a desire to arrive at speculative conclusions before turning to

25. Smith, "Thomas Aquinas' *De Deo*," 130. Smith is here referring to Seckler, *Das Heil in der Geschichte*, 40. Smith rightly argues that Chenu seems to conflate Bonaventure and Thomas when attributing to Thomas an abstraction of the historical into an organized science for theology. Smith, rightly, sees Thomas as concerned with the historical throughout as he unites the events of history with the order of being.

26. Smith, "Thomas Aquinas' *De Deo*," 130.

27. Ibid., 131. Here Smith develops more fully the thoughts of Otto Pesch in the latter's "Um den Plan der *Summa Theologiae* des hl. Thomas von Aquin," 128–37.

the secure knowledge of revelation. Instead, Thomas believes he must maintain the eternality and freedom of God by avoiding the tendency to reduce the cause of acts to the acts themselves.

> Thomas presents a study of God prior to and apart from the acts by which we know God before discussing those acts because revelation imparts a more full and certain knowledge of the cause, thereby allowing one to speak about the cause directly . . . In the context of eternity it makes perfect sense to discuss God prior to or abstracted from any consideration of creation . . . The purpose for discussing cause before effect , even though the reverse is the order of learning (the order of rational investigation is from effect to cause), is to separate the being from the necessity of the act and to prevent the error of reducing the being to these acts only. In other words, specific acts have a limiting power on the agent. To speak of God as Creator or Savior (only) is to reduce the possible to the actual at a specific point in time. God's power extends beyond the horizon of God's acts; hence, *Deus potest aliae facere quam quae facit.*[28]

For the sake of our discussion regarding Thomas and systematicity, Thomas approaches ordering theology with specific philosophical/theological presuppositions already in place. The reasoning Thomas seems to use for ordering his *Summa* as he does centers on his own doctrinal commitments regarding the eternality and freedom of God. As Smith notes,

> In treating all things *sub ratione Dei*, Thomas subordinates the history of human salvation to the eternity of God. The temporality of human affairs does not become meaningless as all is seen at once *sub ratione Dei*. On the contrary, everything is thereby seen in its proper context, that is, as created by and ordered to God. Regardless of whether we choose to use Chenu's *exitus–reditus* terminology, we must recognize the pedagogical organization of Thomas' *Summa*. This *ordo* represents a scientific structuring in which the order of being contextualizes the events of salvation history. The order in which things must be understood corresponds to the order in which they exist, the order of being: *Deus* first as cause and all else, *sub ratione Dei* as effects. This pattern of organization also corresponds to Aristotle's suggested manner of

---

28. Smith, "Thomas Aquinas' *De Deo*," 131–32.

proceeding scientifically: one must treat the subject first according to *an sit* then *quid est* and finally *quomodo*.[29]

Such a correspondence to Aristotle's conception of science seems to indicate more than simply a familiarity with Aristotle's method. Thomas relies
on a philosophical scheme in his organizational approach to natural and
revelational knowledge. While this may imply a form of systematicity
(reliance on a philosophical scheme for theological prolegomena), the
difference between Thomas' approach and modern systematics remains
rather broad. Thomas' movement from cause to effect in his knowledge
of God in the *Prima Pars* is but his way of limiting the possibility of
human understanding. While it is true he wishes to convey truth about
God, it is not the same type of knowledge or truth obtained through the
study of effects. As we shall see below, Thomas does his best to give us
parameters for understanding the cause, but in the end, parameters are
all he can give us.

The question of systematicity and a comparison between Thomas
and modern systematics hinges on the expected outcome of his theology.
Thomas certainly saw his theology as an expression of Scriptural meditations coordinated with Aristotelian ontology. However, Thomas does
not seem to be engaged in metaphysical speculation. He is attempting to
order his theology according to his perception of salvation history combined with the chain of being, which amounts to an ontological explanation. At the same time, this is not an explanation based in philosophical
sources, nor is it an attempt to go beyond revelation.

Keeping Philosophy and Theology in the Instruction at Paris

Once again the definition of system with which one begins a study looms
large over our discussion of Thomas thus far. We have seen that he was
very concerned with orderliness and the logical progression of subjects
in the *Summa Theologica*. If this is our definition of systematics, then
certainly Thomas fits within this category. Such an order seems born out
of a pedagogical concern for novices and their clear instruction. Thomas
wished for the instruction of theology, in preparation for study of the
Scriptures, to be done in a manner conducive to what he believed was
the most logical order and plainest explanation. However, if our defini-

29. Smith, "Thomas Aquinas' *De Deo*," 132.

tion of system is more specifically directed toward philosophical notions like absolute or universal knowledge in a rationalistic system and the use of philosophical categories as foundational to theology, then further examination of Thomas' *Summa* seems necessary in order to ascertain if he can be said to have anticipated such Enlightenment notions.

Universal Knowledge and the Mystery of God

First, on the notion of absolute or universal knowledge, Thomas is fairly clear that he wishes to maintain room for mystery within our knowledge of God. Thomas uses analogy as the primary tool to open up the secrets of God hidden in Scripture and theology. But analogy for Thomas does not do the work that some modern theologians have assumed it does, or want it to do.

Many contemporary theologians have picked up on Thomas' modesty with regard to descriptions of God. Perhaps the best way to engage the discussion surrounding Thomas' use of analogy is to examine the debate from within, looking at both the interpretation of Aquinas' use of analogy and the implications of such an interpretation. One of the more astute theologians to comment on Thomas' use of analogy is Nicholas Lash. Lash believes Aquinas has suffered historically due to the neo-scholastic interpretations of his use of analogy. Typical of eighteenth and nineteenth (and twentieth) century positivist thought, the neo-scholastics believed that Aquinas had a 'theory' of analogy. This theory could subsequently be used—albeit in a limited fashion due to the recognition of the apophatic "side" of analogy—to positively furnish us with knowledge of God, perhaps even a doctrine of God. Such a heritage of interpretation of Thomas has caused even some twentieth-century scholars to posit a similar expectation. "St. Thomas's doctrine, because it is rooted in the act of being which is analogically common to God and his creatures, gives us a process by which we can transform the *via negativa* into the *via eminentiae* and . . . can achieve a real knowledge of God in this life."[30] Lash counters that if analogy was a theory, that theory could not function analogically.[31] Following the thought of David Burrell, Lash states that "'Aquinas is not attempting to describe God at all' and 'a perceptive reader [of Aquinas' first part of the Prima Pars of the *Summa Theologica*]

---

30. Mascall, *He Who Is*, 225–26.
31. Lash, "Ideology, Metaphor and Analogy," 110.

would think twice before identifying a deliberate consideration of what God is not with a teaching presuming to say what God is."[32] Aquinas' thought in no way provides for a means to transcend the *via negativa*. In fact, his whole discussion of analogy directly confirms that only in the recognition of difference can theological discourse proceed regarding knowledge of God's essence.[33] Lash's description of Aquinas' theology accordingly reflects the dialectical relationship he believes best holds the "is" and "is not" of analogy together. Aquinas' dialectic reflects interplay between the 'way of analogy' and the 'way of metaphor', and includes a sense of primacy for the metaphorical. As Lash states,

> Theology neither reinforces nor supplants the "image" of God built up through Christian living—in prayer, work, suffering, relationship—an image which, for the Christian, finds its focus in consideration of the person, words, work and death of Jesus the Christ. The role of theology, as Aquinas conceives it, is to "exercise critical control" over this image, and over the narratives in which it finds expression, . . . On this account, then, metaphysical theology stands in a critical relationship to religious practice similar to that which I have already suggested obtains between the "hermeneutical" theological disciplines and the practice of religion.[34]

Following this interpretation of Aquinas, Lash believes that theology's primary, perhaps sole, function is to act as the critical conscience for construction of the Christian narrative. Such construction is not the building of a theoretical system of doctrines. Instead, it is the guidance of the Christian community in her practices. Lash still recognizes the need for reflection, but only in so far as it serves to correct errant practice.

The import is twofold for Lash's interpretation of Aquinas' use of analogy. First, it reduces reflection on language to a functional, rather than a foundational, or representative, role. In other words, linguistic description is moved to the periphery and functions as a monitor of meaning, instead of serving to ground meaning in some literally real or descriptive sense. The second consequence of his interpretation is that it allows the void left by the reduction of language to be filled by practice. Action becomes the locus of meaning prior to any descriptive account

32. Ibid., 109. Lash is here quoting Burrell's *Aquinas: God and Action*, 16; 13.

33. Lash, "Ideology, Metaphor and Analogy," 110.

34. Ibid., 109.

of the activity. This second consequence accords well with Lash's belief that, at best, our 'knowledge' of God is referential and never descriptive. Linguistic representation is merely our attempt to help mold and appropriately delimit our prior experience of God encountered in communal relatedness. Nevertheless, even the meaning discovered in action remains referential and in no way 'captures' the essence of God.[35]

Lash believes that what he has established is a "dialectic between construction and the disciplined quest for discovery, between narrative and metaphysics, between making sense and assessing the cost of the operation."[36] The advantage of promoting such a dialectic is that narrative can be constructed within the context of a community that will conscientiously guide it along the appropriate path of specifically Christian discourse. Likewise, Lash also preserves a usefulness for doctrine. Adopting the language of George Lindbeck, Lash is prepared to engage doctrine in its "regulative" capacity.[37] Doctrine functions to direct the focus of theological discourse and to set the boundaries within which discourse takes place.

Of course, Lash's depiction of Aquinas becomes problematic when he encounters Aquinas' analogically positive predications of God as "wise, good, and living."[38] His answer to this dilemma is to focus on the openness that is evident even in Aquinas' perfectionistic language.[39] Lash is forced to interpret these perfectionistic terms in such a broad sense that they are finally devoid of any descriptive value.

35. Lash, *Easter in Ordinary*, 223ff.

36. Ibid., 118.

37. "[T]he *primary* function of Christian doctrine is regulative rather than descriptive." (Lash, *Easter in Ordinary*, 260. Italics Lash's.) Lash explicitly acknowledges his indebtedness to Lindbeck for this insight. Through his use of a dialectic, Lash is attempting to circumvent the problem discovered in Lindbeck, i.e., the inability to develop an ontological foundation for narrative. Cf. Lindbeck, *The Nature of Doctrine*.

38. Thomas refers to God in these terms in his *Summa Theologica*, I.13.2.

39. Indeed, it appears as though one of Aquinas' primary intentions is to expand our vision of who and what God is by challenging the limits of our language. He does this by expanding our notions of perfection to their utmost height. Only at this point can they be predicated of God. But these ascriptions do not originate with us since they pre-exist in God. We only participate in them.

Lash appears to be attempting to follow Aquinas' intentions by creating an openness in his theological discourse that would allow for expanded horizons. Unfortunately, Lash's conception of openness is engulfed by the void he creates through his rigorous apophaticism. Language cannot challenge us to expand our vision of the Christian God when it consistently drives us further into emptiness.

While it seems obvious that Aquinas, due to his muted discussion of the perfections of God, is not attempting to arrive at a 'catalogue' of doctrines about God, Lash still seems to have misconceived Aquinas' use of analogy. Indeed, Lash appears to have subsumed analogy into metaphor. He cannot allow that analogous language be used positively to predicate perfectionistic terms of God, something Aquinas is willing to do, albeit in an nondescript manner from our creaturely perspective. For Lash, both metaphor and analogy function only apophatically.[40] Lash seems entrapped in the very notion he wishes to refute regarding Aquinas. He is, rightly, attempting to defend Aquinas against those who would make the latter out to be a positivist. In other words, Lash seems bent on demonstrating the unsystematic nature of Thomas' work, at least from a more modernistic perspective. Lash appears to see the neo-Thomists as fundamentally anachronistic. However, in so doing, he finally ignores the characteristics of Thomas' theology that make it unphilosophical.[41] Thomas is well aware of the positive language used to "describe" God in Scripture. He is attempting to account for such language without falling into the trap of reducing the mysterious nature of God to the mere human language of natural reason. To accomplish such a walk on the tightrope between reason and revelation, Thomas uses analogy to open the door on possible positive predications regard-

40. Lash, "Ideology, Metaphor and Analogy," 112. Lash recognizes the danger in attempting to describe analogy according to his interpretation of Aquinas. As he states, Aquinas "does go on to talk *less negatively*" about God (Lash, "Considering the Trinity," 188; and "Ideology, Metaphor and Analogy," 110–12, italics mine). At this point he attempts to grant the possibility of positive terms being applied to God, though certainly not in a literal sense. Aquinas would go along with Lash's restriction of analogy this far, but Lash appears to go a step further when he broadens these predications (wise, good and living) so much that they become nebulous, unrecognizable as analogous predications of God. Cf. Lamadrid, "Is There a System in the Theology of Nicholas Lash?" 409–10.

41. Lash is not original in following an historical rendering of Thomas according to a medieval "philosophical theology." E.g., see Burrell, *Knowing the Unknowable God*, 2–3. Lash appears to be relying heavily on Burrell's assessment of the pluralistic context surrounding Thomas' writings.

While I must agree that a pluralist rendering admits several similarities for comparison of Thomas to his Jewish and Islamic counterparts, I remain unconvinced that Thomas had anything other than apologetic concerns in mind in any comparisons or borrowing that may have occurred along more philosophical lines, and he would have seen such a comparative endeavor as somewhat reductionistic in that it ignores what he believed to be the defining characteristic of Christian theology: the pinnacle of revelation in Jesus.

ing God. He is not saying our language can capture God. In this, Lash has rightly discovered the protective nature of Thomas' use of analogy in conveying the mystery and otherness of God as He is in His essence. However, Lash seems to ignore the way in which Thomas is also willing to recognize the accommodation to human language God makes in revelation, albeit an accommodation that remains limited in its scope for accomplishing real knowledge. Thomas seems to want to take the human reader as far as revelation will go; no more than this, but certainly no less either. Thomas definitely sees the value in silence, toward which Lash believes the mystery of God drives humans. However, if silence is all we have, finally, then why write the *Summa*, at least, why write it in the way it's written? Thomas wrote to prepare theological novices for commenting on the Scriptures, not only to meditate in silence, necessary as that may be at times as well. Lash seems to engage the *Summa* as though it were for masters lecturing on certain knowledge, rather than seeing it as a way to maintain the modesty of novices by limiting their use of and confidence in natural reason.

Lash attempts to escape the dilemma of the positive versus the negative in analogy by allowing positive predication to be communally referential. Perfectionistic terms can still refer to God as they are spoken in our communal relationship with God. In the context of relatedness, Lash believes we can speak of God positively without making descriptive claims about the essence of God.[42] But this relatedness appears to be specifically located in human relatedness to one another. Lash asks:

> How might we come to know the unknown God? How might we know him with a knowledge which is, *as* knowledge of *God*, redemptive—and hence in some measure transformative of our contemporary crisis of meaning (which is a crisis of *human* meaning, of culture and politics and institutions, and by no means merely a problem about ideas)? And how might such knowledge as we can attain be knowledge that displays the *difference* between the world and its creator, and thus be knowledge of the *unknown* God? How, in Rahner's formulation, "can the incomprehensible and nameless be the meaning that *we* have?" The answer is as easy to *state* as it is difficult and demanding to "realize" and to understand: through the occurrence of human community.[43]

42. Lash, *Easter in Ordinary*, 221ff.

43. Ibid., 230–31. Italics Lash's. The quote of Karl Rahner is taken from his *Theological Investigations*, vol. 18, 94.

But does 'human community' translate so easily into Christian narrative? In other words, is there anything in Lash's work to prevent his *theology* from lapsing into a mere *anthropology* or *sociology of religion*? Perhaps he would not find these terms offensive. However, I see no reason to find them distinctively Christian. Lash seems to propose that for knowledge of God to be redemptive, it must be "other," or language that is more than a mere human reflection on ideas qua human. However, by rooting his answer in human community, has he really escaped anthropology? It would seem he still searches for the possibility of the divine in the *merely* human practices, albeit human practices divinely ordained. How does one know the language regulating the practices reaches the otherness of the divine if it remains entirely entrenched in human reflection? Is this not still, merely, a sociology of religion, or perhaps even a reductionistic turn toward immanentism?

With such a broadly sociological purview, Lash seems to acquiesce to the egalitarian nature of knowledge typical of modernity. Aquinas was not nearly so egalitarian in his approach to knowledge. God remains unavailable to natural human reason, dependent as it is on the senses (I.12.7). God's essence cannot be sensibly known in this life (I.12.12). As will be discussed further below, knowledge of Him is limited to those to whom He has given the light of revealed knowledge (I.12.13). Lash does not differentiate the kinds of knowledge in Aquinas. While still holding humbly and modestly to any claims of knowing, Aquinas believes revelation affords those who are graced an opportunity to understand a higher knowledge than that of natural reason. Thus revealed knowledge is higher than analogous knowledge, dependent as the latter is upon the sensibility of created objects. Lash is, on this point, perhaps due to a more modern theistic conception of knowledge of God, leaving revelational knowledge out of the equation. On the other hand, Aquinas seems to ascend in his understanding of religious epistemology from natural knowledge to Christological knowledge as supreme, causing one to ask, "Where do we begin?"

Lash's understanding of Aquinas rightly takes strong issue with the positivistic interpretation of Aquinas' use of analogy. But his solution is distinctly post-modern in its dependence upon Wittgenstinian anthropology for use of language in discovering how descriptive statements might still maintain some value in a community committed to upholding the tradition these statements have embodied for centuries. Likewise,

Lash seems to think of knowledge in a more pluralistic sense than does Aquinas. In other words, Lash conceives of knowledge as available to all. Certainly, it must be granted that both Thomas and Lash are working from within a very Catholic context. They can perhaps assume that tradition will regulate the way in which the church assimilates its doctrinal heritage, providing a way for the community to use doctrine in its regulatory role while at the same time not expecting doctrine to somehow define God in any "real" sense.[44] However, it seems that Thomas' context may not have been quite so open to such a pluralistic frame of mind, allowing novices to be satisfied with only the via negativa when discussing God, particularly in the face of Islamic teachings about humanity's inability to know God. Even granting tremendous humility in theology and modesty concerning its accomplishments, Thomas feels compelled to state that it must be possible for us to know God in some real sense, for if we could not, then what we do see with our highest intellect would be an idolatrous image.[45]

Thomas, Philosophy, and Revelation

Thomas is quite evidently not original in his conception of a design for the *Summa Theologica*. First, he gives every indication that he is borrowing his organizational plan from Aristotle's conception of science. Second, he makes no claim to originality in the limited theological substance he offers his readers. For substance, he simply turns to revelation. In order to bring our study of Thomas to a conclusion, we must first take up an explanation of how his organizational structure impacts and shapes what he does theologically. After this brief discussion of organizational method, we will then turn our attention to what Thomas believes we can know and how we can know it.

As will be illustrated below, Thomas demonstrates that his organizational method is derived from Aristotle's science. His frequent explicit reference to "the philosopher" indicates that Thomas was knowingly

44. Interestingly, such an assumption would be unusual for Lash, given the Constantinian implications. Perhaps he would wish to limit the size of the community to individual local churches, but this simply relocates the problem to deciding who really represents the Tradition. Pluralism would flourish in such a context, but this might be better described as a second Reformation, of sorts. The difference would be that this time the factions would be far more numerous.

45. Thomas Aquinas, *Summa Thelogica*, I.12.1.

and approvingly subjecting the organization of pedagogical material for novice theologians to the prescriptions of Aristotle. Even further, in Aristotle, Thomas enlists an altogether pagan philosopher. The novelty and risk of such an approach is borne out in the subsequent history of Thomas' life, teaching, and the use of his work for training novices. To say that he and his work suffered hardship for a time is putting it rather mildly.

The question naturally arises, "If so much difficulty could (and did) arise from using Aristotle's scientific method, why pursue it?" Thomas answers this question by demonstrating his understanding of what may or may not constitute real knowledge of God and by showing how specific claims to more comprehensive knowledge derived from the activities of God sensed by humans may in fact be more detrimental than helpful in discovering substantive or essential knowledge of God. Thomas believed he was protecting the knowledge of God from an equivocation with the effects found in creation. As Smith pointed out earlier: "In the context of eternity it makes perfect sense to discuss God prior to or abstracted from any consideration of creation . . . The purpose for discussing cause before effect, even though the reverse is the order of learning (the order of rational investigation is from effect to cause), is to separate the being from the necessity of the act and to prevent the error of reducing the being to these acts only."[46] To pursue knowledge from effect to cause is to attempt to construct a doctrine or understanding of God based on what can be seen in His creatures. While Thomas would agree that such knowledge is analogically possible, it does not give us comprehensive knowledge of God's essence—it is imperfect knowledge.

> [Good, wise, and living] signify the divine substance, and are predicated substantially of God, although they fall short of a full representation of Him. Which is Proved thus. For these names express God, so far as our intellects know Him. Now since our intellect knows God from creatures, it knows Him as far as creatures represent Him. Now it was shown above (Q. 4, A. 2) that God prepossesses in Himself all the perfections of creatures, being Himself simply and universally perfect. Hence, every creature represents Him, and is like Him so far as it possesses some perfection: yet it represents Him not as something of the same species or genus, but as the excelling principle of whose form the effects fall short, although they derive some kind of likeness

46. Smith, "Thomas Aquinas' *De Deo*," 132.

thereto, even as the forms of inferior bodies represent the power of the sun. This was explained above (Q. 4, A. 3), in treating of the divine perfection. Therefore the aforesaid names signify the divine substance, but in an imperfect manner, even as creatures represent it imperfectly. So when we say *God is good*, the meaning is not *God is the cause of goodness*, or, *God is not evil*; but the meaning is, *Whatever good we attribute to creatures, pre-exists in God*, and in a more excellent and higher way. Hence, it does not follow that God is good, because He causes goodness; but rather on the contrary, He causes goodness in things because He is good; according to what Augustine says (*De Doctr. Christ.* i. 32), *Because He is good, we are.*[47]

Thomas finds the knowledge of effects imperfect and of a totally different order.[48] This does not mean we can have no knowledge of God, as he said of words like good and wise, they "are predicated substantially of God, although they fall short of a full representation of Him." This means that we can have knowledge, and can even name that knowledge according to our creaturely signification.[49] However, such signification is limited to the extent that it is never equivalent to the perfection of the cause. "Univocal predication is impossible between God and creatures. The reason of this is that every effect which is not an adequate result of the power of the efficient cause, receives the similitude of the agent not in its full degree, but in a measure that falls short, so that what is divided and multiplied in the effects resides in the agent simply."[50] What we can see here in Thomas is that he was not merely aware of the limitation of knowledge that proceeds from cause to effect; rather, he constructed his understanding of knowledge on the basis of such limitation. Following Aristotle, Thomas believed we must first discover knowledge of the cause and then proceed to the knowledge of the effects.[51] Thomas could not allow that the effects of the primary cause be determinative of the essence of the cause. Instead, the effects must remain in their right relationship

47. Thomas Aquinas, *Summa Theologica*, I.13.2.

48. Ibid., I.1.1, reply to objection 2.

49. Ibid., I.13.3.

50. Ibid., I.13.5. Such multiplicity could be reduced by Lash's understanding of communal, or narrative, construction through practice. In other words, the communal nature of the narrative could alleviate a certain amount of multiplicity. However, any community will remain so limited by both time and space as to make it impossible to argue for a knowledge by means of cumulative effects.

51. See Aristotle, *Posterior Analytics*, 12:71b9–72b4.

to the cause—as effects. The multiplicity of the effects remained an in-surmountable obstacle to arriving at comprehensive knowledge, not to mention Thomas believed knowledge by means of the effects is knowl-edge of a different order than knowledge of the cause.

We can see how Thomas follows Aristotle to arrive at an organiza-tional method that considers the knowledge of the cause as primary and knowledge of effects as secondary. The knowledge gained through effects is not purely speculative, since effects do bear similitude to their cause. However, the similarity is only discovered analogously. Thus, Thomas does not conceive of a "theology from below" that affords his readers any sure knowledge based in the effects. This leads us to Thomas' answer to discovering theological knowledge: theological knowledge is best set in the context of disclosure, rather than discovery.

Thomas' overarching purpose in the *Summa Theologica* is to pres-ent novices with an initiation into the study of sacred theology. Such an initiation must ground them in the basic questions of studying the highest science. However, they will not engage the study of the high-est science until they have completed their initiation. It is only masters who are able to comment on the Scriptures, and masters must first have command of the basic questions. Likewise, Thomas wants masters to be fully aware of the limitations of natural reason, pressing them to regard revelation more highly.

A major emphasis in this initiation by Thomas seems to revolve around limitation. Thomas believes that the reason of humans can ob-tain knowledge of God, but as we have seen, it can obtain only limited knowledge, and even that cannot occur without assistance from God. As Thomas makes clear in two articles of Question 12,

> I answer that, it is impossible for any created intellect to see the essence of God by its own natural power . . . [T]he created in-tellect cannot see the essence of God, unless God by His grace unites Himself to the created intellect, as an object made intel-ligible to it. (I.12.4)

> I answer that, everything which is raised up to what exceeds its nature, must be prepared by some disposition above its nature; as, for example, if air is to receive the form of fire, it must be prepared by some disposition for such a form. But when any cre-ated intellect sees the essence of God, the essence of God itself becomes the intelligible form of the intellect. Hence it is neces-

sary that some supernatural disposition should be added to the intellect in order that it may be raised up to such a great and sublime height. Now since the natural power of the created intellect does not avail to enable it to see the essence of God, as was shown in the preceding article, it is necessary that the power of understanding should be added by divine grace. Now this increase of the intellectual powers is called the illumination of the intellect, as we also call the intelligible object itself by the name of light of illumination. And this is the light spoken of in the Apocalypse (Apocalypse xxi:23): "The glory of God hath enlightened it"— viz., the society of the blessed who see God. By this light the blessed are made "deiform"—that is, like to God, according to the saying: "When He shall appear we shall be like to Him, and [Vulg., 'because'] we shall see Him as He is" (1 John ii:2). (I.12.5)[52]

God "gifts" humanity with knowledge of Himself, because He wishes for humanity to know Him. Indeed, this is the highest good attainable and expressible: the knowledge of God. Thomas must remain open to such an infusion of real knowledge so that the knowledge the man Jesus has of the Father may be understood as real, even, or perhaps especially, while He was Incarnate.[53] God wishes to reveal Himself, because that is the greatest thing He could do. Further, such knowledge (i.e., goodness) is supremely communicated not in words or propositions, but in the communication of the divine person in the Incarnation.

To each thing, that is befitting which belongs to it by reason of its very nature; thus, to reason befits man, since this belongs to him because he is of a rational nature. But the very nature of God is goodness, as is clear from Dionysius (*Div. Nom.* i). Hence, what belongs to the essence of goodness befits God. But it belongs to the essence of goodness to communicate itself to others, as is plain from Dionysius (*Div. Nom.* iv). Hence it belongs to the essence of the highest good to communicate itself in the highest manner to the creature, and this is brought about chiefly by "His so joining created nature to Himself that one Person is made up of these three—the Word, a soul and flesh," as Augustine says (*De Trin.* xiii). Hence it is manifest that it was fitting that God should become incarnate.[54]

52. Thomas Aquinas, *Summa Theologica*, I.12.4, I.12.5.
53. Ibid., III.9.4.
54. Ibid., III.1.2.

Thus, we see that Thomas believes revealed knowledge is the supreme form of knowledge of God (i.e., God's own self-expression). For the theologian, this means a hierarchy exists when it comes to knowledge. The Incarnation is the supreme revelation of God. His expression of Himself in the words of revelation found in the Scriptures follows closely as the subject to be considered by human reason in sacred science. It is the only authoritative knowledge to which the theologian can appeal for certainty when answering questions of faith. "The principles of other sciences either are evident and cannot be proved, or are proved by natural reason through some other science. But the knowledge proper to this science comes through revelation and not through natural reason. Therefore it has no concern to prove the principles of other sciences, but only to judge of them. Whatsoever is found in other sciences contrary to any truth of this science must be condemned as false: "Destroying counsels and every height that exalteth itself against the knowledge of God" (2 Corinthians 10:4–5)."[55] Thomas is standing within the orthodox tradition of the church when he attributes such a high view of authority to revelation. He regularly appeals to both church fathers and the Scripture as authoritative. However, it is only the opinion of church fathers and his contemporary theologians that come under scrutiny within the objections and answers to objections. Scripture is beyond question and beyond dispute. "Sacred doctrine . . . properly uses the authority of the canonical Scriptures as an incontrovertible proof, and the authority of the doctors of the church as one that may properly be used, yet merely as probable."[56] Certainly interpretations may occasionally vary when it comes to the Scriptures. However, even within the possibilities obtained through varying interpretations, Thomas does not allow for a plurality of interpretations to resolve the issue. He appeals to the literal interpretation as supreme.

> The author of Holy Writ is God, in whose power it is to signify His meaning, not by words only (as man also can do), but also by things themselves. So, whereas in every other science things are signified by words, this science has the property, that the things signified by the words have themselves also a signification. Therefore that first signification whereby words signify things belongs to the first sense, the historical or literal. That significa-

55. Ibid., I.1.6, reply to objection 2.
56. Ibid., I.1.8, reply to objection 2.

tion whereby things signified by words have themselves also a signification is called the spiritual sense, which is based on the literal, and presupposes it.[57]

Further, he does not believe that the Scripture itself allows for multiple interpretations, since anything taught allegorically in one place is discovered literally in another.

> The multiplicity of these senses does not produce equivocation or any other kind of multiplicity, seeing that these senses are not multiplied because one word signifies several things, but because the things signified by the words can be themselves types of other things. Thus in Holy Writ no confusion results, for all the senses are founded on one—the literal—from which alone can any argument be drawn, and not from those intended in allegory, as Augustine says (*Epis.* 48). Nevertheless, nothing of Holy Scripture perishes on account of this, since nothing necessary to faith is contained under the spiritual sense which is not elsewhere put forward by the Scripture in its literal sense.[58]

The whole of Thomas' work in the *Summa Theologica* may be explained as a means of leading novices to a humble acceptance of their role in sacred science. Revelation remains as the primary authority over all they do and propose. This does not negate the use of their reason; however, it does indicate that reason is always in service to revelation.

> Thomas' ordering principle, *ordo rerum*, however, does not entail a philosophical discussion of the doctrine of God. The unity of this science, *sacra doctrina*, demands that all remain under or within the *ratio* of being divinely "revealable." As Thomas attempts to find a rational basis for some of those beliefs, he is pursuing a deeper understanding with the belief that the object of faith is intelligible in itself, if not to us in this life. The reasoning upon the faith will typically, but not exclusively, involve the manifestation of that faith where reason cannot attain of its own accord. Revelation, however, provides the more certain and complete knowledge. The argument from authority never gives up its place to rational argument, though rational argument may be employed where the authority of revelation is retained . . . The argument from authority, that is from the authority of revelation, always reigns as the more certain and complete.[59]

57. Ibid., I.1.10.

58. Ibid., I.1.10, reply to objection 1.

59. Smith, "Thomas Aquinas' *De Deo*," 135–36. Smith is here referring to Thomas' *Summa Theologica*, I.1.3, and I.1.8.

Thomas expects that revelation will guide and limit the study and conclusions of theology. In this, he expects revelation to serve as an authority above and beyond the interpreter. In other words, revelation serves as an external authority over the theologian and his/her reason or speculation. Thomas remains orthodox in his regard for revelation and his limitation of human knowledge. I suspect he would regard such limitation of knowledge gained through reason and his respect for revelation as but a "natural" expression of humility in light of what confronts the theologian in study. As we shall see in chapters that remain, such humility is lost after the Enlightenment. This is not to say that post-Enlightenment students of theology, or theism, lost their respect for the nature of the subject. Instead, the limitation of human reason, when compared to the authority of revelation, seems to have been relativized according to the Constantinian presumptuousness of scholastic humanism. In other words, since everyone within the known world existed within the parameters of Christian redemption through the sacraments, beginning at infancy, theologians could easily assume an anthropology that released human reason from its limitations. Reason was "naturally" good and reliable. Further, reason was sufficient to replace all external authorities, such as revelation. Such a conclusion is foreign to Thomas, but resides comfortably in the thought of Rene Descartes.

Conclusion

Thomas' use of philosophy seems clear within his *Summa Theologica*. He followed a pattern of knowing according to the science of Aristotle, where knowing the effect, which is the normative beginning point for learning according to the senses, is secondary to knowing the cause. Thomas follows this pattern so that he might prevent God from being reduced to merely His effects. At the same time, Thomas is also quite careful to indicate that limitations to our knowledge cannot be overcome by reason. Thus, God needed to disclose Himself in means available to humans. He does this by providing knowledge of a different order: revelation. God has given humanity representation of Himself in the text of the Scriptures, but this representation stands as only a witness to the greater revelation of Himself in the person of Jesus. Ultimately, in Jesus, humanity can be graced with knowledge that is both reliable and higher than natural knowledge. Of course, we will not be able to have complete knowledge of Jesus until we are able to stand before Him and see Him face to face. In this, the *exitus–reditus* pattern is complete for Thomas. Knowledge is begun by God and enhanced through illumination during the Christian's creaturely existence. Knowing finally culminates in the beatific vision when the believer is present with God.

This pattern used by Aquinas was not an arbitrary organization of topics, nor was it designed based on the nature of the knowledge only (analogous knowledge based on the chain of being). Thomas was writing for a specific audience and organized his material according to their needs. What is somewhat distinct about the *Summa* is that the audience is an academic audience, of sorts, requiring an organizational pattern well-suited to their specific needs. Since they were studying subjects from a somewhat more academic frame of reference, Thomas organized and presented his material in the current academic format. The question is, "Does this format constitute a system?" According to the post-Enlightenment notions of systematic knowledge as universal knowledge available to anyone that provides real and comprehensive knowledge of "the way things really are" on the subject of God, Thomas does not seem to have devised a system. He may be closer to it than others, due to his use of a philosophical pattern for organization. However, such organizational borrowing has occurred in others prior to Thomas. He is simply using a new pattern in Aristotle. Is Thomas highly organized and efficient in his discussion? Yes, by all accounts he is well organized and does not attempt to respond to historical concerns found in his current circumstances. Is he attempting to give an account of knowledge that is beyond history? It does not appear that he is, nor can he do so in light of his high regard for revelation.

5

Wycliffe in a Philosophical Mold

Introduction

As theology progressed through the Middle Ages, not every question was settled by commenting on Lombard's *Sentences*. In fact, the *Sentences* seemed to raise several questions not addressed previously, or at least it provided the context for raising various questions. Questions came from many quarters, including other areas of the university (e.g., philosophy, science, etc.). Incongruities within and between theologies needed to be settled. Typically the church had a ready answer for each issue, but schism was very alive, even within the church hierarchy.

Theological investigation at this point seemed largely concerned with demonstrating the truths of doctrine and the creeds as they were spelled out in the various manuals, particularly Lombard's *Sentences*. However, other issues occasionally arose that needed to be addressed on an individual basis. It is through one of these issues that we see perhaps most clearly what was the theological method of the Middle Ages, especially as it relates to a doctrine that was still developing. Far from insisting upon the defensibility of a position only because it was philosophically logical and consistent with other doctrines, both sides of the debate attempted to demonstrate their historicity. Tradition, in the form of the Fathers and an appropriate interpretation of Scripture, was the field where many battles were fought. One such notable battle was the issue of transubstantiation for John Wycliffe (ca. 1330–1384). Though by no means the only issue to arise in the fourteenth century, or even the most politically dramatic, Wycliffe illustrates well the ground on which theological debates were staged. Let us turn our attention to how this battle was fought, and then analyze how Wycliffe's response depicts the theological method of the Middle Ages.

The Transubstantiation Debate

The year 1378 was a turning point in the career of John Wycliffe. Having been told through a papal bull and subsequent trial that his views on civil lordship were not in accord with those of the magisterium in Avignon, he became well aware that his battles were no longer being fought inside the confines of "historical Church teaching."[1] Pope Gregory XI had made his views concerning the rights of the papacy clear by condemning eighteen of Wycliffe's propositions on civil rights in bulls sent in 1377 to Oxford university, where Wycliffe was lecturing, as well as to the clerical authorities of England, and to Edward III (though he died and the bull needed to be re-addressed to Richard II, the child king). The ensuing trial resulted in Wycliffe being enjoined to abstain from arguing disputed positions in the schools or in sermons, largely a slap on the wrist since Richard's mother had issued an order that no judgment should be passed on his case. The crowds at the trial also helped deter any action against Wycliffe since the trial was perceived as an attempt by a French Pope to control English liberties.

However, death removed Gregory before he could press toward further action against Wycliffe. This was the beginning of what has commonly been termed the Great Papal Schism.[2] Certainly the new pope in France, Clement VII, was not inclined to rile the English, thereby paving the way for their support of the new pope in Rome, Urban VI, although the English were already largely supportive of the latter. Urban VI also could not afford to ruffle the feathers of his English supporters by suppressing one of the more vocal advocates for English liberty. Therefore, the bulls against Wycliffe were soon forgotten and the matter of enforcing them put behind the two rival popes.

Nevertheless, Wycliffe had been told in no uncertain terms that what he taught was erroneous. He could no longer expect his arguments to persuade the papal hierarchy of what he believed to be un-Christian policies.[3] If he was to continue in the favor of the pope, some type of re-

1. McFarlane, *John Wycliffe and the Beginnings of English Nonconformity*, 80.

2. Ibid., 82.

3. McFarlane believes Wycliffe fully expected his teachings to have a reformatory impact on the magisterium prior to the condemnations of some of his doctrines, cf.

cantation would be necessary, but Wycliffe never appears to have considered this as an option. Indeed, perhaps the option became rather obscure since the battle was now to be forced upon him by local ecclesiastical authorities.

Urban VI could not take a direct hand in the matters surrounding Wycliffe and his teaching; however, this does not mean they went unnoticed. The monks and local authorities to whom Wycliffe had unfavorably addressed many of his tracts were continually seeking a way to silence the "heretic." The evidence began to accrue in 1379 when Wycliffe turned his attention to an exposition of the Eucharist.

It is a question as to what gave rise to Wycliffe's expositions on the Eucharist, which placed his teaching very much in opposition to the widely held belief of transubstantiation. Earlier in his career, he had espoused a form of the quantitative view held by Aquinas, and could even be found in support of the Scotist view of transubstantiation, which was the popular view to which he later found himself in opposition.[4] His realist philosophy could certainly have led him to conclusions that denied the possibility of transubstantiation.[5] It is also conceivable that his arguments were still politically motivated. Believing he had demonstrated the un-Christian position of the contemporaneous Church and its authorities, he may have been turning his attention to the remaining powers of the clergy evidenced by their supernatural capacity to turn bread and wine into the body and blood of Christ.[6] Whatever led him to his conclusions, they most certainly did not accord with the current

---

McFarlane, *John Wycliffe and the Beginnings of English Nonconformity*, 81ff. Shirley is also convinced that Wycliffe was faced with a crisis point by the condemnation of his views and the election of two popes, causing him to abandon hope that he would be able to cause any type of reform inside the church. Cf. Wycliffe, *Fasciculi Zizaniorum*, xliiff.

4. Workman, *John Wyclif*, 31ff. Matthew also gives a fairly good overview of Wycliffe's early teachings on the Eucharist in *The English Works of Wyclif*, xxiff.

5. Workman, *John Wyclif*, 30. Workman believes that Wycliffe's metaphysics is what led him to his conclusions on the Eucharist, denying any influence of the abuses that had given rise to many of his other conclusions, e.g. lordship. Also cf. Leff, "Wycliff and Hus: A Doctrinal Comparison," 117.

6. McFarlane, *John Wycliffe and the Beginnings of English Nonconformity*, 93–94, and Keen, "Wyclif, the Bible, and Transubstantiation," 9ff. Both of these authors cite the progression of Wycliffe's thought in his writings of 1379 and the manner in which Wycliffe had arrived at many of his other positions as evidence he was continuing his program of reform.

teaching of the church. Such a position of theological variance provided the clerics with the ammunition they needed to attack Wycliffe.

Wycliffe's lectures on the Eucharist during 1379 comprised the materials afterwards embodied in his book, *De Eucharistia*. Up until this point, Wycliffe could simply be numbered among the many spokesmen of the anti-clerical interests. However, with the revelation of his views on the Eucharist, he was now to be singled out as something other than a political malcontent. By late 1380 or early 1381, his views on the Eucharist were evidence enough to pursue action against him.[7] The opposition came this time, as would be expected, from local quarters, since the pope was in no position to interfere. The current chancellor of Oxford, William Barton, who had constantly opposed the teachings of Wycliffe, appointed a commission of twelve doctors to report on their colleague's Eucharistic teaching. A seven to five vote found the charge against Wycliffe of teaching erroneous doctrines proved, which afforded Barton the opportunity to threaten imprisonment, suspension, and even excommunication for those who held to such beliefs. Only a few moments after Barton's pronouncement, Wycliffe, though at first surprised, seemed undaunted, and replied with an appeal to the king.[8] The appeal went seemingly unnoticed by the king, and the Peasants' Revolt of June, 1381, with which the teachings of Wycliffe became associated, left Wycliffe with little support from the nobility.[9]

The activity at Oxford served to draw up the battle lines for future discussion of the issues. Displeased by the ecclesial interference into the independence of the university, the seculars sought, particularly through

7. The date of the commission is somewhat uncertain, but obviously prior to Wycliffe's defense of his position in the *Confession* which is dated May 10, 1381. For documentation of what took place in this commission and the activities following it, see Wycliffe, *Fasciculi Zizaniorum*, 110ff.

8. This appeal may seem somewhat unusual in that he did not appeal to an ecclesiastical court, even though by English law, the jurisdiction in matters of faith belonged within the confines of such a court and not to the king. However, Sergeant points out that the control of teaching in the university was not an ecclesial matter, but a secular matter for the king to decide since the university was not under ecclesial authority. Cf. Sergeant, *John Wyclif: Last of the Schoolmen and First of the English Reformers*, 248–51.

9. The Peasants' Revolt, as McFarlane argues, was not caused or supported by Wycliffe and his teaching. However, the connection to Wycliffe was made through John Ball, a former pupil of Wycliffe, due to the similarities of some of their teachings, especially that the 'just' alone had a right to their possessions. See McFarlane, *John Wycliffe and the Beginnings of English Nonconformity*, 99.

elections, to demonstrate their displeasure.[10] Having supporters of his views in power at Oxford kept Wycliffe hopeful that his battle could continue to be waged against the clerics and appealing to the upper-class laity. He continued to solicit support from the anti-clerical quarters; however, with less success than previous attempts. One of the enemies he had created during his many rampages against the pope had recently been elevated to Archbishop of Canterbury. Archbishop William Courtenay was quick to use his authority as an opportunity to squash the "Lollardy" from his province, and the place to begin was at Oxford with the followers of Wycliffe and the positions espoused by Wycliffe himself.[11] The so-called 'Earthquake Council' of May 17, 1382, and the subsequent pursuits against the followers of Wycliffe's views left him little room for hope that reform or change was going to happen in his lifetime. Having been relieved of his position at Oxford and now being systematically effaced from the memory of political and ecclesial interests, coupled with failing health, Wycliffe returned to his residence in Lutterworth from which he continued a prolific writing campaign against the views of the clerical authorities on many fronts, including transubstantiation.[12]

It is in this context that Wycliffe composes the work with which this study is mainly concerned, his *Trialogus*, most likely written in the latter half of 1382 or early in 1383.[13] As the title indicates, this Latin work was a colloquy amongst three speakers. The names of these speakers are Alithia, Pseudis, and Phronesis—or Truth, Falsehood, and Wisdom. Following a scholastic pattern of disputation which outlines the views of the opponent in as full an explanation as possible and proceeds to refute

10. For an excellent treatment of the activity at Oxford during this time, see Hudson's, "Wycliffism in Oxford 1381–1411," 67–84.

11. Vaughan outlines the program undertaken to eradicate the influence of Wycliffe after he left Oxford. Wycliffe's teachings, and eventually Wycliffe himself along with a number of followers at Oxford, were condemned as heretical, but Wycliffe was never really accosted during his remaining years at Lutterworth. Cf. Wycliffe, *Tracts and Treatises of John de Wycliffe*, lxxiff.

12. Wycliffe was seriously ill in 1379 at Oxford. In 1382, he suffered his first stroke which left him with some paralysis. It was a second stroke on December 28, 1384, that led to his death on the 31st.

13. Certainly this work was subsequent to the "Earthquake Council" (May 17, 1382) since this is referred to in the text, and presumably prior to the crusade of Spenser (April, 1383), bishop of Norwich, who raised support for his crusade chiefly through papal pardons and indulgences, since no mention of this outstanding use of papal power is given. Cf. Wycliffe, *Tracts and Treatises of John de Wycliffe*, 13; and Workman, *John Wyclif*, 309.

every point, Wycliffe attempted to recount many of the quarrels he had with the papacy through the four books that comprise this work. Written in Latin and in a style becoming of the academic skills of Wycliffe, it is unlikely that this work was intended for the ears of the common folk, nor does it appear to be an appeal for the support of the gentry. It is more probable that the work, being somewhat of a compendium of Wycliffe's beliefs with nothing particularly new being introduced, was intended for use in academic teaching and discussion. This is supported by the later (1397) examination by Arundel, the Archbishop of Canterbury, of its purported reading in the schools as a textbook, particularly at Oxford and Cambridge, and the teaching of some of its doctrines.[14] The views of Wycliffe espoused in this text found their most capable transmission through the teaching of the Lollards of the fifteenth century. Though the works of Wycliffe were condemned to be burned in 1413 by the Council of Constance, it is quite evident that many of his texts were spread abroad. The searches made of the rooms at Oxford produced a number of copies, but by this time the popularity amongst the lesser classes had aided in a fairly wide distribution of his thought, if not also his writings.[15] It is significant to note that the *Trialogus* was the first of Wycliffe's writings to be printed (at Basel in 1525) and provides one of the few direct links with the continental reformers of the sixteenth century.[16]

The text of the *Trialogus* that treats the matter of the Eucharist is found in the fourth book, occupying the first nine points of disputation. It is the first of the sacraments treated in the list of disputations relating to the sacraments. The nine points for discussion are as follows:

I.   On the Eucharist

II. What is denoted by the pronoun "this" in the words of consecration

III. Showing that the bread remains bread after consecration

IV. The preceding statements confirmed by argument

14. Workman, *John Wyclif*, 340.

15. Anne Hudson provides the most complete account of how Wycliffite texts survived in her *The Premature Reformation*, 82ff. Also cf. Stacey, *John Wyclif and Reform*, 133ff; and Genet, "The Dissemination of Manuscripts Relating to English Political Thought in the Fourteenth Century," 217–37.

16. McFarlane, *John Wycliffe and the Beginnings of English Nonconformity*, 117.

V.   How and from what cause the heresy concerning the sacrament
      of the Eucharist has grown up

VI.   In what way the bread is the body of our Lord, and not the iden-
      tical body itself

VII. On the identification of the bread with the body of Christ

VIII. Showing that the body of Christ does not corrupt (decay)

IX.   Whether two bodies may be at once in the same place

In the first seven of the points, Phronesis (Wycliffe) is explaining to
Alithia the errors of the heretics and the truth of his own position.
Pseudis, who has fallen asleep, finally awakens in the eighth question to
test the theses of Phronesis.

As can readily be detected from these nine points for disputation,
Wycliffe, in his discussions on the Eucharist, was often arguing against
transubstantiation more than he was arguing for some alternative.
Disproving transubstantiation was his primary goal. Secondarily, he
would make some claims for what he considered an appropriate understanding of what took place when the "body and blood" were offered
to believers, but these claims were often short and unclear. It might be
helpful at this point, before delving into the arguments set forth in each
of these points, to outline the view of transubstantiation against which
Wycliffe is arguing.

According to Wycliffe's understanding of transubstantiation, as the
elements of the Eucharist were consecrated, the "touch of that more glorious Substance which takes possession of them"[17] causes the substance
of the bread and the wine to be lost. What is left behind is the appearance
of the bread and wine which serves to indicate the presence of another
substance. Therefore, a twofold movement can be seen in this process—
the cessation of the bread and wine, although not completely, and the
creation of the body and blood of Christ. Of course the next issue needing attention is how the accidents, the appearance of bread and wine
which mysteriously remain, can be explained. Aquinas had a complex
theory of quantity, but it was not the most prominent view in Wycliffe's
lifetime. The more prominent explanation of the accidents was that of
Duns Scotus. The Scotist view held that the accidents were "maintained
and multiplied as verities without substance by the unconditioned will

17. Workman, *John Wyclif*, 31.

of God. The Eucharist is thus the constant repetition of a stupendous miracle."[18]

As was mentioned above, Wycliffe held to both of these views at various points early in his career. However, Wycliffe's realist philosophy could not allow for the 'annihilation' of the substance of the bread and wine, and the subsequent mystery of the accidents without substance. His belief in the Scriptures, which taught that Christ was bodily in heaven, would not permit him to find Christ offered at the altar. He was especially unwilling to accord such a power of re-creation to the priests who thereby commanded the awe of the laity and produced a sort of idol worship of the elements as something magical and wondrous, since the elements themselves were considered to be God, a definite detraction from the exalted Christ.[19] In this context, the subject matter of the nine points of disputation in the first part of book four of the *Trialogus* becomes almost self-evident.

Throughout his discussion on the Eucharist in the *Trialogus*, Wycliffe is concerned to demonstrate the discord between a realist view of Scripture and the doctrine of transubstantiation. What is somewhat more difficult to discover is what Wycliffe offers as an alternative. Speaking of the bread he says that "this sacrament is the body of Christ in the form of bread,"[20] and that "Christ, who cannot lie, said that the bread he took in his hands was really his body."[21] The 'this' which Christ used when he said "this is my body" referred not to his own body, but to the bread in his hands.[22] Yet Wycliffe wishes to maintain that the bread *is* the body of Christ in some sense.[23] He finds his answer by comparing Scriptural references concerning figurative predication to the statements about the body of Christ. Reminding his readers of the figurative sense in which Christ represented Elijah, and of the ears of grain and the fat cows and lean cows of prophecy representing years (Gen 41), Wycliffe moves on to say that "Beyond all doubt, then, the expression 'this is my body,' is *figurative* as are those in the Gospel of John: 'unless ye eat the

18. Ibid., 33.

19. John Wycliffe, *Trialogus*, 151. Wycliffe believed such a creation of God in the elements meant that "every church would have its own God."

20. Ibid., 133.

21. Ibid., 134.

22. Ibid., 135.

23. Ibid., 138.

flesh of the Son of man,' with many like them, which Christ spake in another sense."[24] Nevertheless, Wycliffe wants to maintain a reality present in the bread as he goes on to state that "the body of Christ is there spiritually,"[25] or "sacramentally."[26] This has caused some to believe that Wycliffe held to a view similar to Luther's consubstantiation,[27] or to a view of receptionism, a position which "makes the nature of the thing received, namely the consecrated elements, depend upon the state of the communicant receiving it."[28]

Much of Wycliffe's early career had been spent taking the battle to the enemy. As one of the many voices who spoke for English liberties, he often found himself in opposition to the ecclesiastical hierarchy to which he was also accountable. At this late stage in his life, the tables were turned. The battle had been brought to him, and in many ways he had lost. Declared heretical, he was forced to live the remainder of his short life without the large and forceful audience to which he had grown accustomed. He was fortunate to have the opportunity to die of natural causes in his residence at Lutterworth on December 31, 1384. Those who followed his teachings in the early fifteenth century would not find life, nor death, as comfortable.

24. Ibid., 149, emphasis mine. Leff wishes to take this in a strong sense, understanding the Christ to be present in the host as a quality or an influence, maintaining the miracle of transubstantiation, but in a way that minimizes the activity of the priest. Cf. Leff, *John Wyclif*, 179.

25. Wycliffe, *Trialogus*, 154.

26. Wycliffe's first chapter of *De Eucharistia* is devoted to discussion of the body being present sacramentally. Spinka believes this to be the best denotation of what Wycliffe believed, but understands him to be espousing a view of consubstantiation, cf. Spinka, *Advocates of Reform*, 30. Workman discusses the distinctions made by Wycliffe when he wished to explain Christ's presence sacramentally. Wycliffe differentiated between *in signo* and *ut in signo* declaring the former to be indicative of Christ's real presence. He appears to have wanted Christ's presence to be understood as more than a simple figure, although it is unclear as to exactly what is meant. Cf. Workman, *John Wyclif*, 36, where Workman comments on Wycliffe's *Apostasia*.

27. Workman, *John Wyclif*, 37. Stacey wavers a bit by calling Wycliffe's view "a doctrine having some affinity to Consubstantiation." Stacey, *John Wyclif and Reform*, 108.

28. McFarlane believes that Wycliffe appears to have approached this view, but is never explicitly clear as to what was his explanation. Receptionism seems to fit Wycliffe's statements, but McFarlane believes that Wycliffe wrestled with the issue for the remainder of his life, never actually settling on an answer that would satisfy him. Cf. McFarlane, *John Wycliffe and the Beginnings of English Nonconformity*, 94–95.

Approaches to Wycliffe's Theological Viewpoint

A great deal of discussion amongst commentators has arisen around both what Wycliffe actually believed and what gave rise to that belief. Since it would be impossible in a few pages to deal with the whole of Wycliffe's theology, this study is restricted to a survey of the arguments of a few commentators to delineate representative viewpoints on these issues. The aim of this survey is not necessarily to resolve the issues being discussed, although resolution may present itself. The primary objective is to discover what are the points of contention in the discussion and how these points are understood by Wycliffe scholars.

The first area to be discussed centers around what gave rise to Wycliffe's contention with ecclesial authorities over transubstantiation. Two somewhat differing opinions have been articulated with regard to why Wycliffe denied transubstantiation as it was propounded by his contemporaries. Gordon Leff has been the most articulate of a thesis that has perhaps prevailed since Wycliffe's lifetime, although he is largely following in the footsteps of biographers such as Herbert Workman and J. A. Robson.[29] According to this view, Wycliffe's arguments against transubstantiation were primarily the product of his metaphysical inquiries. His philosophical realism, as he conceived it, led him inevitably to deny the belief that the bread and wine were substantially the body and blood of Christ. In the development of Wycliffe's thought, it was his commitment to metaphysics that gave rise to his views on transubstantiation and not his previous debates with the ecclesial hierarchy over lordship, since these debates also could be demonstrated to be a consequence of his metaphysics. Wycliffe's metaphysics was the foundation and presupposition for all his beliefs, especially regarding the Eucharist. As Workman has stated, "[Wycliffe] approached the Eucharist from the standpoint not of abuses, but of a metaphysical system. The discovery of abuses came later."[30] Leff likewise cites that "[Wycliffe's] view of the Eucharist grew directly out of his metaphysics."[31] Of course, both Workman and Leff reflect a presumption common to a distinctly modern preoccupation with system and foundations. They are assuming Wycliffe would think

29. Both Workman and Robson demonstrate a reliance on Woodford, Wycliffe's contemporary, who gave a developmental description of Wycliffe's Eucharistic thinking. Cf. Workman, *John Wyclif*, 30, 34ff.; and Robson, *Wyclif and the Oxford Schools*, 190ff.

30. Workman, *John Wyclif*, 30.

31. Leff, "Place of Metaphysics in Wyclif's Theology," 230.

of the Eucharist first in terms of coherence with the rest of his doctrinal position, including both theological and philosophical doctrines. The error in this assumption is discovered in Wycliffe's appeal to the authority of Scripture. Wycliffe's choice of authority is pertinent. Though he may use logic and the rules of his own understanding of epistemology and ontology, his authority is always Scripture and an appropriate interpretation of Scripture. This is even the case when Scripture seems illogical, or at least obscure. Any systematic, or "system-like," considerations seem secondary to Wycliffe's and the historical church's reading of Scripture. To aid in understanding how all this fleshes out in Wycliffe's argument, it is perhaps best that further elucidation be given of his metaphysics.

It has been widely accepted that Wycliffe was a realist. What is generally meant by such a statement is that Wycliffe believed universal categories existed by which subsequent definition and distinction could be made. As Leff has demonstrated, in Wycliffe's system, there were "three main gradations of being: eternal intelligible being in God; essential or universal created possible being, subdivided into the more and less universal causes of particular beings; and finally those individual beings as they exist actually and temporally as substances, appearing and disappearing in time. To them can be added the fourth kind of being, the accidental or non-essential properties, such as size or colour, which individual substances have."[32] This was a distinct departure from the metaphysics of his opponents, the nominalists, who only held to the last two categories of individual existence. Wycliffe regarded all the parts sharing in "the same universal being which had its origin in the intelligible being of all possible beings in God."[33] As Wycliffe states, "We must hold everywhere to Catholic doctrine even if we reject the technical terms; for there cannot be a creature which does not first have a mental or intentional existence in God before it has being in general and secondary being in its created causes. And in this way its potentiality must precede its actuality . . . And every created genus takes its essence from the eternal ideas in God, and thus every creature is a sharing in mental being."[34] This was certainly not a new conception of being. Wycliffe's view of the

32. Leff, "Place of Metaphysics in Wyclif's Theology," 220. Leff is relying heavily on the work of Anthony Kenny and is attempting an explication of Wycliffe's recently edited *De Universalibus*. Cf. Kenny, *Wyclif*, 80–90.

33. Leff, "Place of Metaphysics in Wyclif's Theology," 220–21.

34. Wycliffe, *De Universalibus* as quoted by Leff in "Place of Metaphysics in Wyclif's Theology," 221.

secondary cause participating in the primary cause could be found much earlier and comes to him perhaps through Pseudo-Denis and the *Book of Causes*, both of which are cited by him. The archetypal notion of being, that it is the most universal reality of all, derived from Avicenna and could be traced through Duns Scotus, who separated substance and its properties, a notion Wycliffe used to demonstrate the universality within each individual being rather than leave them in separate existence as Scotus had done. Wycliffe's unique application of this metaphysics came as he bound the participation of the individual in the universality of God as a necessary postulate of God's being. As Leff has explained: "Where Wycliffe was singular was in endowing God's eternal ideas of all possible beings with his own attributes of necessity and eternity as part of his essence rather than as objects of his knowledge of what could exist outside him, as Ockham had done."[35] The consequence of postulating the intelligibility of being in God's essence meant that existence was dependent upon God. As Wycliffe states, "For every creature is, in its intelligible being, identical with God, and it cannot therefore be thought of as existing for a moment unless it is supported by God."[36] It follows that since God was eternal, so the intelligibility of being in Him must also be eternal. It was also therefore indestructible and could not be annihilated. For God to annihilate some substance would entail the annihilation of Himself, an absurdity Wycliffe was quick to point out.[37] When such a view of being was applied to the doctrine of transubstantiation as Wycliffe understood it, it becomes quite evident why Wycliffe could not bear an explanation of "accidents without substance"—substance cannot be annihilated.

Since Wycliffe had developed his metaphysics fairly early in his career (*De Universalibus* was written in the late 1360s), it has been understood as the foundation for much of his later thought, including his views on the church and civil government, but particularly as it related to the Eucharist. Wycliffe's own admissions about the Eucharist demonstrate his thought had some development.[38] As a young man learning under strong nominalist influence, Wycliffe had held to the doctrine of

35. Leff, "Place of Metaphysics in Wyclif's Theology," 221.

36. Wycliffe, *De Universalibus* as quoted by Leff in "Place of Metaphysics in Wyclif's Theology," 223.

37. Wycliffe, *De Universalibus*, ch. 13.

38. Loserth surveys several of Wycliffe's statements that demonstrate he held to and even at times taught the prevailing view of transubstantiation. Cf. Wycliffe, *De Eucharistia*, ivff.

transubstantiation as it was taught by Scotus. As his metaphysics developed and he came to recognize that he could not hold to a view of
accidents without substance in the Eucharist, he moved to a position
espoused by Thomas Aquinas. Thomas suggested that what took place
at the time of consecration changed the substance of the bread and wine
and that the accidents which remained were upheld by what he called
"quantity." As Dziewicki explains: "Quantity is not a mere substance, not
a mere mode of being; it is different from extension for it is what makes
extension, and may be defined as a force that extends material substance.
Thus, after the words of consecration, the substance of bread is no longer
there, but quantity takes its place naturally, being itself upheld by God's
supernatural power: and therefore whatever the bread could do, even to
the feeding of the body, is now performed by the quantity that remains."[39]
The next step for Wycliffe was to recognize that even the quantitative
theory did not completely accord with his conception of the eternal intelligibility of being. Though the accidents were being supported by God
and the substance did not appear to be technically annihilated, it was
still changed into something that could not accord with the reality of
the accidents or the universality of substance. Bound to his metaphysical
foundations, Wycliffe had then to move to a position which would allow
for the remanence of the substance of bread and wine. This evolution
of Wycliffe's view is traced explicitly by a contemporary of Wycliffe, the
friar William Woodford. Once a friend, but like so many of the friars,
an eventual opponent, Woodford had read the *Sentences* with Wycliffe
when they were bachelors of theology at Oxford. This allowed each to
respond in his own lectures to the arguments of the other. Woodford
recalls the development in Wycliffe's view thusly,

> When the said Master John was first lecturing on the *Sentences*
> [1371 or 72], he asserted that though the sacramental accidents
> had a subject, yet the bread ceased to exist at consecration. And
> being much pressed as to what the subject of those accidents was,
> he replied that it was a mathematical body. Afterwards, when this
> position had been much argued against, he answered that he did
> not know what the subject of the accidents was, yet he asserted
> clearly that they had a subject. Now [Woodford was writing in
> 1381] he lays down expressly that the bread remains after conse-
> cration and is the subject of the accidents.[40]

39. Wycliffe, *De Apostasia*, xv.
40. Wycliffe, *Fasciculi Zizaniorum*, xv, n.4. I am citing here the translation by Keen,

This statement seems to make it clear that Wycliffe moved from an early Scotist position, through a puzzlement *via* Thomas 'quantity,' to his eventual position of the remanence of the bread and wine. The means that led to his abandonment of Scotus and Thomas was the academic argumentation that was a part of every learning scholars program. Wycliffe's already developed metaphysics left him early in his career with conclusions that did not accord with the accepted view of transubstantiation. Leff is following Woodford's argument closely when he asserts that Wycliffe, due to his metaphysical commitments, could have reached his final position "at any time within the previous fifteen or more years."[41] With this view, he is following closely the earlier assertions and development of Woodford's opinion by Workman and Robson.[42] Trusting that Woodford accurately portrays the development of Wycliffe's view on the Eucharist, they believe that it was only a matter of time before the consequences of his metaphysical realism would be revealed completely.

Unwilling to accept Woodford's comments *prima facie*, Maurice Keen has taken issue with the developmental theory implicit in the former's statement. Keen raises three objections to Woodford's analysis. First, it imposes an uncomfortably long gap between Wycliffe's first grapplings with the Eucharist and his final conclusions. Second, though Wycliffe denied transubstantiation, he was never sure what he wished to put in its place. His efforts were spent arguing against transubstantiation, rather than for something else. If ignorance had gotten him off the hook before, why not continue to use it as a haven from his accusers? Finally, if all that was at issue was a point of metaphysics, why does Wycliffe tie all his arguments concerning transubstantiation to the abuses in the Church he had delineated in his works immediately prior to his writings against transubstantiation?[43]

Resting on these objections, Keen does not believe it possible that Wycliffe simply arrived at his Eucharistic conclusions as a result of metaphysical reflection. Arguing particularly from the timing of Wycliffe's arguments, i.e. after his disputes against many of the abuses in the Church

"Wyclif, the Bible, and Transubstantiation," 10. For more discussion of this quotation, see Robson, *Wyclif and the Oxford Schools*, 192–93.

41. Leff, *Heresy in the Later Middle Ages*, 499, 550.

42. Workman, *John Wyclif*, 34ff.; and Robson, *Wyclif and the Oxford Schools,* 190ff.

43. Keen, "Wyclif, the Bible, and Transubstantiation," 10–11. Loserth appears to strengthen Keen's argument by demonstrating Wycliffe's maintenance of transubstantiation at a late date, possibly even 1378. Cf. Wycliffe, *De Eucharistia,* iv–v.

had already been written, Keen states that "[Wycliffe] believed that on this one point of accidents without substance he could make those whom he regarded as the pillars of abuse, the followers of Antichrist or 'western Mahomets' as he made them out to be, look ridiculous and fraudulent (as he believed they really were). In other words, I believe almost the opposite of Workman's view, that Wycliffe attacked transubstantiation rather from the point of view of abuse than of a metaphysical system."[44] Keen proceeds to support this view with recourse not to Wycliffe's negative accounts of transubstantiation, but to his positive statements for the remanence of the bread and wine. Wycliffe's voluminous arguments against transubstantiation had been used to support the view that it had grown out of his metaphysics, academic debate forcing his hand; the overwhelming negativity in Wycliffe's argument, it is thought, finally demonstrates his foundational commitment to a metaphysical position. However, Keen wishes to demonstrate that Wycliffe's beliefs regarding the *remanence* of the bread and wine were founded not primarily on metaphysical argument, but on Scripture and the Fathers. Keen sees the Scriptural studies of Wycliffe's life directly prior to his conclusions on the Eucharist, alongside his arguments regarding the power of the clerics, as what settled the question of the Eucharist for him.[45] Granting that metaphysics was the ground for the questions about the Eucharist and in large part responsible for his rejection of transubstantiation, Keen wishes to view Scripture and the Fathers as the answer to the problem. Focusing more heavily on Scripture later in his life, which gave him stronger warrant to posit the remanence of the bread and wine, and reflecting on the abuses of the ecclesial authorities, Wycliffe used the Eucharist to once again supply an argument against the papal powers. Regarding transubstantiation to be a new doctrine that arose during the terrible reign of Innocent III, Wycliffe attempted to demonstrate papal discordance to the believing public once again.[46]

While it is not within the scope of this study to attempt to settle this issue, a few comments may be helpful. Keen does seem convincing in

44. Ibid., 11.

45. Ibid., 12–13. Keen is giving strong weight to the fact that Wycliffe has just completed his commentary on the whole Bible, *Postilla super totam Bibliam*. For a dscussion of the significance of this commentary, see Smalley, "John Wyclif's Postilla super totam Bibliam," 186–205.

46. For a more complete discussion of this thesis, see Keen, "Wyclif, the Bible, and Transubstantiation," 11–16.

regard to the timing of Wycliffe's writings on the Eucharist. It seems to answer the questions about why Wycliffe would wait until the end of his career to write so forcefully and so extensively on the subject. Wycliffe's appeal to the king for support in the face of the charges surrounding his teachings also appears to support the thesis that his explication was driven by political concerns more than metaphysical or doctrinal. However, Keen does not consider the possibility that the magisterium had simply overlooked Wycliffe's previous denials of transubstantiation, hoping to pin him with something stronger in regard to his tirades against the papacy, only later realizing that Wycliffe's views on the Eucharist was its strongest case against him. This may simply have fueled the fire for Wycliffe to write profusely on the subject. It is also possible that Wycliffe was using Scripture as a popular form for the argumentation since it may have been more accessible to his hearers than some abstract metaphysical development of the argument. Nonetheless, Keen does demonstrate the inadequacy of Woodford's strictly flat reading of Wycliffe's development. It seems unreasonable, though certainly not impossible, to postulate that Wycliffe was arguing in a strictly academic sense when he was chastising the papacy over transubstantiation. Perhaps a combination of the two views may be more adequate to both the personality and scholastic propriety of Wycliffe.

The second area needful of further study is what exactly was Wycliffe's view of the Eucharist. Though everyone agrees that Wycliffe did not explicitly spell out what was his belief, none have failed to give at least a modest opinion. While not attempting to be exhaustive, we must now turn to a brief overview of the proposals.

The distinctions amongst the various commentators is minimal, considering they agree on most points. Wycliffe believed that the bread and wine remained in their substance after the consecration, but he also held that Christ was somehow present. The question regarding what Wycliffe actually believed centers around how Christ was present at the Eucharist.

Commentators have attempted to piece together a coherent view attributable to Wycliffe, a task perhaps more difficult than one would imagine. Wycliffe's own statements on the subject are somewhat unclear. This has left commentators with the unfortunate task of drawing together the few disparate statements that he does make. A general consensus has prevailed that when Wycliffe declared Christ was present in the elements in a "figurative" sense, he was not proclaiming them to be a simple sign.[47] This would contradict his further delineation of Christ being present "spiritually."[48] But just what this presence of Christ was in some real sense is uncertain. Some have suggested that Wycliffe's view was constantly developing and that he had not arrived at a substantial conclusion when he died.[49] Others have defined Wycliffe's views according to the terms used by Wycliffe himself, comparing the statements he made on the presence of Christ in the elements and observing that he uses terms he expects to be explanatory, but that are in some ways equivocal.[50] Vaughan has attempted to give some perspective by comparing the terms according to their applicability. Citing Wycliffe's defense in his Latin confession, Vaughan summarizes that there are "Six modes of subsistence which may be attributed to the body of our Savior: three of these may be affirmed of that body as it is present in the Eucharist, and three of the state in which it exists in heaven. In the Eucharist, the body of Christ is virtually, spiritually, and sacramentally present; but his substantial, corporeal, and dimensional presence is said to be restricted to his mode of existence in the celestial state."[51] Still others have used a conception of consubstantiation, defining the term as the co-existence of two substances, to provide a reference point, explaining Wycliffe as holding something similar though impossibly identical.[52] Unfortunately, the definitions cited thus far do not solve the problem of identifying Wycliffe's view. They simply relocate it.

It appears easier to identify what Wycliffe did not believe than what he actually held. Certainly this is understandable since he spent more

47. Wycliffe, *Trialogus*, 149.

48. Ibid.

49. Workman, *John Wyclif*, 37ff.; Keen, "Wyclif, the Bible, and Transubstantiation," 15; and McFarlane, *John Wycliffe and the Beginnings of English Nonconformity*, 94–95.

50. Though perhaps not intending to leave the reader wondering as to what Wycliffe meant by his statements, or simply not having the resources to accomplish a definition, many authors are forced to leave a definition to the reader. Cf. Robson, *Wyclif and the Oxford Schools*, 194–95; Kenny, *Wyclif*, 88–89; Leff, "Place of Metaphysics in Wyclif's Theology," 231; and Stacey, *John Wyclif and Reform*, 107.

51. Wycliffe, *Tracts and Treatises of John de Wycliffe*, lxxxviii.

52. Workman, *John Wyclif*, 37; and Leff, "Place of Metaphysics in Wyclif's Theology," 231. Spinka and Stacey do a more complete job of defining both consubstantiation and receptionism and offering reasons as to why Wycliffe could not be classified strictly according to either conception. Cf. Stacey, *John Wyclif and Reform*, 108; and Spinka, *Advocates of Reform*, 30.

of his effort arguing against transubstantiation than arguing for another view. However, some attempts at description have shown promise. Leff has described what took place for Wycliffe contrasting the natural and the supernatural. What took place was "a sacramental conversion, in which the bread and wine at once remained naturally the same and became something new. It was an essentially spiritual transformation which Wycliffe did not attempt to explain naturally. It took place through a miracle."[53] This statement helps to locate the reality of the presence in the miraculous. While not allowing for subsequent explication, it does at least make an attempt at definition.

Spinka has attempted to clarify the issue by venturing a definition of Christ's sacramental presence. To speak of Wycliffe's view as sacramental means that the bread is "a material substance symbolizing a spiritual content or, as Augustine phrased it, an outward symbol of an inner grace."[54] What is particularly useful in this description is that Spinka is attempting to relate what Wycliffe meant to perhaps the strongest influence on his view, Augustine. What is needed in Spinka's linkage is a clearer definition of what Augustine meant by 'symbol' and how Wycliffe would have understood it. Keen also touches on Wycliffe's comments regarding Augustine's view of the Eucharist. Keen attempts to understand how Wycliffe interpreted the faith that is displayed in Augustine's statement: "What we see is the bread and the chalice that the eyes announce: and faith receives that the bread is the body and that the chalice is the blood of our Lord. These are sacraments, since one thing is seen, another understood."[55] Likewise, Stacey puts the debate within the framework of Augustine's view of the Eucharist, which is itself not a settled issue.[56] Unfortunately, none of these authors pursue further parallels between Wycliffe's view of the Eucharist and what he understood as the view of the Fathers. Certainly all the commentators do give mention of Wycliffe's use of the Fathers, but do not appear to give sufficient attention to the influence they had on his view of the Eucharist. Perhaps further attention to Wycliffe's Eucharistic heritage may provide more insight into what exactly Wycliffe believed in his development of Eucharistic doctrine.

---

53. Leff, *John Wyclif*, 179.

54. Spinka, *Advocates of Reform*, 30.

55. Keen, "Wyclif, the Bible, and Transubstantiation," 12.

56. Stacey, *John Wyclif and Reform*, 107ff.

Resolution of Wycliffe's Supposed Unfinished View

It is the aim of the final section in this chapter to present an interpretation of Wycliffe that continues various portions of previous discussions, but also allows his own developments on the Eucharist to be seen in a larger historical context. It is hoped that such a task will alleviate much of the tension plaguing students of Wycliffe as they attempt to piece together what were Wycliffe's actual Eucharistic beliefs.[57] Such tension is caused by a presumption that Wycliffe was attempting to argue a complete, or developing, systematic viewpoint that was demonstrably unique to himself, or at least as something proposed by Wycliffe that could replace the existing view of transubstantiation. To presume Wycliffe was engaged in such a task, though not without merit in view of Wycliffe's many treatises on the Eucharist, appears to overlook the intent of Wycliffe's historical citations and his own primitivist ends. Indeed, it is the aim of this study to demonstrate that Wycliffe believed his view was plain to be seen in the views held by the Fathers, particularly Augustine, the Church, as he interpreted it until the period following the Fourth Lateran Council (1215), and the authors of Scripture. Wycliffe could not hope to proffer a new or more developed view than existed in these manifold witnesses. His own work was not intended to give an alternative explication, although he continually made positive references to what was his view. He was not laying out a systematic treatment he believed logically (or perhaps epistemologically) superior to all other options Instead, he wished for his writings to demonstrate the ahistorical stance of the Church, and to call believers back to what he believed was the appropriate view. To attempt to piece Wycliffe's own view together is to misread his intentions. To understand what Wycliffe believed, one must retrace the historical views of the Eucharist and attempt to identify how Wycliffe understood and

57. Many authors have attempted to identify Wycliffe's beliefs only to end in frustrated and incomplete descriptions. Often the disclaimer is given that Wycliffe's own view was still developing when he died. Cf. Workman, *John Wyclif*, 37ff.; Keen, "Wyclif, the Bible, and Transubstantiation," 15; McFarlane, *John Wycliffe and the Beginnings of English Nonconformity*, 94–95; and Matthew's "Letter to Michael Henry Dziewicki," xxxvi. Here everyone agrees that Wycliffe knew what was the wrong view, but had no idea with what he wished to replace it. Such disclaimers assume he was aiming at a full explanation of the Eucharist, entirely missing the polemical intent of Wycliffe's writings and Wycliffe's own belief that he was defending what he regarded as a completed historical view against the novelty of transubstantiation. This being the case, Wycliffe would never have felt the necessity to give a full explanation of *his* view of the Eucharist. He believed it had existed for centuries, observable to all who rightly read the Scriptures and the Fathers.

interpreted them. Wycliffe assumed that his own view corresponded to his reading of the Fathers and Scripture, which he believed had already been explained in full prior to the "heresies" of recent centuries. Resting on this, he presumed that his brief statements of belief would be read in the larger context of historical belief and that the burden of proof was upon those who held to the "new" belief, transubstantiation.[58]

Obviously, it is not within the scope of this chapter to examine every historical figure or development of Eucharistic doctrine. The primary focus of the following discussion will center around Wycliffe's own view of doctrinal development. Attention will then be given to the way in which Wycliffe was using historical argument and what he hoped to gain from citations of the Fathers and Scripture. It is hoped that such an endeavor will help to uncover a path to understanding Wycliffe's view concerning the Eucharist, and provide the reader with an appropriate context in which to interpret his statements. Further, such a study will help to reveal the way in which theological investigation proceeded during this period. This will help provide clearer answers to questions such as: Is internal consistency important for Wycliffe's theology? Where does philosophy fit in his theology? Is his disagreement with transubstantiation due to its incompatibility with other doctrines in his theology (i.e., it is systematically incoherent), or his understanding of Scripture and the Fathers? Though greater detail may be given by means of reference to the whole of Wycliffe's works on the Eucharist, the *Trialogus* will be treated as representative for the sake of brevity.[59]

58. It is certainly admitted that Wycliffe may have introduced new elements into the discussion which require specific treatment as owing to Wycliffe. Likewise, it could be argued that Wycliffe's view may not have been an accurate reading of the Fathers or of Scripture, making his view something unique. The intent of this study is not primarily to discredit such possibilities, but simply to demonstrate that Wycliffe saw no need to delineate a careful systematic presentation of his own view since he already understood himself to be standing squarely within the tradition. Indeed, for Wycliffe to engage in such a task would have been read by his opponents as development of a new view, tantamount to an admission of heresy. (This is exactly the interpretation given by the friar William Woodford when Wycliffe posits the remanence of the bread and wine according to metaphysical demonstration. Cf. Wycliffe, *Fasciculi Zizaniorum*, xv n. 4.) New ideas or arguments regarding the Eucharist attributable to Wycliffe do not require that he was engaged in something historically novel, necessitating exposition of his total "view," only that he was nuancing, whether consciously or other, what he understood as *the* historical position.

59. Most certainly specifics of the arguments from *De Eucharistia* and *De Apostasia* could nuance the thesis of this study, as would a treatment of his Scriptural commentar-

Wycliffe's own view of the historical development of Eucharistic doctrine is quite flat until the controversies surrounding the Fourth Lateran Council caused a great chasm to open up between the view he understood to be taught by the Fathers and Scripture, and the current view of transubstantiation. While discussing the errors of his contemporaries, Wycliffe attempts to demonstrate the purity of the 'court of Rome' prior to the adoption of transubstantiation. "This very court, before the loosing of Satan, was plainly in agreement with the ancient doctrine aforesaid, as is evident from Con. Dis. II. c. Ego Berengarius, and so were all the holy doctors who treated of the subject prior to that time. After that time, however, the Scriptures were neglected, and many heresies were circulated on this subject, especially among the friars, and the disciples of that school . . ."[60] The Fourth Lateran Council (1215) marks the turning point for Wycliffe. Pope Innocent III, being "led away by his madness,"[61] was the first to adopt the view of transubstantiation officially. Though the view itself had been taking shape well before the time of the council, the word transubstantiation was first found in official documents at this time.[62] Wycliffe points to this as the beginning of the

ies, but from this author's readings, it is felt that they would more assuredly confirm the manner in which Wycliffe's view is herein interpreted more strictly according to the *Trialogus*.

60. Wycliffe, *Trialogus*, 133–34. The discussions of the Eucharist involving Berengarius took place in 1037–1059. Berengarius was arguing for a figurative presence of Christ's body in the bread and was later compelled to advocate a real presence. Wycliffe's reading of Berengarius does not seem completely accurate in this instance, although he may be referring more strictly to the early Berengarius. One also wonders if Wycliffe is aware of the previous debates in the middle of the ninth century in which Paschasius Radbert's thesis, which amounted to a form of Ambrosian realism and is now considered to be the progenitor of transubstantiation, was presented to the emperor Charles the Bald and was later countered by Ratramn of Corbey, who argued for a figurative presence. This appears to be the beginning of formal controversy between what have been called the Augustinian and Ambrosian traditions. For a good discussion of Augustine's and Ambrose's views in comparison, see Crockett, *Eucharist*, 88–98.

61. Wycliffe, *Trialogus*, 144–45.

62. The word 'transubstantiation' had only begun to appear in writings around the year 1140. Dugmore points to the quick approval for the term and the subsequent Bull of *Unam sanctam ecclesiam* of 1302, which made Catholic teaching on any doctrine the official doctrine to be held if one wanted to be considered a part of the Christian Church and qualified for salvation, as evidence that the authorities were simply choosing one view from among many to solidify the position of the papacy and impose a uniformity upon all who belonged to the Church. Cf. Dugmore, *Mass and the English Reformers*, 24–25.

end. "The reason why men fall into this heresy, is that they disbelieve the Gospel, and embrace in preference the papal laws and apocryphal sayings. And of all the kinds of infidelity that ever grew up in the church of God, this draws men down deeper and more imperceptibly into the vortices of error, and causes more to apostatize from our Lord Jesus Christ."[63] Wycliffe's treatment of the schism identifies the official adoption of transubstantiation as the point at which the schism began and attributes it to rebels who discovered something novel. He bases much of his argument upon the fact, as he understands it, that everyone prior to this point had believed in a uniform doctrine. Whether this is a rhetorical device or Wycliffe is entirely sincere in his belief is uncertain. However, it is crucial to note the means by which Wycliffe sets himself up in congruence with the entirety of history prior to the time of Innocent III.

It is widely held today that the positions of a realist interpretation, which understood the body as somehow really present in the bread, and a symbolic interpretation, which viewed the presence more figuratively, have existed at least since the time of Ambrose and Augustine.[64] As each particular view developed within the medieval Church, certain conflicts arose, but each view was more or less tolerated until the period of the tenth and eleventh centuries. Subsequent to the Fourth Lateran Council, the more symbolic view was denounced as opposed to the official teaching of the Church. Wycliffe does not seem to recognize the two streams of thought running through the centuries of the Church's teaching. He cites some authors, particularly Ambrose, alongside of Augustine, displaying their agreement.[65]

Obviously, those who held to transubstantiation were also appealing to Scripture and the Fathers in support of their view. However, Wycliffe is careful to demonstrate that his is the true interpretation of the Fathers, and especially of Scripture. He spends a great deal of time refuting the citations made by his opponents, reinterpreting them according to his

63. Wycliffe, *Trialogus*, 144. Immediately following this statement, Wycliffe launches into an implication of Innocent III as the leader of the apostasy.

64. Both Crockett and Dugmore outline the development of these views from their reading of the New Testament through the early Fathers to Augustine and Ambrose. Cf. Crockett, *Eucharist*, chs. 1–2, esp. pp. 39ff.; Dugmore, *Mass and the English Reformers*, 3ff. These authors are here using the term 'realist' in a sense quite different from that attributed to Wycliffe in previous paragraphs.

65. Wycliffe, *De Eucharistia*, 33; and a citation of Ambrose alone in Wycliffe, *Trialogus*, 72.

own view.[66] His conception of the historical development of Eucharistic doctrine is strictly linear, in that from the time of Scripture, one view predominated throughout with schismatic branches appearing only recently. It is evident throughout his discussion that he is attempting to defend *the* historical view against a novel interpretation. With this in view, attention must now be given to the question, "Why did Wycliffe believe his interpretation was *the* correct one?"

As has been widely accepted, and is obvious from the nature of Wycliffe's writings, most of his effort in studies on the Eucharist is devoted to the refutation of transubstantiation. Wycliffe has carefully constructed his argument against the notion of "accidents without substance." Such negativity is often viewed as deriving specifically from his positive universal conceptions of being and participation of reality in the archetypal being of God, which cannot allow for any type of annihilation of substance leaving only the visible accidents.[67] It must certainly be granted that much of Wycliffe's aim in his writings was to refute the predominant view of transubstantiation, and this could only be done through metaphysical argumentation. As was seen above, this was particularly true early in his life when he was willing only to refute the position according to metaphysical debate concerning annihilation and did not offer an alternative. However, later in his career, Wycliffe was prepared to state unequivocally that the substance of the bread and wine remained, requiring him to offer some explanation of how Christ was then present in the sacrament. This has led many students of Wycliffe to search through his writings to "put together" his view on the subject. The conclusions of such a "hunt" have offered only despair and frustration as no one seems to have a definitive answer. From this, many have surmised

66. Chapters V–VIII of Wycliffe, *De Apostasia* are devoted to this task. Dziewicki points out that Wycliffe is mainly concerned with following Scripture and is willing to simply admit that some of the Fathers could have been mistaken. However, Dziewicki also makes it clear that Wycliffe pushed each authority quite hard to make him fit with his own view. Cf. Wycliffe, *De Apostasia*, xxiiff.

67. Gordon Leff outlines Wycliffe's metaphysics nicely in his "Place of Metaphysics in Wyclif's Theology," 219ff. Unfortunately, Leff places inordinate emphasis on Wycliffe's metaphysics as the sole source for all subsequent development in Wycliffe's thought, simply overlooking, or at the least giving too little credence to, social and Scriptural warrants for Wycliffe's later stance on the Eucharist. From Leff's position it would be extremely difficult to identify Wycliffe's Eucharistic understanding since the identifiably metaphysical arguments of Wycliffe are used negatively against transubstantiation. Wycliffe looks more specifically to Scripture and the Fathers to identify his own view.

that Wycliffe did not have a completed view and died before he could develop it.[68] However, it is the contention of this study that Wycliffe did have what he understood to be a completed view and was defending it against the attacks of the schismatics. This view was that which was held by the Fathers, particularly Augustine, which Wycliffe believed could plainly be seen if one read Augustine and Scripture appropriately.[69]

Wycliffe's metaphysics and Scriptural interpretations seem quite complementary to the neo-Platonism of Augustine, one could even argue the neo-Platonism of Paul, and allows him to fit much of what Augustine stated *prima facie* into his schema of belief.[70] Indeed, Wycliffe was such a proponent of Augustine that he earned the title "John, son of Augustine" from his contemporaries.[71] Leaving aside the question of whether Wycliffe accurately portrayed Augustine or simply read him through fourteenth century Wycliffite metaphysical eyes, this study is concerned with the manner in which Wycliffe used Augustine.

As is evident from Wycliffe's citations, Augustine is considered to be a luminary authority. In the text of the *Trialogus* itself which pertains to the subject of the Eucharist, Augustine is quoted ten times compared to three of Jerome, the next most preeminent authority for Wycliffe in this text. But of course for Wycliffe, the Fathers are only further witnesses

68. See note 57 above for representative views decrying Wycliffe's lack of a complete doctrinal development of the Eucharist.

69. Such a belief derives in part from Maurice Keen's thesis that Wycliffe discovered in his Scriptural commentaries arguments which gave him the impetus to put forth the remanence of the bread and wine, something he had previously been unwilling to do. Keen may well be right that this was part of a grander scheme to demonstrate the hypocrisy and illegitimacy of the contemporaneous papacy. Keen believes that this intention drew most of his effort and never allowed Wycliffe to complete his own views on the Eucharist. See Keen, "Wyclif, the Bible, and Transubstantiation," 11–16. My contention is that Wycliffe was in fact asserting the view of Augustine, as it represented the view of the whole Church prior to Innocent III, and was an accurate portrayal of Scripture as Wycliffe read it. Wycliffe had no need to develop the view further since his task was to get his audience to simply read the Fathers and Scripture appropriately, and observe the incongruity of this reading with the papacy's views.

70. Though Wycliffe himself did not know Plato firsthand, he does state that "Plato's view of ideas was sound and in accordance with our own sacred Scripture as Augustine testifies." Wycliffe, *De Universalibus* as quoted here by Anthony Kenny in his "Realism of *De Universalibus*," 25. In this study, Kenny spends considerable time discussing whether Wycliffe was more avowedly Platonist or Aristotelian, allowing Wycliffe to draw from both in his metaphysics, and pointing out that whatever Wycliffe is, he is most certainly not a nominalist.

71. Robson, *Wyclif and the Oxford Schools*, 25.

to the truth of Scripture as he read it. Indeed, the Scriptures were the terrain in which the conflict must proceed, but Augustine appeared on the battlefield as the general before which no foe could stand. Wycliffe used Augustine and other Fathers to substantiate his criticisms of transubstantiation as well as to support his positive statements regarding remanence of the bread and wine. It is on this point of positive support that another distinction in the use of the Fathers, particularly Augustine, must be highlighted.

Wycliffe was arguing against transubstantiation, and the annihilation it appeared to entail, on ground that was foreign to the vocabulary of the Fathers and Scripture. The very words in which the debate was couched were only recently discussed in relation to the Eucharist.[72] Wycliffe took up the challenge and fought his battles on the grounds defined by his foes, using their terminology and arguing against their particular definitions of Scriptural and Patristic quotations. It is on this level that most commentators have looked for Wycliffe to explain his own view. However, when Wycliffe made positive statements concerning what he believed, he often simply restated his reading of the Fathers and Scripture, or gave explanations that amounted to paraphrases of how the Fathers interpreted Scripture. It appears as though Wycliffe expected explanations using the Fathers' language to be enough. His expectation that Scripture's meaning was in a sense "self-evident" seems to have found root in his Eucharistic teaching as well.[73] An overview of Wycliffe's own positive teachings will help to clarify the point that Wycliffe was not attempting to teach anything new or different, or even to give a substantially "modern" rendering (i.e., in the language of his contemporaries) of his reading of history.

In the text of the *Trialogus*, Wycliffe's positive statements are intermingled with arguments against transubstantiation. This does not allow

---

72. Dugmore discusses the new language that had developed in relation to the Eucharistic doctrine. In this new language, he observes the disappearance of Patristic terminology, even citations of Patristic authority, and the emergence of a metaphysical language more in line with the thought of the twelfth century. Cf. Dugmore, *The Mass and the English Reformers*, 37ff, esp. 39–40.

73. This does not mean that Wycliffe held to some modern conception of perspecuity. This statement is simply meant to point out that Wycliffe expected some teachings would be clear if read appropriately. Indeed, much of his argument against the novelty of transubstantiation is that it was simply a misreading of Scripture, for which the remedy was corrective "lenses."

for a simple exposition of what were Wycliffe's positive statements since they are often given in the context of a contrast with transubstantiation. However, the following is a somewhat representative listing of positive statements that can be garnered from a reading of the *Trialogus*. Each point, while being the most accurate portrayal of Scripture, is also attributed to the Fathers explicitly by Wycliffe, or can easily be seen as derivative of his reading of the them, especially Augustine:[74]

1) the distinction between the sacrament and the "thing" of the sacrament[75]

2) the bread remains after consecration[76]

3) the bread is Christ's body "sacramentally"[77]

4) Christ is present in the host "figuratively"[78]

---

74. It must be granted that such a method, which does not treat the totality of the work and each particular point in its context, is not without some shortcomings. The intention of such a sketchy presentation of the points is necessary for the sake of space. Though not expecting the thesis of this study to be fully demonstrated by only outlining the warrant, it is hoped that at least the probability, or possibility, of such a proposal finds merit.

75. Wycliffe, *Trialogus*, 132; and in Wycliffe, *De Eucharistia*, 11. This appears to be directly derivative of Augustine's distinction between *sacramentum* and the *res sacramentum*. For a more comprehensive discussion of Augustine's distinctions, see Dugmore, *The Mass and the English Reformers*, 13ff; and Crockett, *Eucharist: Symbol of Transformation*, 90.

76. On this point, Wycliffe cites Augustine, "And according to Augustine, on this passage in our Lord's sermon on the mount, by daily bread, Christ intends, among other happy significations, this venerable sacrament . . . In the same manner the apostles recognized Christ with breaking of bread, as we are told in Luke xxiv. And Augustine, with the papal enactment, De Con. Dist. III. *non omnes*, tells us that this bread is the venerable sacrament." Wycliffe, *Trialogus*, 139–40. Also see Wycliffe, *De Eucharistia*, 33, where Wycliffe quotes Augustine's *Decretum*, pars III, dist. II, c. 58, I, 1336.

77. Wycliffe attributes this conception to Jerome as the latter had accurately interpreted the words of Christ. Wycliffe, *Trialogus*, 138.

78. Wycliffe uses the conception of the "figurative" sense throughout much of his argument. When he finally develops what figurative predication means, in contradistinction to formal or essential predication, he exegetes Augustine's use of figure alongside Scriptural quotations that make reference to figurative interpretations. The crux of his explanation of how figure is to be understood is more than as a simple sign, but as an effectual sign. The effectiveness is found in the eating of the bread spiritually, a concept more thoroughly treated by Augustine, but on which Wycliffe hinges his whole doctrine of the Eucharist, see Wycliffe, *Trialogus*, 147–49. Augustine spoke quite readily of the figurative sense of the bread (see especially his sermon on Psalm III partially translated by L. Murdock Smith III in his "Influence of the Eucharistic Theology of Augustine

5) Christ's physical body is ascended, He is present in the elements "spiritually"[79]

6) the Church is the body of Christ into which the Eucharist draws all believers into unity[80]

This list could be lengthened if we were to consider Wycliffe's conceptions of Christ being present in the whole world, as the soul is present in all the members of the body, or his treatment of the activity of the Spirit in the consecration of the elements. However, it must suffice that brief delineation of some of the major tenets that enter into the discussion of what was Wycliffe's view have been identified as deriving from, or at least paralleling, Augustine. The last point mentioned above, number six, is perhaps the most crucial to aiding in our understanding of what both Augustine and Wycliffe believed concerning the Eucharist. Crockett has stated that "Like Paul, [Augustine] interprets participation in the body of Christ in both its Christological and ecclesiological senses. The ultimate gift of the Eucharist is the building up of believers into union with Christ their head in a unity of peace and love. The *res*, or reality that is signified by the sacramental signs, is not simply an individual relationship with Christ attained by faith, but community in love between Christ and all the members of his body."[81] Augustine makes this conception clear as he addresses the newly baptized at length:

> If you wish to understand the body of Christ, listen to the Apostle's words: "You are the body and the members of Christ."

of Hippo on the Eucharistic Theology of Thomas Cranmer," 109). But Augustine, like Wycliffe who followed him, did not posit this figure as a simple sign. It was also much more than a sign which was realized as the faithful ate the elements. Spiritual nourishment took place as well as physical nourishment. For Augustine, this Spiritual nourishment connected the believer not only to Christ spiritually, but physically to his body as it was represented in the community of the Church. For a more complete discussion of Augustine's conception of the Eucharist, see Smith, "Influence of the Eucharistic Theology of Augustine of Hippo on the Eucharistic Theology of Thomas Cranmer," 108–12, 117–18.

79. Wycliffe, *Trialogus*, 132, 154. Augustine also addressed the question of where Christ's body was located, see Smith, "Influence of the Eucharistic Theology of Augustine of Hippo on the Eucharistic Theology of Thomas Cranmer," 109, 112.

80. Augustine makes this plain in his Sermon 272 as is quoted by Crockett in *Eucharist*, 94–95. Wycliffe makes use of this quotation in his exposition of how the bread is the body of our Lord. Cf. Wycliffe, *Trialogus*, 148.

81. Crockett, *Eucharist*, 94.

If you are the body and members of Christ, it is your mystery which is placed on the Lord's table; it is your mystery you receive. It is to that which you are that you answer, "Amen," and by that response you make your assent. You hear the words "the body of Christ"; you answer, "Amen," Be a member of Christ so that the "Amen" may be true. Why then is he in the bread? Let us not put forward any suggestion of our own, but listen to the repeated teaching of the Apostle; for he says, speaking of this sacrament: "We are many, but we are one loaf, one body." Understand and rejoice: unity, truth, goodness, love. "One loaf." What is that one loaf? "We many are one body." Remember that the bread is not made from one grain of wheat, but of many. When you were exorcised you were, in a manner, ground; when baptized you were, in a manner, moistened. When you received the fire of the Holy Spirit you were, in a manner, cooked. . . . Many grapes hang in a cluster, but their juice is mixed in unity. So the Lord has set his mark on us, wished us to belong to him, has consecrated on his table the mystery of our peace and unity. If anyone receives the sacrament of unity, but does not "keep the bond of peace," they do not receive a sacrament for their benefit, but evidence for their condemnation.[82]

Wycliffe makes use of this quotation when he is attempting to identify how the bread is the body of Christ figuratively understood (here using figure as something more than a sign):

For as Augustine teaches, in what he says on John—corn is collected of a multitude of grain, and ground; secondly, water is poured on it, and it is kneaded; and thirdly, it is taken as the food of the body for nourishment. In a similar way believers receive the sacramental bread in fragments; it is afterwards watered by evangelical faith, and kneaded in the heart; and when baked by the fire of charity, is spiritually eaten. Accordingly, Augustine says, on John, "Believe with a faith molded by charity, and thou hast eaten"; and this must be understood of eating spiritually.[83]

Without giving any further qualifications or explanations, Wycliffe believes this statement of Augustine is self-evident and quotes it as representative of his own beliefs. To understand what Wycliffe believed, one must attempt to interpret how he was reading Augustine. Wycliffe is demonstrating, in this passage, belief in a twofold sense of eating,

82. From Augustine's sermon 272 as quoted in ibid., 94–95.

83. Wycliffe, *Trialogus*, 148.

physical and spiritual, which was also certainly present in Augustine. As Augustine states, "So then the Eucharist is our daily bread; but let us in such wise receive it, that we be not refreshed in our bodies only, but in our souls. For the virtue which is apprehended there, is unity, that gathered together into His body, and made His members, we may be what we receive."[84] Wycliffe further appears to be adopting some form of Augustine's conception of the "virtue of the Sacrament," which Augustine equates with eating spiritually. "For even we at this day do receive visible food: but the sacrament is one thing, the virtue of the sacrament another . . . See ye then, brethren, that ye eat the heavenly bread in a spiritual sense, bring innocence to the altar. Though your sins are daily, at least let them not be deadly."[85] The *res* of the sacrament for Augustine is active when one virtuously partakes in this spiritual eating. The feeding of the soul takes place as one faithfully receives the elements and is drawn into the community of the faithful, the "body of Christ." For Augustine, the spiritual feeding envelopes both the grace imparted to the believer and the completion of that grace as the believer is drawn into the body. Unity and love of community is the goal of the Eucharist for Augustine. Wycliffe may be referring to this when he speaks of the union of Christ with his Church.[86] He may also have had this in mind as he reckons the heresy spread by his foes to be the most diabolical of heresies.[87] It seems improbable that Wycliffe merely reflected on the Eucharist for the sake of metaphysics, which could have left his view incomplete. From his arguments against the divisiveness of the transubstantiation heresy, it may well be surmised that Augustinian unity was his ultimate goal and the completion of "Wycliffe's" view of the Eucharist. Perhaps, this also being the goal of those who held to transubstantiation, Wycliffe did not see the need to go beyond arguing for a specific means to that end. Whatever the case, as Wycliffe reminds his readers of Augustine's statement, "Believe

---

84. Augustine, *Sermons on New Testament Lessons*, IV.7, 282.

85. Augustine, *Homilies on the Gospel according to John, and his First Epistle*, XXVI.11, 171.

86. Wycliffe, *Trialogus*, 133. Although one may certainly wonder how Wycliffe understood his efforts to be useful for 'peace and unity', he viewed his task as one of calling the heretics back into the larger community of the faithful throughout history. However, to make such a statement is somewhat ironic in view of Wycliffe's ultimate state, being condemned as a heretic himself and cast out of the fold of the unified Church.

87. Ibid.

with a faith molded by charity, and thou hast eaten,"[88] he aligns himself with what he believes is Augustine's view, including the efficacy of spiritual eating. Having said this, he feels he has said enough.

Conclusion

It is important to remember that this is pre-Reformation theology. In other words, Wycliffe, like the early Luther, still believes himself to be a part of the church. His struggle with the hierarchy is taking place with the intent of changing the church, not leaving it. There is more at stake than simply the truth of a statement regarding the reality of the substances. Wycliffe's argument, though it may have arisen from a desire for correct doctrine and an appropriate understanding of Scripture, has as much to do with his life in the church as a practicing Christian as it does his life in the university as a student/professor who may challenge and pursue various ideas. Theology, and every other discipline within the university, is not a totally free discipline. Though the university was not finally under the authority of the church, challenging doctrine in the university was still a challenge to the church itself, particularly in this case since transubstantiation had been declared the official church teaching. More than simply the truth of a statement or its place in the system is at stake in this debate.

With that in mind, Wycliffe would most certainly have wished to offer the strongest defense possible for his position. As has been seen in the study above, he did just that. He argued from the Fathers, Augustine being preeminent, and from Scripture. Certainly his philosophy was at work in his defense, but to turn to his philosophy for a defense would have left him open to attack from his opponents on ground that was less secure within the church. Philosophy had its place and was certainly a part of the discussion in this period of theology, but it was not the arena in which theology was finally discussed or decided. With this in mind, we cannot apply a narrow definition of system to Wycliffe. Though he was well aware of the philosophical issues and these may even have been what finally changed his mind about transubstantiation, he could not use a more purely philosophical approach to defend his position. Nevertheless, he was quite orderly and precise in his presentation of what the Fathers taught and what he believed Scripture taught. He sees an

88. Ibid., 148.

inconsistency in the theology of the church and wishes to correct it. His method is certainly not a modern one, but it is a method nonetheless. He appealed to authorities he believed displayed congruity, but he never developed a demonstration of that congruity. Systematic tendencies may have been at work in Wycliffe at various points in his debates and writing, but there is, finally, no system here; nor should we expect one.

6

The Rigid System in Rhetorical Dress?

Calvin's Construction in the Institutes

Introduction

> The theologian's task is not to divert the ears with chatter, but
> to strengthen consciences by teaching things true, sure, and
> profitable.[1]

WHEN JOHN CALVIN WROTE THESE WORDS CONCERNING SPECULATION
about angels, he poignantly summarized his understanding of the work
to which he had been called and would devote the greater part of his life.
Calvin did not primarily understand himself to be a philosopher or a
politician. His main office in life, his calling, was to serve the living God
by teaching His people. He was first and foremost a theologian whose
responsibilities included pastoral care and preaching. It was with these
responsibilities constantly in mind that he pursued an outline of his beliefs in the *Institutes*. Amongst the pressures and concerns of preaching
and teaching, Calvin sought to give a coherent account of what would
eventually come to be known as the Reformed faith.

This focus on the pastoral duties of Calvin's life has become a
prominent feature of some contemporary Calvin biographies. The concern to contextualize the writings of Calvin within his life as a pastor is
captured quite eloquently in the work of William Bouwsma, *John Calvin:
A Sixteenth-Century Portrait*. In this study, Bouwsma carefully attempts
to analyze Calvin's personality and pastoral agenda without falling into
psychological speculation. He presents a very plain, and at times even
distraught, Calvin who was both an inheritor of the humanistic culture

---

1. Calvin, *Institutes*, I, xiv, 4.

in which he had been raised and a fellow-reformer of the tradition with which so many had become dissatisfied.

In the midst of an analysis of Calvin's pastoral program and his contextualized identity, the issue at stake concerns the purpose and program of his writings, particularly the *Institutes*. It is debatable whether Calvin can rightly be classified as a "systematic" theologian. Bouwsma has attempted to paint Calvin as more rhetorically inclined, and as such, less a systematician than has often been suspected.[2]

This chapter is an attempt to understand Calvin's theological method in light of his pastoral responsibilities and the apologetic nature of his writing. Though it will be impossible to provide a comprehensive summary of his thought, this study will attempt to examine the foundations of Calvin's theological investigations, particularly as they are portrayed in Bowsma's biographical work. Some of the questions to be considered in a study of this nature are: Was there a dominant theological system in the sixteenth century? What is the relationship of Calvin's doctrine to the notion of system? What was the intention of the *Institutes* throughout the various editions and do the changes represent something other than a restatement for rhetorical purposes? Can Calvin rightly be called a systematic theologian?

Biblical and Systematic Theology

At the outset of our study of Calvin, a modern distinction seems in order. The twentieth, and twenty-first, century has seen a great deal of debate concerning the appropriate methodology to apply in theological investigation. Such discussions have generally advocated one of two particular methods. The first is most often called Biblical theology. Biblical theology limits its investigative scope to a particular text or author under study, often deriving doctrinal formulations only from the material being considered, if any derivations are to be made. The second method generally used by theologians is systematic theology. As discussed in previous chapters, this method may employ a wider range of sources to formulate its particular doctrinal assertions according to a coherent pattern, including at times terms and categories found outside specifically Scriptural sources. These are rather general definitions with which some

2. Bouwsma is not unique in his approach to Calvin as a rhetorician. In many respects, he has recounted the argument of David Willis in his article "Rhetoric and Responsibility in Calvin's Theology," 43–63.

may wish to take issue; however, they provide us with a reference point to which we can compare various definitions and nuances as we turn our attention to the subject with which this study is specifically concerned, an accurate understanding of Calvin's method.

Bouwsma's Understanding of Systematic Theology

Bouwsma makes it very evident at the beginning of his work that he does not believe Calvin to have followed any systematic agenda. He states emphatically that his understanding of Calvin cannot allow for the systematic inclinations often connected with Calvinist theology:

> The approach by way of tensions and contradictions makes it clear that I cannot accept the received version of Calvin as a systematic thinker. I do not believe that Calvin even aspired to the construction of a system, as the term "system" is commonly understood; as a biblical theologian, he despised what passed for systematic theology in his own time. He sought, like other humanists, to develop as effective a pedagogy as possible, and this meant arranging what he had to communicate in the most readily apprehensible and effective manner; the urgency of the crisis of his time required it. Beyond this, the intellectual and cultural resources available to thinkers of the sixteenth century made the production of "systematic thought" almost inconceivable, a circumstance that students of Calvin's thought have not always kept in mind. A systematic Calvin would be an anachronism; there are no "systematic" thinkers of any significance in the sixteenth century.[3]

What this lengthy quotation makes readily apparent is Bouwsma's narrow definition of system as it is applied to theological pursuits. Bouwsma's rejection of Calvin as a systematic thinker is based on the "commonly understood" definition of what constitutes a system or systematic thought. Unfortunately, he leaves his readers with little specific detail of his definition of system.[4] Later in the study, Bowsma makes some reference as to his conception of system when he states that "Calvin did not conceive of his task as the exposition of a 'theology' for the ages. He had more

---

3. Bouwsma, *John Calvin*, 5.

4. Holtrop uses this point to question Bouwsma's actual support of his thesis that Calvin is "unsystematic." He asserts that Bouwsma is simply stating conjecture without giving necessary support. Cf. Holtrop, "Reply," 10.

urgent matters to attend to."[5] This statement appears to give insight as to the view to which Bouwsma is opposed concerning Calvin's writings. Bouwsma's definition of systematic thought seems to include three distinct elements. First, he believes that a systematic thinker is endeavoring to give an account of Christianity which represents eternal truth in such a way as to remain valid for successive generations. Second, he believes that the primary purpose of a system of theology is something other than pedagogical. Third, he assumes that systematic thought is somehow bound to the rise of modernity, presumably modern science.[6] Bouwsma's contrasting of Calvin as a Biblical theologian in opposition to systematic theologians indicates that he understands Calvin's theological work to have been subordinated to a more pressing purpose. Bouwsma understands this purpose to be rhetoric.

Before turning our attention to a more complete understanding of Bouwsma's characterization of Calvin, let us further discuss the notion of system as it was used in the theological investigations of the sixteenth century. What methods were available to Calvin?

Theological Method in and around the Sixteenth Century

Calvin as Inheritor and Innovator

Calvin used a great deal of the thought of Thomas and Lombard, amongst other theologians of centuries past.[7] It could be argued that Calvin's use of theological questions from a wide range of the sources of previous centuries constitutes a systematic agenda as he attempts a re-ordering and compilation according to a specific purpose. However, Bouwsma wishes to classify Calvin more precisely as a humanist because of this wide use of varying philosophical and theological material and his pursuits in the office of pastor.[8] While it may be true that Calvin used

5. Bouwsma, *John Calvin*, 191.

6. Bouwsma hints at this last point as he discusses Calvin's rejection of any sense of scientific discourse. Cf. Bouwsma, *John Calvin*, 160, esp. n. 100.

7. Wendel, *Calvin*, 19, 126–27. Wendel makes it clear that Calvin was exposed to the *Sentences* by John Mair while at the College de Montaigu. Calvin is quite dependent in many respects on the works of Duns Scotus and Bucer. For a more complete discussion of the influences upon Calvin's thought in the *Institutes*, cf. Wendel, *Calvin*, 122–44.

8. A major premise of Bouwsma's work is to prove that Calvin was at base a humanist, and as such could not have pursued a systematic agenda. Cf. Bouwsma, *John Calvin*,

a wide range of sources and did wish to make an effective presentation of his work, it does not appear obvious that Calvin was unconcerned with presenting a well ordered, even systematic, work according to what appeared to him to be a logical presentation of the Christian faith. Let us examine three particular areas of Calvin's thought in support of the contention that Calvin used logical construction in the *Institutes*, even to the point of attempting a modest systematic design.

CALVIN'S STATED PURPOSES

The first area for discussion is Calvin's own explanation of the overarching purpose employed in his work. Calvin was very definite in his desire that his writing and his life be used to further Godliness. In his 1559 Introduction to the *Institutes,* he states, "[S]ince I undertook the office of teacher in the church, I have had no other purpose than to benefit the church by maintaining the pure doctrine of godliness."[9]

Calvin clearly desired that his work be useful in the furthering of obedience and fruitfulness in the church. To help accomplish this end, he followed a specific purpose in his writing of the *Institutes*. It was not intended to be a speculative work worthy of isolated study and distinguishable honor. Indeed, it was a secondary source of instruction and guidance into the teachings of Scripture. For Calvin, Scripture was the primary source of sound doctrine and was to be studied to provide clear understanding of the doctrines of the Christian church. He affirmed this in a statement concerning the subject matter of the French edition of 1560. "Holy Scripture contains a perfect doctrine, to which one can add nothing, since in it our Lord has meant to display the infinite treasures of his wisdom."[10] As he proceeded to clarify, Calvin believed his work was a guiding reference to Scripture.

> Moreover, it has been my purpose in this labor to prepare and instruct candidates in sacred theology for the reading of the divine Word, in order that they may be able both to have easy access to

---

5, 113ff. Bouwsma's reasoning is largely derived from Calvin's use of divergent sources; however, he does not rely on this evidence alone to prove Calvin's humanistic tendencies. He also discusses Calvin's use of language (cf. 114ff.). This is perhaps his most crucial evidence as he points to Calvin's "humanistic" use of rhetoric and his rhetorical understanding of how language was to be used.

9. Reprinted in McNeill's edition of the *Institutes*, 4.

10. Ibid., 6.

it and to advance in it without stumbling. For I believe I have so
embraced the sum of religion in all its parts, and have arranged
it in such an order, that if anyone rightly grasps it, it will not be
difficult for him to determine what he ought especially to seek in
Scripture, and to what end he ought to relate its contents.[11]

Calvin obviously did not wish his work to supplant the Scriptures in
theological training. He believed his primary purpose in writing was
to allow Scripture to teach the authoritative doctrine of the church, to
which he was giving helpful guidance.

In what way, however, will Scripture teach this doctrine? In the
statement above, Calvin maintained that his purpose was not only to
give candidates "easy access" to Scripture and to help them "advance,"
but he also wished to "prepare and instruct" them in such a way that
"if any one rightly grasps [Calvin's sum of religion], it will not be difficult for him to determine what he ought especially to seek in Scripture,
and to what end he ought to relate its contents." Calvin did not wish for
God's people to grope around for instruction from the Scriptures, but
he wished to guide them into that for which they *should seek*. "Although
Holy Scripture contains a perfect doctrine, to which one can add nothing, since in it our Lord has meant to display the infinite treasures of his
wisdom, *yet a person who has not much practice in it has good reason for
some guidance and direction, to know what he ought to look for in it.*"[12]
And Calvin believed his work could fulfill this need for guidance, since
it gave extensive insight into Christian doctrine. Calvin's role as teacher
compelled him to write instructively, though certainly this didn't exclude
construction as well. "Perhaps the duty of those who have received from
God fuller light than others is to help simple folk at this point, and as it
were to lend them a hand in order to guide them and help them to find
the sum of what God meant to teach us in his Word."[13] Calvin further
promised that his work "can be a key to open a way for all children of
God into a good and right understanding of Holy Scripture."[14]

All these statements seem to indicate that Calvin had a very specific
view in mind concerning the *Institutes'* role as Scriptural guide. Two

11. Ibid. Note the similarities here to the intentions and program of Thomas Aquinas
in his *Summa Theologica*.
12. Ibid., emphasis mine.
13. Ibid.
14. Ibid., 7.

related points are made in these statements which must be identified. First, Calvin believes the *Institutes* constitute a "sum of religion in all its parts." This fits with the apologetic purpose with which he was writing the work, i.e., it is in his response to those who accused him of heresy that he would necessarily wish to include a clear outline of all his beliefs. Calvin's intentions, though apologetic, were also comprehensive. As a parallel intention, he wished for his work to serve as a manual of instruction for "candidates in sacred theology." An instruction manual of such a nature must be comprehensive. He claims explicitly "I have here treated at length almost all the articles pertaining to Christianity."[15] He further believes that his work has been arranged in "such an order" that if understood appropriately, it will serve as the perfect guide to capturing the teaching of Scripture. While this is obviously not the same thing as claiming to have comprehensively captured all knowledge of God, when coupled with Calvin's understanding of revelation, he does seem to be striving to arrive at sure knowledge. This would put his intentions in parallel with those of some modern systematicians, though their sources and confidence in their conclusions may vary.

Along these lines, a second point needing clarification is implied in Calvin's description of the *Institutes* as a *preparatory* guide to the Scriptures. He appears to be assuming here that Scripture cannot be rightly understood by the masses without assistance, or at the very least, not rightly applied to living. Undoubtedly, he is also criticizing the guidance of some doctors of the church as well. Calvin's epistemological foundations make it quite clear that only those who are rightly related to God can rightly understand Him.[16] It appears that he believes his "guide" to the Scriptures also serves a similar purpose, opening up a right understanding of them.. Knowing God and being appropriately in service to Him presupposes faith. Knowing the Scripture and how to rightly interpret it also seems to presuppose a knowledge of the doctrines of Christianity as they are outlined in the *Institutes*. Unlike modern systematic theology, at least, unlike most theology after Kant, Calvin's thought is not meant to be egalitarian.

These purposes of Calvin serve to illustrate the point that his work was very orderly and constructed in such a way as to provide students of Scripture with a scheme to which they could refer when making

15. Ibid.
16. Calvin, *Institutes*, III, ii, 6.

judgments concerning the appropriate understanding of passages of Scripture. Indeed, Calvin believed he could avoid long digressions in his comments on Scripture since he had here given detailed explanation of the way in which it rightly contributed to Christian doctrine.[17] Calvin believed he had succeeded in providing the Reformed church with a comprehensive summary of its Christian beliefs, rightly ordered.

THE REVISIONS OF THE *INSTITUTES*

The development of Calvin's thought in the *Institutes* throughout its several revisions illustrates his concern for logical construction. Beginning as a relatively brief catechism, the *Institutes* followed the order of Luther's *Catechism*. As it began to take shape and expand as a work more specifically of Calvin's molding, Calvin followed a pattern based on a quadripartite division of the Apostle's Creed in dealing with various subjects. This remained generally true of all successive editions; however, Calvin was not attempting to give a simple commentary on the creed. He was attempting to give a comprehensive outline of all Christian doctrine. Later, as time became a more pressing issue for a prematurely aged Calvin, he gave his attention to the appropriate inclusion of doctrinal detail and the correct order of the material. Francois Wendel argues that by 1560 Calvin "paid no great attention to form, although this remains very fine. What mattered to him above all in his last editions was to give strict precision and as logical a structure as possible to his thought."[18] Believing Calvin's emphasis to be primarily constructive, Wendel further explains that "The principal changes are due to the new arrangement of the material, according to a more systematic plan and a stricter internal logic."[19] Calvin's concern for logical coherence was a continual factor in the development of the *Institutes* throughout its various editions.[20] Such concern betrays not only a desire to be effectively convincing, but also to be accurate. As Scripture was recorded that God's truth might "abide

17. Calvin's introduction to the 1560 French edition, reprinted in McNeill's edition of the *Institutes*, 7.

18. Wendel, *Calvin*, 119.

19. Ibid., 120.

20. For a more detailed account of the development of the *Institutes* throughout the various editions, cf. Wendel, *Calvin*, 112–22.

forever in the world,"[21] so Calvin desired that his work would serve successive generations in the instruction of true Christian doctrine.[22]

THE STRUCTURE OF THE *INSTITUTES*

Following closely the matter of logical coherence, another related area that represents the use of modest systematic thought in Calvin is his structure of the *Institutes*. Thomas Aquinas had structured his *Summa* in a manner reflecting a circular pattern which represented the way in which he viewed the grace of God to proceed: from God, to man, and back to God. Likewise, Calvin gave a very definite structure to the *Institutes*. As was mentioned above, Calvin made use of a pattern based on the Apostle's Creed. Such a patterning could be said to have polemical or perhaps mnemonic usefulness, or even pedagogical value. Whatever its usefulness, the fact remains it is a pattern entailing a logical order. Just as the creed was designed to give a coherent explanation of very basic doctrines of the Christian faith, so Calvin's exposition of the Christian faith was designed to follow a logical progression from God the Father to the person of Christ and his work, and eventually to the Holy Spirit and His work within the church. The inclusion of a doctrine like providence created problems for Calvin as to where to include it. Calvin was perplexed not by what constituted the doctrine, but by its logical placement in his scheme.[23] Appropriate relationship amongst doctrinal claims and teachings was a primary concern for Calvin as he attempted to rightly instruct believers.

It seems readily apparent from the discussion above that logical construction of the *Institutes* was a major concern for Calvin. His purpose in producing the work required a coherent and instructive format. His constant reworking and reconstruction of the work indicates the ever present need for assimilation of new information, new presentation, or different phrasing into his overarching scheme. The overall structure follows a pattern not found in Scripture, but is derived and constructed on beliefs and doctrines chosen from various Scriptural sources. These factors would appear to provide ample evidence that Calvin was a sys-

21. Calvin, *Institutes*, I, iv, 2.

22. Calvin's introduction to the 1560 French edition, reprinted in McNeill's edition of the *Institutes*, 8.

23. For a brief discussion of this problem see Calvin, *Institutes*, I, xvi, 1, note 1; and Wendel, *Calvin*, 115–16.

tematic theologian according to the modest or general definition given previously in the chapters above. He makes extensive use of logical ordering and has a distinct concern for how the doctrinal claims he makes from Scripture fit with other claims. However, before discussing this further and before returning to a more complete description of Bouwsma's understanding of Calvin, let us turn our attention to some of the peripheral issues with which our discussion of systematics, particularly as it developed, must be concerned.

Theology after Calvin

In the years after Calvin's death, it came to be less and less clear who was the enemy of the Protestant faith. The reformers had always had in the papacy a common foe; however, the sundry groups that had arisen since the days of Calvin and Luther often found themselves in opposition with one another. This was not only limited to bickering amongst the Lutheran, Reformed, and Anabaptist factions; it also came to be a problem within each group, particularly within the Reformed church at the Synod of Dort.

In 1618–1619, the Reformed Church of the Netherlands felt the repercussions of a theological debate based on doctrines found specifically in the creeds and in the very teachings of Calvin himself. The teachings of Calvin had evolved into more rigid statements of doctrine, which lent themselves to formulations of doctrinal standards not originally espoused by Calvin. The Canons of Dort set forth the official teaching of the Reformed Church in opposition to those discussed in the *Remonstrance* of 1610. The Canons were doctrinally forthright and were often understood, especially by the Remonstrants, to represent an unyielding systematic expression of the Christian faith as it had been depicted by Calvin. Calvinism began to take shape as a set of beliefs in opposition to other belief systems in a way not so firmly expressed by Calvin.

At the same time, the apologetic responses of the Christian faith were being challenged by questions never before raised. The university and its instructors in the sciences were growing in their skepticism concerning the traditional Christian answers to the questions of cosmic origin and the physical sciences. The Protestant church was too involved in its own turmoils to give explicit attention to the problems being raised in the university, though certainly it did give attention to the matters at hand within Protestantism. The church's authority, both Protestant and Catholic, was also being challenged by the increasingly powerful political bodies that could now constitute much of their existence apart from church recognition or Christian establishment. This meant that the questions being raised were more appropriately answered by the philosophers and scientist who were raising them; and the answers were very much bound to be expressions of the scientific agenda in which they arose. Theology was being practiced not only by theologians, but also by scientists within scientific frameworks. As will be seen in the following chapters, the notion of system within these frameworks made theology more of a theistic movement outside the bounds of necessarily Christian distinctions. Demonstrating rational thought and devising systems of doctrine became the dominant agenda in establishing a verifiable belief, often to the exclusion of any notion of the distinctly Christian God who was revealed in Scripture.[24]

As these two streams of thought (the rational scientific stream and the doctrinal stream already existent in the church) converged, it became possible to take Calvin's outline of theology and reconstruct it according to an overarching theological scheme, deriving doctrinal formulations from one or two pre-eminent doctrines and conceiving doctrines in terms foreign to Scripture. This became the agenda of the systematician as theology was more inclined to follow a scientific method. With this as a very brief background of current systematic thought, let us renew our conversation with the notions of Bouwsma on Calvin.

Calvin versus Calvinism

As was made clear earlier, Bouwsma does not believe Calvin to be a systematician in the contemporary sense of the word. Instead, he understands Calvin to be a representative of the humanist tradition that proceeded in theological investigation according to an entirely different agenda.

Bouwsma believes Calvin was in a turmoil of anxiety caused by his fear of the Abyss, a state represented by disorder, unrestrained evil-doers, and the uncertainty of the future. Further, Calvin labored under a growing dissatisfaction with the failure of all the institutions to order life aright and the suffocating sense of having no way out, a dissatisfaction

---

24. For an excellent discussion of this historical development, cf. Buckley, *At the Origins of Modern Atheism.*

and suffocation represented by the Labyrinth. This tension in Calvin, Bouwsma argues, gave him no opportunity to rest comfortably in the surety of a theological system. Instead, he was constantly at war within himself to satisfy his earthly longings for order and to faithfully live up to his office of teacher and role as a local pastor to those embodying imperfection, often including himself in this group.[25]

With this picture of Calvin in mind, Bouwsma turns to a description of Calvin's theological task. As a product of Renaissance humanism, Calvin was inspired to write not according to any scientific agenda, but solely according to his desire to see people moved by the power of God. The overarching goal of Calvin's work therefore became 'persuasion' as it could be accomplished through the use of rhetoric. Bouwsma thus claims that Calvin is a proponent of the rhetorical nature of theology as it could be used to aid in persuading people to act according to the accepted standards of the Christian faith.

It is not hard to see why Bouwsma cannot allow Calvin to be a systematician. Bouwsma has devised a more modern definition of systematics, one based on a monolithic scientific methodology and logical progression. As he compares this with the tensioned humanism he finds in Calvin, the two seem incompatible.[26] But is Bouwsma correct in defining systematic theology as necessarily bound to scientific development and doctrinal connectedness? As has been argued above, it seems likely that a modest sense of system may be present in pre-modern theology. Is it not possible to understand Calvin as orderly in his development of doctrine, yet also concerned with the most convincing presentation?

Calvin as a Modest Systematician/Biblicist

Much of the preceding study has been devoted to providing background knowledge with which to begin the discussion of whether Calvin is rightly described as a systematic theologian. Having made some prelimi-

---

25. For a thorough discussion of Bouwsma's view of Calvin as a humanist, cf. Bouwsma, *John Calvin*, 113ff.

26. Holtrop has outlined the possibility for a different understanding of Calvin's worldview which allow for both Calvin's orderly desires and his pastoral realities to converge in simply different methods of constructing theological teaching. This would allow for Calvin to write to two different audiences at the same time, rather than writing with a constant anxiousness. Cf. Holtrop, "Between the 'Labyrinth' and the 'Abyss'—a review article," 26–27.

nary remarks regarding his method, we will continue here the discussion concerning the nature of systematics as it may be applied to Calvin. In particular, we will interact with specific points in Bowsma's depiction of Calvin. It has been demonstrated that Calvin was intent on giving a logical presentation of his theology and that he believed the *Institutes* to be representative of the doctrines of the eternal Word. In such a pursuit, he was following a path already laid by theologians before him. Calvin was certainly methodical in his presentation, revising often for the sake of precision. However, Bouwsma disagrees that such method constitutes a systematic effort.

Perhaps the best place to begin is with a brief restatement of Bouwsma's description of system and the reasoning with which he supports his opposition to calling Calvin a systematician. As was stated above, it is difficult to ascertain an exact definition since Bouwsma does not wish to allow himself to be pinned down on this subject. However, it can be surmised from his brief comments that it likely includes three elements: representing eternal truth in such a way as to maintain validity for successive generations, pedagogical purpose expressed in a method derived from sources external to Scripture, and certain contemporary facets of modern science.[27] With this brief description of system in mind, Bouwsma approaches Calvin as a man of the sixteenth century, as one who knows little of the systematic agenda with which later theologians would pursue such an enterprise. Calvin is a humanist and a pastor who desires to move his people with the power of presentation. Rhetoric is the medium with which Calvin proceeds to persuade those who have been entrusted to his care.

The portrait Bouwsma paints of Calvin as a humanist is very compelling in light of his evangelical fervor and his pastoral responsibilities. However, Bowsma seems to exclude too much by limiting Calvin's purposes to rhetoric. Bowsma seems to have developed a false dichotomy

27. The closest one can come to a gaining a specific understanding of what Bouwsma means by system may be found in a transcript of responses to his "Calvinism as Theologia Rhetorica," 72. Here Bouwsma comments on the usefulness of Ramus for Calvinists after Calvin's death, stating hypothetically that "Ramism promised a kind of integration, to draw the two sides of Calvin together so that people could persuade themselves that he was a systematic thinker in a mode that seemed increasingly attractive as the sixteenth century advanced." Bouwsma indicates in further comments that he may believe the systematic nature of theology under Ramus includes a singular identity of purpose and non-contradiction. Both of these concepts are rightly included in the first element of Bouwsma's definition above.

by believing Calvin must either a humanist or a systematician. Indeed, as has been seen in other theologians in the chapters above, Calvin may have delved into both without compromising either. Bowsma is undoubtedly right that the seventeenth century took Calvin's theology in directions Calvin never envisioned or intended. However, in a manner similar to Emlightenment rationalism, Calvin certainly believed his knowledge was sure. On the other hand, he was pre-modern, due to his strong sense of the nature of knowledge provided by revelation. Let us attempt to tease out some of the differences and similarities by examining several objections to Bouwsma's description, which excludes any systematic tendencies in Calvin.

1. System in Infancy

The first objection to Bouwsma's characterization relates to his definition of a system and how it is used in theology. It must be agreed that Calvin was not the systematizer that many have often accused him of being. Later generations of Calvinists and the scientific and philosophical use of Calvinist categories in establishing or defending theistic systems have surrounded the works of Calvin with a cloud of rigid and quixotic logic. Bouwsma appears to have this type of Calvinism in mind when he objects to the use of the term "system" as descriptive of Calvin.[28] This study must certainly agree with Bouwsma on this historical clarification. Calvin was not a Calvinist according to the contemporary perception of the belief system.[29]

However, this does not mean that Calvin could not have displayed certain systematic leanings in his theological work. Bouwsma excludes from his description the possibility of a pre-sixteenth century depiction of system in theology. He all but ignores the fact that Calvin was just as much an inheritor of earlier theological thought as he was philosophical thought. Bouwsma has not attended to the fact that systematic thought existed in Protestant circles as much as it did in Catholic circles well before Calvin's *Institutes*. Calvin was not intentionally avoiding any

---

28. Bouwsma, *John Calvin*, 233–34.

29. For further discussion of the issue of systematization in Calvinism as compared to Calvin's own thought, cf. Dowey, "Book Review, 'John Calvin: A Sixteenth Century Portrait,'" 847; and Leith, "Calvin's Theological Method and the Ambiguity in His Theology," 107–8.

tendency toward systematization as Bouwsma has supposed.[30] He was correcting what he understood to be a mistaken approach to systematic theology. The *Institutes* was intended to be as much a manual for theological instruction as the *Summa*. Bouwsma does not consider that perhaps Calvin was re-doing the system according to what he understood was the appropriate method.[31] The *Institutes* was not intended as something new. It dealt with consistently historical theological themes as they were represented in other author's theological works. Systematic intentions regarding order and comprehensiveness most certainly existed in sixteenth century, and pre-sixteenth century, theology, bounded of course by Scripture. Calvin was not only aware of other theologies, but he also used and discussed many of the questions with which these theologies were concerned, indicating not only systematic awareness, but an apparent *systematic* apologetical concern.[32] Calvin originally ordered his theology according to a catechismal pattern and it evolved into a formulation based on the Apostle's Creed. Calvin was demonstrating the historicity of his claims as they related to the Creed and as they answered the questions raised by previous systematicians. Granted, he believed all his claims to be based on Scripture, but they were not all simple deductions from a clear outline of doctrine explicitly set forth in Scripture.

The nature of theology in the sixteenth century, at least as it is represented by Calvin, appears to have included at least one element distinctly systematic: the theological ordering of doctrine according to a scheme not revealed in Scripture. This is certainly not a new practice, but does indicate that Calvin made use of elements somewhat systematic, since

30. Bouwsma, *John Calvin*, 5.

31. I do not mean to infer here that Thomas' *Summa* was a system in the modern sense of the term. I am merely observing that Calvin viewed the *Summa* as comprehensive in its doctrinal scope and wished to provide Protestants with something just as comprehensive.

32. Again, a simple perusal of the *Institutes* will indicate that Calvin was not an innovator in his thought. He used much of the material developed and discussed before him. Perhaps his greatest accomplishment is the order with which he presented the material. Cf. Wendel, *Calvin*, 122ff. Bouwsma is certainly aware that Calvin was not constructing something new, but he chooses to ignore the theological concerns of Calvin in favor of the humanistic (cf. Bouwsma, *John Calvin*, 232). Both were there, but the structure of Calvin's theology depended upon the systematic endeavors of previous theologians. Even when Calvin is critical of them, he is still granting their products credence by giving a detailed response and offering an alternative.

his work did not follow a strictly exegetical pattern. This leads to the second objection to Bouwsma's characterization of Calvin.

2. Calvin and Biblical Theology

By identifying Calvin as a "biblical theologian,"[33] Bouwsma seems to be making a distinction that is also somewhat anachronistic. Just as it would be inappropriate to identify Calvin as a systematician after the fashion of the later Calvinists, so it is inappropriate to label him a Biblical theologian, since this characterization represents a modern classification of a branch of theological study somewhat in opposition to modern systematic theology. To introduce the categories of systematic and Biblical theology as they are understood in contemporary terms foists a characterization upon Calvin that does not appear to be appropriate. Calvin concerned himself with both Biblical materials and materials that could be classified as systematic. Calvin was both systematic and Biblical in his theological aspirations, but could be neither according to strictly contemporary definitions since the distinctions were not at all clear in the sixteenth century.

Even if the categories are allowed to stand for the sake of identification, it does not at all appear that Bouwsma is correct in his analysis of Calvin as a Biblical theologian. Bouwsma may wish to argue that Calvin could be categorized more strictly as a Biblical theologian since he dealt more explicitly with Scriptural materials. However, this introduces a problem. To describe Calvin as more strictly limited to Scriptural materials and thought when dealing with doctrinal development seems to undermine Bouwsma's whole premise that Calvin was a humanist who used several and varying sources for the purpose of persuasion. While such nomenclature may fit his commentaries, the *Institutes* is organized around concerns other than strictly exegesis of Biblical passages. The contemporary definition of Biblical theology is much too restrictive to allow such an equivocation.

In his attempt to demonstrate the rhetorical as opposed to the systematic nature of the *Institutes*, Bouwsma believes Calvin did not give extensive attention to logic, a primarily systematic concern. "The *Institutes* is not logically ordered; it consists of a series of overlapping topics generally following the order of the Apostles' Creed. This organiza-

33. Bouwsma, *John Calvin*, 5.

tion allowed Calvin the flexibility for a variety of persuasive strategies."[34] On the contrary, Bowsma seems to be overstating the issue. To say that Calvin did not use logic but yet followed the order of the Apostle's creed is tantamount to saying the authors of the creed did not use logic in its presentation.

More to the point, Calvin's order and logical structure, even as it proceeded according to the Apostle's Creed, was an overarching approach not found explicitly in Scripture, but used to make a logical and convincing presentation of the material. Bouwsma may wish to debate whether the Apostles' creed proceeds according to a logical structure, but the fact that Calvin used it counters Bouwsma's claim that Calvin was strictly a Biblical theologian. Calvin was using a structure not revealed in Scripture to order his theology. This scheme indicates a freedom to leave the revealed categories of Scripture for the purpose of ordering theology around something chosen according to the arranger's desires. Calvin was not a Biblical theologian according to the contemporary definition. Certainly he made extensive use of Scripture. However, he exercised a freedom not consistent with the modern standards of Biblical theology. Perhaps, he is best characterized as a modestly systematic and Biblical theologian.[35]

3. Calvin and Logic

The third objection relates more specifically to Bouwsma's depiction of Calvin as inattentive to logic. Continuing the quotation cited above, Bouwsma believes logic and rhetoric cannot cohabitate in Calvin's theology. "The *Institutes* is not logically ordered; it consists of a series of overlapping topics generally following the order of the Apostles' Creed. This organization allowed Calvin the flexibility for a variety of persuasive strategies. His hortatory letter to the King of France establishes at the outset the rhetorical character of the work, and the text is throughout a complex mixture of demonstration, advocacy, and apologetics

---

34. Ibid., 125–26.

35. It is possible that Bouwsma's definition of Biblical theology is referring to Calvin's self-limitation to those doctrines explicitly discussed in Scripture and his commenting only on statements found in revelation. If this is more strictly Bouwsma's focus in defining Calvin as a Biblical theologian, Bouwsma has not given enough attention to Calvin's use of non-Scriptural materials, e.g., the eventual inclusion of trinitarian language.

... the Institutes exploits numerous rhetorical devices in order to teach, to move, and to delight."[36] This statement infers that the use of logical thought in the rhetorical process could not occur. Bouwsma appears to believe that rhetoric is necessarily opposed to system, a dichotomy that seems rather implausible. In this, he could be remembering the statement of the great humanist Erasmus when he remarked that Christian philosophy was only adopted by a few and "seated in emotions rather than in syllogisms, a life rather than an argument, inspiration rather than erudition, a transformation rather than a system of reason."[37] Such thinking would exclude the explicit use of a systematic or logical agenda when developing theological propositions.

However, it does not appear that Calvin was so opposed to the use of a reasonable approach to Scripture, nor was he opposed to the use of logic in the learning of theology. His conception of Christian philosophy certainly downplayed the capacity of human reason, but instead of throwing it out, he subjected it to the renewal of regeneration and the direction of the Holy Spirit.[38]

Calvin was not opposed to the use of reason, even as it was applied to the construction and appropriation of doctrine. In fact, it may be appropriate to say that Calvin's use of rhetoric presupposes a systematic scheme to which one may refer for substance and order. As Karl-Heinz zur Muehlen has stated in response to Bouwsma's thesis, "It is correct that without rhetoric the communication of Biblical truth remains without effect. But it is equally correct that without dialectic, i.e., the systematic illumination of the substantive theological interconnection, rhetoric threatens to become merely verbal."[39] It is certainly true that the apologetic nature of the Institutes required that it use some rhetorical devices; however, this presupposes rather than excludes the use of system. Logic and doctrinal harmony (i.e., non-contradiction) are necessary elements in a rhetorical work for coherence and persuasiveness. Bouwsma does not appear to have recognized the implications of his study, or perhaps has overestimated his findings. The use of rhetoric is certainly a tool of Calvin, but it is subservient to his work as a theologian who believes

36. Bouwsma, John Calvin, 125–26.

37. Erasmus, Paracelsis, id est adhortatio ad Christianae philosophiae studium, V. 141ff., cited by McNeill in his edition of the Institutes, 6–7 n. 8.

38. Calvin, Institutes, III, vi, 4; I, xi, 7; I, xii, 1 n. 1.

39. Muehlen, Response to Bouwsma's "Calvinism as Theologia Rhetorica," 55.

the truths of Scripture must always agree.[40] To lift rhetoric to the fore as *the* overarching structural guide, as Bouwsma has done, seems to be a somewhat selective presentation of Calvin, or at the very least a superficial reading according to presupposed humanistic interests. Bouwsma fails to recognize his own systematization of Calvin's work according to an extra-Biblical scheme of rhetoric. Bouwsma's work could even be considered self-defeating if the use of a rhetorical scheme is understood to be a systematic endeavor, aligning all the teachings according to the overall "doctrine" of persuasiveness.[41]

Final Reflections

The systematic tendencies of the *Institutes* are not best understood as a systematic endeavor according to contemporary standards. However, this does not mean that it is not systematic in its own right. Calvin worked as a theologian of the sixteenth century, and as such, he presented his material according to the accepted logical and theological procedures of that period. He was not largely innovative in this task, but he was extremely comprehensive, including in his work a constant dialogue with the patristics, the humanists, and his contemporaries as he attempted to outline his understanding of a Scriptural Christianity.

Bouwsma set out to prove that Calvin was a humanist, and perhaps he has accomplished that task. However, it is not apparent that Calvin's humanism demanded he give up any systematic tendencies as he progressed in his theological development. Calvin's continued work on the various editions of the *Institutes* did include a strong concern for rhetorical persuasiveness. But his persuasiveness centered around coherence and historicity. Calvin believed he was espousing what was recorded in Scripture, only in a more orderly fashion.

40. As is evident throughout this study, I do not accept Bouwsma's two Calvin's thesis. Such psychologizing does not do justice to the very definiteness apparent throughout Calvin's lifetime. The antinomies that may exist within his work are not the product of an anxious mind. Instead, they simply reflect a scholar who is trying to be honest with the historical questions set before him and the Scripture to which he appeals for authority. Bouwsma correctly believes that Calvin was aware of the distance between doctrine and "real life." Calvin's logically ordered scheme of Christianity was an attempt to bring the two together in a manual for Christian training.

41. Dowey, "Book Review," 846. It may even be plausible to say that rhetoric inherently involves a theological claim about the nature of Christianity, which, if developed, may reveal a very modern, or perhaps post-modern, notion of epistemology and truth.

Calvin desired changed lives, as his pastoral nature would demand, but only as they came into conformity with a *right understanding* of Christ. The *Institutes* was written to guide believers in both reflective thought and deed. The direction of the Holy Spirit did not reject logic, but included reason rightly subjected to the truths of Scripture. Calvin combined reason and action, and, in a very pre-modern manner, would not allow a separation of the intellectual from the affectual and pragmatic character of Christianity. He demonstrated throughout that both were intertwined in the working of the Spirit. Perhaps he summarizes his own intentions best.

> Let this therefore be the first step, that a man depart from himself in order that he may apply the whole force of his ability in the service of the Lord. I call "service" not only what lies in obedience to God's Word but what turns the mind of man, empty of its own carnal sense, wholly to the bidding of God's Spirit. While it is the first entrance to life, all philosophers were ignorant of this transformation, which Paul calls "renewal of the mind" (Eph. 4:23). For they set up reason alone as the ruling principle in man, and think that it alone should be listened to; to it alone, in short, they entrust the conduct of life. But the Christian philosophy bids reason give way to, submit and subject itself to, the Holy Spirit so that the man himself may no longer live but hear Christ living and reigning within him (Gal. 2:20).[42]

---

42. Calvin, *Institutes*, III, vii, 1.

7

System with a Twist
Enlightenment Influences on Theology and Epistemology

Introduction

STUDENTS OF IMMANUEL KANT (1724–1804) HAVE INVARIABLY NO-
ticed that the idea of system functions in a foundational manner in his
philosophy. As Heidegger writes, "It is therefore not just chance that it
is in Kant that one really finds for the first time an explicitly systematic consideration of the essence of system and the determination of its
concept from the essence of reason,"[1] and again "Kant was the first to
discover the inner systematic character of reason."[2] Though for Kant system was primarily a tool to organize reason, the centrality of system was
taken up by later German Idealists and became so dominant that Hegel
asserts, "Philosophizing without system cannot be scientific." [3] But what
exactly is *system* for Kant? How does it function within his philosophy
and what was unique about his use of system? This chapter proposes to
discover what Kant meant when he identified system as a functional notion within his work and how it served to further his entire philosophical
program.

Our study of Kant in this chapter serves to begin a transition from
the historical development of systematic tendencies in pre-modern theologians to the post-Emlightenment nature of epistemology grounded
in reason. The notion of a post-Enlightenment system has generated a

1. Heidegger, *Schellings Abhandlung über das Wesen der menschlichen Freiheit* (1809)
43.

2. Ibid., 46.

3. Hegel, *Enzyklopädie der philosophischen Wissenschaften*, §14. Cf. "Knowing
(Wissen) is real only as science or as system," (*Phän. des Geistes, Vorrede*, vol. 3, 27). And
"Truth (das Wahre) is real only as system," (ibid., 28).

great deal of interest in recent decades, specifically from those seeking its demise as an epistemological foundation. Various narrative theologians and philosophers bemoan the manner in which systematization has characterized all modern, and even some post-modern, thought (thus the nomenclature of structuralism and post-structuralism). They seek a new epistemological grounding in which systematic foundationalism is not the pre-eminent consideration for evaluating meaning. Though their criticism is seldom explicitly historical, it appears to point toward the origination of systematic schemes developed during the Enlightenment. One of the more common foes singled out in light of these particular complaints is Kant.[4]

The following study begins with two historical illustrations of how system had been used in philosophy prior to Kant. This will provide us with some idea of how Kant's use was unique and allow us to move directly into his own work. The main focus of the study is to examine Kant's conception of system as it is represented in his *Critique of Pure Reason*. Brief comparison will also be made to his later discussions of system in the *Critique of Judgment*. Ultimately, both discussions will help to identify the overarching purposes behind Kant's employment of the idea of system. The final section of this study will place the function of system within the teleological framework in which Kant conceived his whole philosophical project. Though not specifically theological, the impact of Kant's work on theology was tremendous. In this chapter, we will focus primarily on his philosophical impact, with some reference to how he influenced later theological studies.

A Brief History of System in Philosophy

Systematicity is by no means a new conception in philosophy. One could possibly trace it back to Aristotle in his discussion of method in the natural sciences.[5] It is also possible that if systematicity is somehow complementary to mathematical development, the history of a systematic schema could have its origin in Pythagorean or perhaps even in Egyptian or Babylonian roots.[6] Some have pointed to the Summas produced by

4. For an extended discussion of Kant's heritage and a post-liberal critique of Kant, see my *System and Story*, ch. 3.

5. Aristotle, *Parts of Animals*, 1. 1. 639 a 1 sq.

6. For a brief outline of the history of mathematical development and a comparison of various 'systems', see Bunt, et al., *The Historical Roots of Elementary Mathematics*; or

Scholasticism and the works of Suarez and Spinoza as representative of systematic thought.[7] However, everyone agrees that something new took place in Kant's conception of system. Like the theologians discussed above, other philosophers had used an external order or had applied a logical arrangement that constituted a systematic effort in one sense. But Kant internalized the conception of system, making it the very foundation of knowledge, rather than an aid or strategy for communicating knowledge. Kant does not go as far as his successors, like Hegel and other later German Idealists. Nevertheless, system determines for Kant the very notions of philosophy and reason. As he states, "*Philosophy* is the system of all philosophical knowledge," [8] and "The unity of reason is the unity of system." [9] He even goes so far as to assert that system is what defines science: "Every theory (Lehre) if it forms a system is called science (Wissenschaft)." [10] As will be seen below, it is the totalizing nature of system deriving from a singular idea that is new in Enlightenment thought, especially in Kant.

Of course, Kant was not putting his conception of system forth in a vacuum. Other conceptions of science and knowledge abounded. He proposed his epistemological scheme cognizant of the views surrounding him. His task was to demonstrate their futility, while at the same time champion his own project. To understand more fully how he proceeded in his course, we must turn our attention to the competing philosophical schemes. It would be impossible to deal in any depth with every philosopher's use of system. Therefore, we will limit our discussion here to how a few of Kant's predecessors attempted to unify and constitute scientific knowledge. This will provide direct insight into how Kant posited his use of system as a contrast to these figures.

Boyer and Merzbach, *History of Mathematics*. While it is altogether implausible to say that mathematical order and schematization in their earliest developments constitute the idea of a system according to a post-Enlightenment definition, nonetheless, they do represent a sense of orderedness and structure that function in a very systematic manner.

7. O'Farrell, "System and Reason," 5.

8. Kant, *Critique of Pure Reason*, A 838, B 866, emphasis Kant's.

9. Ibid., A 680, B 708.

10. Kant, *Metaphysische Anfangsgründe der Naturwissenschaft*, A IV, as quoted by O'Farrell, "System and Reason," 6.

Descartes and Leibniz

René Descartes (1596–1650) deplored the division of labor in the sciences.[11] As people drew a distinction within the arts, so "they held the same to be true of the sciences also, and distinguishing them according to their subject matter, they have imagined that they ought to be studied separately, each in isolation from the rest. But this is certainly wrong." [12] Descartes believed that in fact there was only one science, a universal one, which was most obvious in the science of geometry. As he explains, "Those long chains of reasoning, simple and easy as they are, of which geometricians make use in order to arrive at the most difficult demonstrations, had caused me to imagine that all those things which fall under the cognizance of man might very likely be mutually related in some fashion."[13] But the mutual relationship could not be grounded on the subject-matter of the sciences. To ground unity in some sense on the subject matter would not grant a unification of the various sciences, but would in fact constitute their isolation according to each discipline as a mere collection of detached truths, hence the necessity to ground the unity in a logical scheme of interconnection amongst the sciences. Descartes makes this clear in a letter to Mersenne, dated December 24, 1640.

> It is to be observed in everything I write that I do not follow the order of subject matters, but only on that of reasons, that is to say, I do not undertake to say in one and the same place everything which belongs to a subject, because it would be impossible for me to prove it satisfactorily, there being some reasons which have to be drawn from much remoter sources than others; but in reasoning by order, *a facilioribus ad difficiliora*, I deduce thereby what I can, sometimes for one matter, sometimes for another, which is in my view the true way of finding and explaining the truth; and as for the ordering of subject matters, it is good only for those for

11. Many opponents may be held out as those who divided the sciences according to their subject matter. Perhaps the most pre-eminent in Descartes' mind were the ancients, particularly Aristotle or the Stoics, who divided the sciences into the three main subjects of Physics, Ethics, and Logic.

12. Descartes, *Regulae ad directionem ingenii*, (1628), I, H.R., I, 1. Cf. the discussion of this text by McRae, *The Problem of the Unity of the Sciences: Bacon to Kant*, 7.

13. Descartes, *Discourse on Method* (1637), II, from *The Philosophical Works of Descartes*, I, 92.

whom all reasons are detached, and who can say as much about one difficulty as about another.[14]

All objects of knowledge are mutually related, allowing the totality of scientific knowledge, organized as it is according to his "order of reasons," to comprise a single science. This whole structure rests on a deductive system, beginning with a small number of first causes or principles which are known *per se*. As Descartes explains, "there are but few pure and simple essences which either our experiences or some sort of innate light in us enable us to hold as primary and existing *per se*, not as depending on any others." [15] The remainder of knowledge is then the combination of these atomistic simple natures. "No knowledge is at any time possible of anything beyond those simple natures and what may be called their *intermixture* or *combination* with one another."[16] Descartes' deductive system is founded on the combination of the simple essences. Unity, or the conception of the whole, is the logical ordering of the constituent elements. The parts of the system determine the whole.

Of course, Descartes was functioning within a context in which theology had typically served as the "Queen of the Sciences." Though the Church after Luther and, more contemporaneously Galileo, was definitely on the decline, Descartes still felt compelled to present his knowledge and appeal to the theology faculty for approval of his work. Descartes himself seemed to believe that his work would be a help in defending the Church against attacks of being unscientific. Thus, he writes to the Faculty of Sacred Theology at Paris, "I have always thought that two issues—namely, God and the soul—are chief among those that ought to be demonstrated with the aid of philosophy *rather than theology*."[17] Descartes could hardly have foreseen the impact such a move would have on theology.

Gottfried Wilhelm Leibniz (1646–1716), like Descartes, believed that only one science exists. The distribution of knowledge according to each individual science, i.e., according to subject matter, was simply an arbitrary convenience, not derived from any necessary unity in the parts of each science. These parts could be classified in an encyclopedic man-

14. Descartes, *Correspondence*, IV, 239.
15. Descartes, *Regulae*, VI, H.R., I, 16.
16. Ibid., XII, H.R., I, 43, emphasis mine.
17. Descartes, *Meditations on First Philosophy*, 1, emphasis mine.

ner according to their subject matter, but every part was still a component of the logically ordered whole.[18] Following Descartes, Leibniz believed the whole or unity of science was the aggregate of the parts. "The fruit of several analyses of different particulars will be the catalogue of simple thoughts, or those which are not very far from being simple. Having the catalogue of simple thoughts, we shall be ready to begin again *a priori* to explain the origin of things starting from their source in a perfect order and from a *combination* or *synthesis* which is absolutely complete. And that is all our soul can do in its present state."[19] Once again combination of the "simple thoughts" constitutes the conception of the whole. The whole is determined by the parts.

This brief encounter with two of Kant's fairly immediate predecessors has given us the opportunity to observe one of the main efforts at conceiving unity within the sciences. The division of labor amongst the sciences according to subject matter was deplored by both Descartes and Leibniz, positing instead their own view of how the sciences were related. Certainly, these were not the only conceptions of unity. Obviously, Descartes and Leibniz had opponents in mind, perhaps even contemporaries.[20] However, the outline provided above affords the best context in which to differentiate the thought of Kant on the unity of the sciences. Two contrasts stand out as particularly useful for our discussion. The first relates to the conception of each science as it exists in itself. The second relates to the manner in which the unity of all sciences is accomplished.

Kant on the Unity of the Sciences

Kant's account of the division of the sciences looks very different from that of Descartes and Leibniz. Descartes had condemned the distribution of knowledge analogous to the division of labor in the arts. Kant on the other hand supported such a division. "All crafts, handiworks,

18. Leibniz, *New Essays Concerning Human Understanding*, (1704), IV, xxi, 4, 623ff. The similarity with the later French Encyclopeadists Diderot and d'Alembert is obvious. The main difference is that Leibniz, in his projected encyclopeadia, made the logical ordering of knowledge primary and introduced the index to provide classification by subject, whereas Diderot and d'Alembert made classification by subject primary and introduced cross-references to establish the logical connections.

19. Leibniz, *On Wisdom*, (ca. 1693), 80, emphasis mine.

20. The last chapter in Locke's Essay *Concerning Human Understanding*, which adopted the ancient classification of the sciences into Physics, Ethics, and Logic, provided Leibniz with an immediate context to outline his own thought on the subject.

and arts have gained by the division of labor, for when one person does not do everything, but each limits himself to a particular job which is distinguished from all the others by the treatment it requires, he can do it with greater perfection and with more facility. Where work is not thus differentiated and divided, where everyone is a jack-of-all trades, the crafts remain at a barbaric level."[21] Further, Kant not only believed that this should be true for the artisan and craftsman, but also for the scientist. "Every science is a system in its own right . . . we must set to work with the science architectonically, treating it as a whole and independent building, not as an annex or part of another building, though we may later construct, starting from either building, a passage connecting the one to the other."[22] The first contrast with Descartes and Leibniz concerning the individual sciences is clear. For Kant, each science is a self-subsisting unity, requiring that it pursue the definition of its own scope and subject.[23] The sciences each preside over a domain of knowledge. And we must remember that Kant defines systematic unity as what determines scientific knowledge: in regard to Kant's system "systematic unity is what first raises ordinary knowledge to the rank of science, that is, makes a system out of a mere aggregate of knowledge . . ."[24] Every science constitutes a systematic unity within its own limits of knowledge. And as just stated, system for Kant is not the aggregate of the parts. System is born out of what Kant calls an antecedent *idea*.

> This idea is the concept provided by reason—of the form of a whole—in so far as the concept determines *a priori* not only the scope of its manifold content, but also the positions which the parts occupy relatively to one another. The scientific concept of reason contains, therefore, the end and the form of that whole which is congruent with this requirement. The unity of the end to which all the parts relate and in the idea of which they all stand in relation to one another, makes it possible for us to determine from our knowledge of the other parts whether any part be missing, and to prevent any arbitrary addition, or in respect of its completeness any indeterminateness that does not conform to the limits which are thus determined *a priori*. The whole is thus

21. Kant, *Foundations of the Metaphysics of Morals*, 4.

22. Kant, *Critique of Judgment*, § 68; p. 261. By "architectonic," Kant means "the art of constructing systems" (*Critique of Pure Reason*, A 832, B 860).

23. *Critique of Pure Reason*, A 842, B 870.

24. Ibid., A 832, B 860.

an organized unity (*articulatio*), and not an aggregate (*coacer-vatio*). It may grow from within (*per intussusceptionem*), but not by external addition (*per appositionem*). It is thus like an animal body, the growth of which is not by the addition of a new member, but by the rendering of each member, without change of proportion, stronger and more effective for its purposes.[25]

This conception of idea functions not only for the unity of each science, but also for the unity of the whole of scientific knowledge. "Not only is each system articulated in accordance with an idea, but they are one and all *organically* united in a system of human knowledge, as members of one whole, and so as admitting of an architectonic of all human knowledge . . ."[26] This has led one author to remark, "The totality of the sciences is an organism comprising lesser organisms."[27] Tom Rockmore notes that idea in Kant is the critical component in his conception of system. "In the *Critique of Pure Reason*, [Kant] defines a system as the unity of the different types of knowledge under a single idea. The idea in question is a concept given by reason that forms a totality. This concept determines on an *a priori* basis the extent of its content as well as the relation between its constitutive elements . . . A systematic unity is the condition *sine qua non* of a science."[28]

The second contrast with Descartes and Leibniz concerning the unity of the sciences in one whole is also now clear. Kant's antecedent idea of the systematic unity of the whole is the foundation for the unity (i.e., scientific knowledge) of each science. Indeed, Kant's conception of the unity of the sciences posits an *organic* whole which determines the parts, rather than relying on the *combination* of the parts to determine the whole, as Descartes and Leibniz had.[29]

We have had occasion to briefly observe the context in which Kant is proposing his conception of system. Though he certainly extended elements of his predecessors' thought, particularly the emphasis on systematic unity, his proposal was in many respects very new. Several questions

25. Ibid., A 833, B 861.

26. Ibid., A 835, B 863, emphasis mine.

27. McRae, *Problem of Unity*, 11.

28. Rockmore, *Before and After Hegel*, 17–18.

29. Interestingly, as is evident from the quotes above, the descriptive terms "organic" and "combination" come directly from the authors, drawing out the contrast quite clearly. For a brief discussion of the use of these terms, see McRae, *Problem of Unity*, 10ff.

concerning the origin of Kant's *idea* of systematic unity and its function in his over-arching philosophical project can no longer be avoided. We must now devote our attention to a more thorough discussion of Kant's own conception of system.

Systematicity in Kant

The Critique of Pure Reason

In the *Critique of Pure Reason*, Kant portrays system as an organic whole that grows by means of extension rather than addition. We have seen that systematicity relies on an *a priori* idea of systematic unity. We must now attempt to further understand how this idea of systematicity is developed by Kant. The lengthy quote from above is worth repeating in this respect.

> In accordance with reason's legislative prescriptions, our diverse modes of knowledge must not be permitted to be a mere rhapsody, but must form a system. Only so can they further the essential ends of reason. By a system I understand the unity of the manifold modes of knowledge under one idea. This idea is the concept provided by reason—of the form of a whole—in so far as the concept determines *a priori* not only the scope of its manifold content, but also the positions which the parts occupy relatively to one another. The scientific concept of reason contains, therefore, the end and the form of that whole which is congruent with this requirement. The unity of the end to which all the parts relate and in the idea of which they all stand in relation to one another, makes it possible for us to determine from our knowledge of the other parts whether any part be missing, and to prevent any arbitrary addition, or in respect of its completeness any indeterminateness that does not conform to the limits which are thus determined *a priori*. The whole is thus an organized unity (*articulatio*), and not an aggregate (*coacervatio*). It may grow from within (*per intussusceptionem*), but not by external addition (*per appositionem*). It is thus like an animal body, the growth of which is not by the addition of a new member, but by the rendering of each member, without change of proportion, stronger and more effective for its purposes.[30]

The idea is the form or principle which unifies the whole, so that it is not simply an aggregate, but an articulated unity. All the parts within the

30. *Critique of Pure Reason*, A 833, B 861.

whole and their relationships to each other are *predetermined* by the *a priori* idea of the unified whole.[31] The idea of system therefore functions to define the extent of the system as well as the parts included in the development of the whole. Thus the idea of system grounds the conception Kant has as the *end* toward which all the parts are directed. As Kant explains, "The *representation* of the whole contains the ground of possibility of the form of the same and the connection of the parts which belong to it . . . [thus the whole's] *representation* is the cause of its possibility."[32] To understand more clearly how the idea of systematicity fits into Kant's larger epistemological scheme, we must place the idea within the context of reason as it relates to the understanding.

Kant explains that

> When a science is an aggregate brought into existence in a merely experimental manner, completeness [of the whole conceptual field of the pure understanding] can never be guaranteed by any kind of mere estimate. It is possible only by means of *an idea of the totality* of the a priori knowledge yielded by the understanding; such an idea can furnish an exact classification of the concepts which compose that totality, exhibiting their *interconnection in a system*. Pure understanding distinguishes itself not merely from all that is empirical but completely also from all sensibility. It is a unity self-subsistent, self-sufficient, and not to be increased by any additions from without. The sum of its knowledge thus constitutes a system, comprehended and determined by one idea. The completeness and articulation of this system can at the same time yield a criterion of the correctness and genuineness of all its components.[33]

Kant makes it clear that the only means by which scientific completion can be accomplished is by positing the constitutive idea of system. This is the template by which the "genuineness" of scientific knowledge can be measured. The advantage of constituting science by means of the idea of system is twofold.

---

31. One might call this the *law of systematicity* or the *principle of homogeneity*, as we shall later see Kant refer to its correlatives, *specification* and *continuity*, as *laws* or *principles*.

32. As quoted by O'Farrell, "System and Reason," 13, emphasis Kant's. O'Farrell references this passage incorrectly. I was unable to finally discover its location in Kant's writings.

33. *Critique of Pure Reason*, A 64–65, B 89–90, emphasis Kant's.

First, it provides for the determination of the division of the pure concepts in the context of the whole (diversity). The place of each concept is determined according to its *a priori* position within the whole. "For these concepts spring, pure and unmixed, out of the understanding which is an absolute unity; and must therefore be connected with each other according to one concept or idea. Such a connection supplies us with a rule, by which we are enabled to assign its proper place to each pure concept of the understanding, and by which we can determine in an *a priori* manner their systematic completeness."[34] Even as the pure concepts are connected in the unified whole, they yet bear the mark of articulation that constitutes them as parts of that whole. This means that the absence of division amongst the parts would be evident by reason of the articulation presupposed by the unity of the parts into the whole.

Second, Kant has established the fact that the pure concepts of the understanding must also form a system (unity). The pure understanding is a "self-subsistent, self-sufficient" unity which no outside additions can increase. It is an "absolute unity" founded in the idea of the whole. This is what leads Kant to great claims for philosophical knowledge. "All pure *a priori* knowledge, owing to the special faculty of knowledge in which alone it can originate, has in itself a peculiar unity; and metaphysics is the philosophy which has as its task the statement of that knowledge in this systematic unity."[35]

However, Kant makes it clear that understanding does not function of its own accord in a systematic fashion. Indeed, it is reason which directs the understanding to the unity found in system. As was stated earlier, the idea of system is the result of the "legislative prescriptions" of reason. It is reason which provides collective unity for the understanding.

> Reason is never in immediate relation to an object, but only to the understanding; and it is only through the understanding that it has its own [specific] empirical employment. It does not, therefore, *create* concepts (of objects) but only *orders* them, and gives them that unity which they can have only if they be employed in their widest possible application, that is, with a view to obtaining totality in the various series. The understanding does not concern itself with this totality, but only with that connection through which, in accordance with *concepts*, such *series* of conditions *come into being*. Reason has, therefore, as its sole object,

34. Ibid., A 67, B 92.
35. Ibid., A 845, B 873.

the understanding and its effective application. Just as the understanding unifies the manifold in the object by means of concepts,
so reason unifies the manifold of concepts by means of ideas,
positing a certain collective unity as the goal of the activities of
the understanding, which otherwise are concerned solely with
distributive unity.[36]

Reason has as its task the regulative function of the transcendental ideas.
Systematicity, as a function of reason, is therefore regulatory and determinative, never constitutive. Accordingly, Kant maintains that "transcendental ideas never allow of any constitutive employment."[37] Through
its judgments, the understanding, concerned as it is with distributive
unity, subsumes sense impressions under their corresponding concepts
and rules, but does not then proceed to connect the concepts to one another. They are left as dispersed unities. Reason functions to discover
the connectedness among understanding's rules and concepts, bringing
them together into a collective unity. Without the systematic function of
reason, the various parts discovered by the understanding would be left
as an incoherent mass.

On the other hand, we must not be fooled into thinking that reason's
task of ordering the concepts of the understanding is merely a constructed schema, formulated without regard for the objects of experience we
are given in empirical intuition. Kant believes that the systematic organization of knowledge is only possible if we suppose that the objects are
themselves amenable to such a classification, that is, that a continuum of
specific variations and similarities lies in them waiting to be discovered.
Of course, we may not surmise from this that system is then derived
from nature. On the contrary, Kant believes we impose it upon nature.
But at the same time that reason imposes systematicity, it also demands
the presupposition of the existence of system in nature.

> We may not say that [the idea of the systematized whole of
> knowledge] is a concept of the object, but only of the thorough-
> going unity of such concepts, in so far as that unity serves as a
> rule for the understanding. These concepts of reason are not de-
> rived from nature; on the contrary, we interrogate nature in ac-
> cordance with these ideas, and consider our knowledge defective
> so long as it is not adequate to them. By general admission, *pure*

36. Ibid., A 643–44, B 671–72, emphasis Kant's.
37. Ibid., A 644, B 672.

earth, pure water, pure air, etc., are not to be found. We require, however, the concepts of them (though, in so far as their complete purity is concerned, they have their origin solely in reason) in order properly to determine the share which each of these natural causes has in producing appearances.[38]

This last statement intimates how the presupposition of unity in nature functions as the understanding seeks to subsume the empirical intuitions under the categories. By presupposing that nature is subsumable under its concepts and rules, the understanding, guided by the regulative function of reason toward systematicity, is able to identify and classify the various species and subspecies under the appropriate conception of its genus. It is then reason's task to connect these into the unified whole of a system.

Turning his attention to specification, Kant introduces *the transcendental law of specification*, which, in a fashion similar to the systematic ascent to genus and on toward ever-increasing unity, obliges the understanding to descend to discover the manifold that may exist under a particular genus (thereby securing extension for the system), even requiring that it seek "under every discoverable species for subspecies, and under every difference for yet smaller differences."[39] Reason guides the understanding to seek ever increasing diversity. At the same time, reason is guiding the organization of this diversity into a unified whole. Systematicity requires specification. As Kant states, "For if there were no *lower* concepts, there could not be *higher* concepts."[40] The amenability of nature to systematicity is once again displayed, but this time in the opposite direction. Alongside our conception of the unity of nature, we must also presuppose its diversity.

> This law of specification cannot be derived from experience; which can never open to our view any such extensive prospects. Empirical specification soon comes to a stop in the distinction of the manifold, if it be not guided by the antecedent law of specification, which, as a principle of reason, leads us to seek always for further differences, and to suspect their existence even when the senses are unable to disclose them. That absorbent earths are of different kinds (chalk and muriatic earths), is a discovery

38. Ibid., A 646, B 674, emphasis Kant's.
39. Ibid., A 656, B 684.
40. Ibid., A 656, B 684, emphasis Kant's.

that was possible only under the guidance of an antecedent rule of reason—reason proceeding on the assumption that nature is so richly diversified that we may presume the presence of such differences, and therefore prescribing to the understanding the task of searching for them. Indeed, it is only on the assumption of differences in nature, just as it is also under the condition that its objects exhibit homogeneity, that we can have any faculty of understanding whatsoever.[41]

Kant is now prepared to draw together both the ascension to genera and the diversity of species together into the whole of systematic unity. He does this by proposing a third law, the law of *affinity*.

Reason thus prepares the field for the understanding: (1) through a principle of the *homogeneity* of the manifold under higher genera; (2) through a principle of the *variety* of the homogeneous under lower species; and (3) in order to complete the systematic unity, a further law, that of the *affinity* of all concepts—a law which prescribes that we proceed from each species to every other by gradual increase of the diversity. These we may entitle the principles of *homogeneity, specification,* and *continuity* of forms. The last named arises from union of the other two, inasmuch as only through the processes of ascending to the higher genera and of descending to the lower species do we obtain the idea of systematic connection in its completeness. For all the manifold differences are then related to one another, inasmuch as they one and all spring from one highest genus, through all degrees of a more and more widely extended determination.[42]

The law of affinity allows that there will be continuous motion as reason directs the understanding to discover diversity and consequently orders the diversity into its place under the genera of the unified system. All differences between the species will border on one another, thereby not allowing any skips or gaps to exist within the system. The system has reached completion, reason has fulfilled its desire for completeness.[43]

To understand the implications of Kant's systematicity, we must keep in mind that he is not out to prove the diversity or systematicity of nature from empirical evidence. He is not seeking veracity based on empirical grounds, rather he must establish the objective validity of the regulative

41. Ibid., A 657, B 685.
42. Ibid., A 658, B 686, emphasis Kant's.
43. Ibid., A 660, B 688; and A 665–66, B 693–94.

ideas antecedent to the activity of the understanding. Systematic unity is not to be found existent in nature.[44] Indeed, sensible intuitions are only meaningful if the regulative ideas of reason are presupposed. "The law of reason which requires us to seek for this unity, is a necessary law, since without it we should have no reason at all, and without reason no coherent employment of the understanding, and in the absence of this no sufficient criterion of empirical truth. In order, therefore, to secure an empirical criterion we have no option save to presuppose the systematic unity of nature as objectively valid and necessary."[45] Kant believes that the possibility of knowing, indeed, the very possibility of experience, rests on the presupposition of systematic unity. The possibility of experience depends upon being able to situate it according to its place within the system of higher genera after its subsumption by the understanding. Knowledge is only possible by means of extension of the system. Without the principle of unity, all that would be left would be an aggregate mass, indeterminate and indescribable. "For we can conclude from the universal to the particular, only in so far as universal properties are ascribed to things as being the foundation upon which the particular properties rest."[46] Kant perhaps illustrates this concept best when he states:

> If among the appearances which present themselves to us, there were so great a variety—I do not say in form, for in that respect the appearances might resemble one another; but in content, that is, in the manifoldness of the existing entities—that even the acutest human understanding could never by comparison of them detect the slightest similarity (a possibility which is quite conceivable), the logical law of genera would have no sort of standing; we should not even have the concept of a genus, or indeed any other universal concept; and the understanding itself, which has to do solely with such concepts, would be non-existent. If, therefore, the logical principle of genera is to be applied to nature (by which I here understand those objects only which are given to us), it presupposes a transcendental principle. And in accordance with this latter principle, homogeneity is necessarily presupposed in the manifold of possible experience (although we are not in a position to determine in *a priori* fashion its de-

44. Ibid., A 653, B 681.
45. Ibid., A 651, B 679.
46. Ibid., A 652, B 680.

gree); for in the absence of homogeneity, no empirical concepts, and therefore no experience, would be possible.[47]

As we shall see in regard to the critique of Kant by later German Idealists, it is on this point of necessary appearances that Kant's system seems to break down. Kant is aiming at a system that is primarily metaphysical, but he requires an empirical object to accomplish it. It seemed readily apparent to Kant's successors that "the system for which Kant congratulates himself was nowhere present in his own theory."[48]

The Critique of Judgment

While it is obviously outside the scope of this study to give a detailed account of system as it was discussed by Kant in his later *Critique of Judgment*, some mention must certainly be made. First, it is pertinent to note that Kant felt the need to repeat his understanding of system in the *Critique of Judgment*. Substantively, he makes sufficient changes in his later remarks to warrant the conclusion that Kant's system was a work in progress. Though he eventually cuts most of his remarks concerning system out of the final version, the *Critique of Judgment* represents a substantial revision of Kant's thought on the subject.

Kant devoted a large portion of his unpublished First Introduction for the *Critique of Judgment* to the subject of system. His First Introduction was almost twice as long as the Second, which he used in the final publication. His desire to shorten the work appears to be the primary reason for his decision to write the Second Introduction.[49] A difference in subject matter may also be observed in the fact that in the First Introduction Kant uses the word system 66 times and the word systematic 9 times, as compared to 3 times each in the Second Introduction. This does not necessitate a change in the meaning of systematicity, but perhaps indicates a slight shift in emphasis.[50] Nevertheless, Kant believed the First Introduction contained "much that is useful for a fuller un-

47. Ibid., A 654, B 682.

48. Rockmore, *Before and After Hegel*, 19.

49. O'Farrell ("System and Reason," 16) makes it clear from Kant's correspondence that he wished to shorten the length of the introduction from its original 59 pages. The final product was 32 pages in length.

50. O'Farrell ("System and Reason," 17ff.) discusses the differences in greater detail, marking out the intention of each Introduction as Kant wished for it to serve a specific intention for his audience.

derstanding of the concept of nature's adaptation-to-end."[51] With this in mind, let us briefly describe the nature of his development of system in the First Introduction.

The focus on the primacy of systematicity in the *Critique of Judgment* represents a slight shift from the *Critique of Pure Reason*. System is now considered under the faculty of judgment, largely due to the fact that though reason dictates that a system of concepts subsume certain concepts under others, and lower species and subspecies under higher genera, it still falls to the faculty of judgment to actually discover and display them.[52] Kant outlines the distinctiveness of judgment in comparison with understanding and reason as follows:

> Now suppose we are concerned with dividing, not a *philosophy*, but our *ability to cognize a priori through concepts*, . . . the systematic presentation of our ability to think turns out to have three parts. The first part is *understanding*, the ability to cognize the *universal* (i.e., rules); the second is *judgment*, the ability to *subsume the particular* under the universal; and the third is *reason*, i.e., the ability to *determine* the particular through the universal (i.e., to derive [the particular] from principles) . . . Yet judgment is a very special cognitive power, not at all independent: it gives us neither concepts nor ideas of any object whatever, whereas understanding does give us such concepts, and reason such ideas. For judgment is merely an ability to subsume under concepts given from elsewhere.[53]

Judgment functions as the power through which understanding and reason can effect their tasks. Such a conception of judgment causes Kant to speak more thoroughly in the First Introduction about the application of reflective judgment as it seeks systematic unity, and, somewhat less thoroughly, of determinative judgment which applies the categories in the understanding to empirical intuitions. The identification of systematicity with reflective judgment has led some to posit that in fact Kant is describing a new conception of system in the *Critique of Judgment*, perhaps

51. Akad. Ausg. Bd. XI, *Briefwechsel*, Bd. 2, Brief 549 (516) 396; as quoted by O'Farrell, "System and Reason," 16. This quote is taken from a letter by Kant dated December 4, 1792.

52. For a useful discussion of the distinctions Kant makes between regulative and determinative judgment, see Friedman, "Regulative and Constitutive," 73ff; and Makkreel, "Regulative and Reflective Uses of Purposiveness in Kant," 50ff.

53. "First Introduction" to the *Critique of Judgment*, 201–2; 391, emphasis Kant's.

even retracting his original theses as they were laid out in the *Critique of Pure Reason*.[54] However, those who would accuse Kant of equivocation, or perhaps retracting his original work appear to be granting too wide a range to judgment, allowing its task to overlap with that of reason. Kant does not mean to substitute the task of judgment for that of reason. For it is only through the activities of the understanding and judgment that reason can effect its task of systematicity. Likewise, the transcendental ideas, which originate from reason, provide judgment with its end, or *telos*. By means of determinative judgment, the understanding seeks the particulars of nature. In order for this to be accomplished, the power of judgment must presuppose the formal adaptation of nature to the end of systematic knowing. Reason supplies the idea of specificity. Reflective judgment seeks for the universal under which to bring the particular, but again it is reason which brings the species and genera of the understanding together into a unified whole by providing the *a priori* idea of systematicity.[55] Further, it is reason that strives for the eventual completion of system into one totally unified whole. Reason never lets the understanding be satisfied with what it has already discovered. Reason drives the understanding onward toward the unconditioned, even though it may seem a somewhat unrealistic aim. We are now prepared to address how Kant believes the idea of system, as it is applied by reason, functions in the overall project of his philosophy.

The Ultimate End of System

We have up to this point been describing the conception of system as it has its function in theoretical knowledge. We have discovered that Kant posited the idea of systematicity to unify the activity of the understanding into a whole, each part in relationship to the other parts. The end of this system was the completion of our knowledge of nature to the extent that eventually all knowledge could be arranged into this articulated whole. But it is not enough for Kant to simply know the unity of nature. Reason also functions within practical knowledge, and the unity

---

54. This is Paul Guyer's interpretation of Kant's thought in the two works. He posits that Kant "reassigns" the ideal of systematicity from the realm of "reason to reflective judgment," believing them to be antithetical in some sense (Guyer, "Reason and Reflective Judgment: Kant on the Significance of Systematicity," 17ff.).

55. "Second Introduction" to the *Critique of Judgment*, 179; 18–19.

gained by reason in each area must somehow come together into one all-encompassing whole, the unity of theoretical and practical knowledge.[56]

For Kant the philosopher is not simply seeking the unity of system for the sake of logical perfection. Indeed, philosophy is much more than that.

> Hitherto the concept of philosophy has been a merely scholastic concept—a concept of a system of knowledge which is sought solely in its character as a science, and which has therefore in view only the systematic unity appropriate to science, and consequently no more than the *logical* perfection of knowledge. But there is likewise another concept of philosophy, a *conceptus cosmicus,* which has always formed the real basis of the term "philosophy," especially when it has been as it were personified and its archetype represented in the ideal *philosopher*. On this view, philosophy is the science of the relation of all knowledge to the essential ends of human reason (*teleologia rationis humanae*), and the philosopher is not an artificer in the field of reason, but himself the lawgiver of human reason.[57]

The essential ends of which Kant is speaking include both the ultimate end and the subordinate ends which necessarily function as means for the ultimate end. The ultimate end is "no other than the whole vocation of man, and the philosophy which deals with it is entitled moral philosophy."[58] Theoretical knowledge and practical knowledge are directed toward unity within each of their respective realms. We should therefore expect that reason would guide them to a synthetic union. Though scientific knowledge exists self-sufficiently, i.e., it takes no direction from nor is it influenced by practical knowledge, it nonetheless must be coordinated in some respect with practical knowledge to achieve what Kant perceives as the ultimate end. Kant's final recourse is to the *purposiveness* of a supreme reason. "This highest formal unity, which rests solely on concepts of reason, is the *purposive* unity of things. The *speculative* interest of reason makes it necessary to regard all order in the world as if it had originated in the purpose of a supreme reason. Such

---

56. Guyer quite correctly calls this the "unity of reason." See Guyer, "Unity of Reason: Pure Reason as Practical Reason in Kant's early Conception of the Transcendental Dialectic," 160. Guyer offers here a good discussion of the relationship of pure reason to practical reason.

57. *Critique of Pure Reason*, A 839, B 867, emphasis Kant's.

58. Ibid., A 840, B 868.

a principle opens out to our reason, as applied in the field of experience, altogether new views as to how the things of the world may be connected according to teleological laws, and so enables it to arrive at their greatest systematic unity."[59] The teleological system of nature governed by a supreme intelligence has its counterpart in moral philosophy as well. Thus both theoretical and practical knowledge depend upon reason's further presupposition of the highest unity being originated and consequently discovered in a purposive supreme being, and this being Kant calls God.[60]

The difference between Kant's God discovered through reason and the God of the church's theologians as discussed in the various chapters above should be quite plain. Though greater formative and extensive influence is felt in religious studies due to the more strident moves of later German Idealists toward a theistic God discovered solely in metaphysics, one cannot help but notice what Kant's scheme does to the historical affirmations of Christian theology regarding Jesus. The Word made flesh is an absurdity in a world of objectivity discovered only in the theoretical. Jesus could, and did, serve as a prime example of practical knowledge for Kant (a la liberalism), but He could never *be* the supreme being, as the church had affirmed for centuries. Thus, though Kant continued to work from a Christian context, his work represents a decisive turn away from Jesus to something called religion, which has primarily to do with practical, or moral, knowledge (i.e., religion is primarily concerned with making humans better humans).[61] The consideration of the subject (i.e., the human) in Enlightenment thought finds a climax in Kant's dependence on the capacity and priority of the human in knowledge. Though Kant may not have intended such an exhaltation, even deification, of the human, his work is but one representation of the swelling mood in the Enlightenment toward anthropology. Kant did not attempt a work in Christian theology. His concerns were directed more specifically at an underlying epistemology. The dramatic shift evident in Kant is the way in which the systematic qualification of knowledge now precedes revelation in theological knowledge.[62] In other words, reason and the internal

59. Ibid., A 687, B 715, emphasis Kant's.

60. Cf. Ibid., A 826–27, B 854–55.

61. Kant, *Religion within the Limits of Reason Alone*, 102–3.

62. I am here mindful of the pre-eminence, or universality, of pure religion over ecclesiastical faith, as the latter is grounded in historical revelation. E.g., see Ibid., 98, 100.

coherence of theological claims with the larger corpus of knowledge are prior to revelational claims in theology. Indeed, revelational knowledge, under Kant, must be subject to the categories of the human mind, which is in direct contrast to the church's belief for centuries regarding the primacy of revelational knowledge. Certainly Kant is not solely responsible for such a shift, but it is a short step from Kant to Schleiermacher and Hegel, not to mention Ritschl and von Harnack.

Summary

We have now observed, however briefly, but hopefully not superficially, Kant's conception of systematic unity as it takes place in accordance with the ends of reason. It is always an idea that directs this unification of the parts into an organic whole. As a regulative function using the idea of differentiation, reason guides the understanding, through determinative judgment, to seek diversity, discovering species and subspecies under the various genera, subsuming empirical intuitions under the categories. Using the idea of systematization, reason then directs the reflective judgment to locate the genera under ever-higher genera, thereby displaying unity. The transcendental law of affinity then demands that knowledge as it is systematized be connected completely, without gaps in knowledge, thereby establishing continuity. Ultimately, the various realms of knowledge, as they are comprised of unified genera in themselves, are yet directed toward one final end which is displayed in moral philosophy. This philosophy discovers its unity, as do all other philosophies, as they are systematized according to the *a priori* final purposive origination of the supreme reason: God. Kant's system, deepening the trench begun by Descartes, seems to be another step toward rationality as a substitute for revelation.

8

Hegel's Pinnacle

Introduction

NO STUDY OF THE HISTORY OF SYSTEM WOULD BE COMPLETE WITHOUT some mention, at least, of Georg Wilhelm Friedrich Hegel (1770–1831). Hegel represents a pinnacle, of sorts in the use of system as a methodology. Though his substantive contributions to theology/religion may be modest, his methodological influence remains immense.

Many works have been written on the methodology of Hegel's philosophy. Likewise, the substance of his theological/religious and historical contributions have been the subject of numerous studies. We will not attempt to provide any contribution to the overall literature available on Hegel's philosophy, understanding of religion, or influence. Instead, using various histories of philosophy, we will attempt to briefly outline how Hegel's thought represents the pinnacle of system in history by observing his understanding of truth. Then, we will move to demonstrate how his systematic approach to theological knowledge bears fruit in contemporary theological/religious studies.

Hegel's System as Truth

The thought of Hegel stands as an extension of German Idealism. Immanuel Kant (1724–1804) provided later Idealists, like Hegel, with a foundation on which to build their thought, especially their systematic philosophy.

> Kant had strongly insisted on the need for philosophy to be a systematic science. Post-Kantian German idealists, including Hegel, were concerned to produce philosophical systems. Throughout his career, Hegel understood philosophy as fully legitimated and

as systematically developed. According to him, philosophy must be all-inclusive, or encyclopedic, and comprise a whole, or totality, since its parts can only be grasped in terms of the whole. The *Encyclopedia of the Philosophical Sciences* (1817, 1827, 1831), which he quickly composed and later twice revised, was intended as an "official" statement of his philosophical system.[1]

Kant initiated and built much of his own thought on a critique of the empiricism of John Locke (1632–1704) and Francis Bacon (1561–1626). Kant rejected the immediate knowledge derived from experience, which was characteristic of English empiricism. Further, he believed knowledge must be found in the relation between appearances and a cognitive reality that exists independent of perception, i.e., the "thing-in-itself." In other words, though Kant believed that empirical data was necessary for knowledge, true knowledge was not attained until the categories perceived the data and processed it within the human consciousness apart from experience. Hegel follows much of Kant's lead; however, Hegel believed the human consciousness could never step outside of itself to examine an object. Instead, "[Hegel] regards knowledge as resulting from a process in which we progressively narrow and eventually overcome the differences between our views of things and the things of which they are the view, *both* of which are contained in consciousness."[2] One can already see here the beginnings of Hegel's famous dialectical method. Rejecting Cartesian foundationalism, Hegel limits the interplay for attaining knowledge to the dialectic occurring within the human consciousness.

> Post-Kantian German philosophy developed the Kantian view of systematic philosophy in two stages: initially through the attempt to work out a satisfactory form of Cartesian foundationalism through qualified return to Descartes; and only later, after the inability to work out an adequate conception of founded system became clear, in a break with Descartes, by invoking a novel concept of unfounded system. In other words, the effort to restate [Kant's] critical philosophy in systematic form led, initially, toward a linear, foundationalist, "Cartesian" view and then only later, when this effort failed, to a circular, antifoundationalist, "anti-Cartesian" view of knowledge.[3]

1. Rockmore, "Hegel," 284.
2. Ibid., 282, emphasis his.
3. Rockmore, *On Hegel's Epistemology and Contemporary Philosophy*, 21.

This meant that Hegel must likewise limit the scope of his reference as to the kind of knowledge obtained. Knowledge is limited, therefore, within Hegel to only what is discoverable in the dialectic. Knowledge is, finally, metaphysical by its very nature. The appeal to reality outside of human consciousness, which was available, or is a given, to Kant, is intentionally avoided by Hegel. Hegel's *Science of Logic* lays out his method for arriving at knowledge. Contrary to the perception of philosophers from Aristotle to Kant, Hegel believed logic was not "a system of rules characterizing the abstract forms of static objects."[4] In place of such a science, Hegel posits that the purview of logic is objective thought, "which is the content of pure science, or thought as it takes itself as its object."[5] Thus, Hegel devised the means to arrive at an epistemology based in a purely internal dialectic.

It is this internal dialectic that has led to some critiques of Hegel's thought as being circular. He does not provide a "beginning point" from which to start the process of knowing based in a foundation or originating principle. Instead, Hegel simply seems to begin without any place to begin; he simply starts thinking by first removing the necessity of a foundation. "But to want the nature of cognition clarified *prior* to the science is to demand that it be considered *outside* the science; *outside* the science this cannot be accomplished, at least not in a scientific manner and such a manner is alone here in place."[6] Hegel then sees that the only next step at arriving at a beginning is to posit that the beginning must be absolute immediacy, as opposed to anything mediated. Thus, "the beginning therefore is *pure being*."[7] However, lest anyone think that pure being can possibly substitute as a foundation, of sorts, for starting the process of reason, Hegel concludes that the beginning point is not as critical as foundationalists would have it. "The essential requirement for the science of logic is not so much that the beginning be a pure immediacy, but rather that the whole of the science be within itself a circle in which the first is also the last and the last is also the first."[8] Such circularity is

---

4. Rockmore, "Hegel," 284.
5. Ibid.
6. Hegel, *Science of Logic*, par. 92.
7. Ibid., par. 99.
8. Ibid., par. 102.

intentional in that it avoids the possibility of establishing any thought prior to the absolute simplicity of being, or as Hegel would have it, God.[9]

From such an epistemological approach, it is a simple step to understanding Hegel's means for measuring truth. Since all attributes of the process of knowing have been internalized, it is therefore necessary that veracity must likewise be measured internally. The measure of truth cannot be subject to the "feelings" or subjectivity of individual humans. Likewise, it cannot be established on any foundational principles or correspondence to an external reality. Instead, truth can only be measured as the coherence of the whole system is displayed or recognized, and individuated truth claims are coherently organized or systematized with regard to other truths.

Hegel believed that the basic need for philosophy was to resolve the divisions that exist in the mind as it perceives experience. "Division [*Entzweiung*] is the source of the need of philosophy."[10] The mind seeks to construct a unified whole of the divisions so that it may at once unite the finite and the infinite. Of course, a final unity is impossible for Hegel, since a final unification of the finite and infinite would result in a conceptualization of the finite that would exclude the finite. In order to maintain the reality of the finite and infinite in a unified whole, Hegel focuses on the process of synthesis, rather than a synthesized final product. Indeed, a final product is not possible, since, as mentioned, it would collapse either the finite or the infinite. As Frederick Copelston makes clear regarding Hegel, "The whole process of reality is a teleological movement towards the actualization of self-thinking Thought; and in this sense the Thought which thinks itself is the *telos* or end of the universe. But it is an end which is immanent within the process."[11] This process cannot be accomplished in human reason by transcending the finite by means of the absolute, or infinte. Instead, the absolute is accessed only through the finite as philosophy presents the dialectic relationship between the finite and the infinite. Only in the dialectic is the infinite discovered, and here only through the mediation of the finite. "In other words, philosophy has to exhibit systematically the self-realization of infinite Reason

9. Ibid., par. 121. Cf. Rockmore, *On Hegel's Epistemology and Contemporary Philosophy*, 30–31. More will be said below in regard to how such anti-foundationalism has influenced the post-modern philosophical and theological critique of modernism.

10. Hegel, *Werke*, vol.1, 44.

11. Copleston, *History of Philosophy*, vol. vii, 171.

in and through the finite."[12] Thus the systematization of the whole is ciritical for knowledge as the finite and infinite are held together in their relation to one another. "The subject matter of philosophy is indeed the Absolute. But the Absolute is the Totality, reality as a whole, the universe. 'Philosophy is concerned with the true and the true is the whole.'"[13] One can now easily see how system plays the most critical role in establishing knowledge and the veracity of knowledge in Hegel. It is only as the parts relate to each other and to the whole that they become understandable. Further, the totalizing nature of the system is what finally unites the finite and infinite. Copleston summarizes the dialectic well.

> Thus in speculative philosophy the mind must elevate itself from the level of understanding in the narrow sense to the level of dialectical thinking which overcomes the rigidity of the concepts of the understanding and sees one concept as generating or passing into its opposite. Only so can it hope to grasp the life of the Absolute in which one moment or phase passes necessarily into another. But this is obviously not enough. If for the understanding concepts A and B are irrevocably opposed whereas for the deeper penetration of dialectical thought A passes into B and B into A, there must be a higher unity or synthesis which unites them without annulling their difference. And it is the function of reason (*Vernunft*) to grasp this moment of identity-in-difference. Hence, philosophy demands the elevation of understanding through dialectical thinking to the level of reason or speculative thought, which is capable of apprehending identity-in-difference.[14]

Reason's function, accordingly, demands a constant process of identification of relationship between the finite and infinite. Progress is presumed by Hegel as each moment is integrated into the whole. Again, Copleston is helpful. "[T]he most cursory inspection of the Hegelian system reveals his preoccupation with triads. Thus there are three main phases in the construction of the life of the Absolute: the logical idea, Nature and Spirit. And each phase is divided and subdivided into triads. Moreover, the whole system is, or aims at a necessary development. That is to say, for philosophical reflection one stage reveals itself as demand-

---

12. Ibid., 172.

13. Ibid., 170. Copleston is here quoting Hegel, *Werke*, vol. II, 24.

14. Copleston, *History of Philosophy*, 175.

ing the next by an inner necessity."[15] It is, then, the whole that finally displays the dialectic in process. The relationship of the parts to each other and to the whole becomes the means by which knowledge is attainable and verifiable. System becomes the arbiter of true knowledge, in that knowledge is only confirmed as true as it aligns or fits within the system. Though not abstracted and linear, as in Kant, systematic knowledge is now even more important, in that it does not merely provide knowledge of an external reality. Knowledge now only can be found within and in relation to the system. The tool previously used to build the machine has, in fact, become the machine.

History and the Progress of Reason

Of course, reason's relationship to the Absolute, as it moves or progresses from experience to the Absolute, that is from logical idea to Spirit, is one that occurs in time and space. In other words, Hegel must likewise account for the progression occurring within history, or at least, must give an account of the relationship of the Absolute to history. In contrast to Kant, who attempted to remove history, as much as possible, from the process of knowing, Hegel attempts to account for the realization that all such knowing occurs within history. Absolute objectivity on the part of the observer is impossible. Thus, Hegel must develop a philosophical understanding of history.

Hegel is perhaps best known for his philosophy of history. His approach to history is not essentially different from his approach to knowledge. History, and Hegel's philosophy of history, is merely a demonstration that the system includes and emphasizes the reality of the dialectic between the finite and the infinite.

> Hegel's general idea is more or less this. As the philosopher knows that reality is the self-unfolding of infinite reason, he knows that reason must operate in human history. At the same time, we cannot tell in advance how it operates. To discover this, we have to study the course of events as depicted by historians in the ordinary sense and try to discern the significant rational process in the mass of contingent material. In theological language, we know in advance that divine providence operates in history. But to see how it operates we must study the historical data.

15. Ibid., 177.

Now, world-history is the process whereby Spirit comes to actual consciousness of itself as freedom. Hence, "world history is progress in the consciousness of freedom." . . . History, therefore, is the process whereby the World-Spirit comes to explicit consciousness of itself as free.[16]

Hegel believes history follows a plan, even a providential plan; however, he does not believe that plan is obvious or spelled out anywhere except in history itself. In this, the historian must approach study of history expecting a pattern to reveal itself, rather than approach history with a pre-conceived pattern in mind. "The only idea which philosophy brings with it [that is, to the contemplation of history] is the simple idea of reason, that reason dominates the world and that world-history is thus a rational process."[17] Thus, Hegel believes he can avoid revisionist readings of history in which the historian describes a pattern that only exists in the mind of the historian.[18]

One can further see in Hegel's philosophy of history a great concern for the realization of political freedom. Hegel was highly influenced by and observant of the French Revolution.[19] Though the revolution itself did not necessarily produce the kind of freedom envisioned by German Idealists such as Kant and Hegel, they were nonetheless undeterred

16. Ibid., 219. Copelston is here quoting Hegel, *Werke*, vol. XI, 36.

17. Hegel, *Philosophy of History*, 9.

18. Copleston (*History of Philosophy*, 219, 223–25) here provides a helpful critique of Hegel's historical presumption. Not only is it problematic to attempt to justify the objectivity of the historian; Hegel himself does not seem to see the necessary bias he brings to historical study. Copleston outlines the problem of "might is right" in Hegel, demonstrating that "if one nation succeeds in conquering another, it seems to follow that its action is justified by its success" (223). The winners typically write the histories, making it impossible, or at least very difficult, to separate the events of history from the interpretation. Hegel makes no such distinction. Copleston, rightly, demonstrates that the Christian interpretation of events may not be so generous, and may even call into question the very justification offered by the "winners" (224). To equate events of history simply with divine providence is, at best, a somewhat naïve fatalism. At worst, it is a front for political posturing.

Hegel seemed to realize this and wished to guard against it (*Philosophy of Right*, par. 342). However, his remarks seem insufficient to avoid such an interpretation of history, given the mood of the Enlightenment and his own portrayal of history as unfolding toward true freedom (Hegel, *Philosophy of History*, 110).

19. For an insightful discussion of how the French Revolution influenced Hegel's understanding of freedom in both its social and political context, see Ritter, *Hegel and the French Revolution*.

from extolling the eventual evolution of politics into a free state. Hegel envisioned an eventual state in which the process of reason coming to consciousness in the Absolute, or Spirit, would result in a recognition of freedom as the highest political good. His own perception was that history was moving this direction, however slowly. In light of the political experiments in freedom in America and France, he remained optimistic that it would become the predominant ideology of states.

Such optimism is perhaps the most striking element of Hegel's philosophy of history. According to him, it is in the culture of early nineteenth-century Europe that "the empire of thought is established actually and concretely . . . Freedom has found the means of realizing its Ideal—its true actuality."[20] Hegel clearly seems to believe in the inevitability of progress in history, which is coordinate with the evolutionary optimism of his day and the generations of Marxists to follow. In this, Hegel is merely illustrating an underlying anthropology inherited from Kant, or better, from Descartes and the Scholastic humanists. Following Kant, Hegel seems to believe history will naturally produce freedom.[21] The natural progression is due to the innate sense of what is good lying beneath the social constraints humanity has taken upon itself through its own lack of development.[22] Though Hegel does not delve into his confidence in the natural social progress of humans, he paves the way for later thinkers to reduce all thought to the anthropological considerations Hegel is merely introducing in his philosophy of history.[23] The turn to the subject begun in Kant finally comes to full flower in the anthropology of such figures as Ludwig Feuerbach (1804–72). Hegel represents a marked step in this transformation from the object to the subject.

Hegel and Enlightenment Thought

Hegel is quite evidently a man of his times. Along with most of philosophy after Descartes, Hegel was confident in the capacity of reason to accomplish the ultimate ends of philosophy: a comprehensive system of

20. Hegel, *Philosophy of History*, 110. For a good discussion of Hegel's understanding of progress in history, see Avineri, *Hegel's Theory of the Modern State*, 221–38.

21. See Kant, "What is Enlightenment?" 89–91.

22. Ibid., 85. "Laziness" and "cowardice" are Kant's exact words for not "coming of age" in the era of Enlightenment.

23. More will be discussed below with regard to how Hegel's philosophy of history paves the way for Feuerbach's reduction of all theology to anthropology.

all knowledge. Reason, after Descartes, was deemed capable of reaching the height and depth of any science, even providing the Idealists with a platform for devising a metaphysic to adequately articulate the theory of system. Such confidence was inherited from the earliest Enlightenment thinkers and influenced all the philosophers to follow.

> The idea of a systematic science accompanies the rationalist idea that appears in the discussion in the seventeenth century, namely, the idea of a scientific philosophy in systematic form. After Descartes, a new rationalism appears based on the principle of the complete transparency of all phenomena with respect to reason, since in theory at least nothing should be resistant to reason. There is no longer any effort to group together (Greek *systema*, assembly, composition) different parts of the theory, but there is the effort to think the concept of a system without limits of any kind.[24]

German idealism could not have achieved its stature as the high-point of metaphysics in philosophical history without the heritage of Enlightenment thought, especially the critical philosophy of Kant. Though continuing the project of Kant in one respect or another, all the post-Kant German Idealists agreed that Kant had not completed his project of achieving knowledge independent of any object. Kant maintained a place in his thought for the "thing-in-itself," which, though not necessarily derived from empirical experience, left him reliant upon an object presented to human cognition in order for the activity of cognition to take place. The later Idealists believed this to be Kant's fatal flaw. As Rockmore observes,

> Jacobi's critique concerns the crucial Kantian idea of the thing-in-itself. In the critical philosophy, Kant distinguishes in effect between two dimensions, or aspects, of the object: what appears, or the phenomenon; and what does not appear but what can without contradiction be thought, that is, the thing-in-itself or noumenon. In disagreement with Kant, Jacobi submitted the concept of the thing-in-itself to a very rigorous critique. He maintains that we need it to enter into the Kantian system, but in virtue of this concept it is not possible to remain within it.[25]

24. Rockmore, *Before and After Hegel*, 15.

25. Ibid., 20. Rockmore is here referring to Kant, *Critique of Pure Reason*, 467, and Jacobi, *Werke*, vol. 2, 304.

The post-Kantian Idealists, in order to move beyond the dependence upon an object, focused their attention on the act of cognition behind the interplay between mind and object. Their emphasis on metaphysics allowed the later Idealists to focus on the process or act of thought, rather than attempting to engage the world as independent of the mind. "If one had any understanding of the development of philosophy and of the demands of modern thought, one could only go forward and complete Kant's work. And this meant eliminating the thing-in-itself. For, given Kant's premises, there was no room for an unknowable occult entity supposed to be independent of the mind. In other words, the critical philosophy had to be transformed into a consistent idealism; and this meant that things had to be regarded in their entirety as products of thought."[26] It was not sufficient that the Idealist merely depict the conscious workings of the mind as it encountered and categorized, to use Kant's epistemology, objects in reality. Instead, "the idealist philosopher must go behind consciousness, as it were, and retrace the process of the unconscious activity which grounds it."[27] This is distinct from Kant, in that Kant was attempting to know reality in the objective sense of an identifiable object. For the Idealists, the system of knowing within the subject itself was in fact where reality was located. Kant was never so confident in the capacity of metaphysics. "Now if we assume that reality is a rational process and that its essential dynamic structure is penetrable by the philosopher, this assumption is naturally accompanied by a confidence in the power and scope of metaphysics, which contrasts sharply with Kant's modest estimate of what it can achieve."[28] Hegel himself, believed this reality could be discovered in the dialectic of the finite reason with the Absolute Reason, as the latter disclosed itself through the relationship to finally achieve a higher consciousness for reason (i.e., Spirit). Hegel, though still under a belief in the autonomous nature of human reason, further believed that this higher consciousness was achieved as a collective of reason in the history of a community.

A second way in which the later German Idealists, especially Hegel, distinguished themselves from Kant was in the way they identified the veracity of their metaphysical idealism. Kant's theory of truth was again "entrapped" by the "thing-in-itself." Kant must account for the way in

26. Copleston, *History of Philosophy*, vol. vii, 3–4.
27. Ibid., 4.
28. Ibid., 9.

which the thing corresponded to the mind's identification of the thing. Thus, the determination of truth consisted in a measurement of this correspondence.

As was made clear in our discussion above, truth for the post-Kantian German Idealists was a matter of coherence. In other words, the identification of truth was associated, more than this, it was identified with the consistent inter-relationship of the various parts of the system to the whole. Speaking in reference to Heraclitus' *logos* as a holistic logical criterion for truth, Hegel declared, "This whole, the universal and divine understanding in unity with which we are logical, is, according to Heraclitus, the essence of truth."[29] The later Idealists, therefore, had little interest in the objects, save for the way in which they demonstrated, for Hegel for instance, the unfolding of the self-consciousness of the Absolute. This was, after all, his philosophy of history as it displayed his metaphysics for observation in the world of objects, especially political states.

In spite of such differences from earlier Enlightenment thinkers like Kant, the later Idealists nevertheless carried on several lines of thought, or methodology, from the Enlightenment. As has been made clear in the paragraphs above, knowledge for all the Idealists, including Kant, was largely an end in itself. While Kant remained interested in science and providing some scientific grounding for his philosophical studies, he still pursued knowledge largely for its own sake. In other words, though Kant was skeptical of the achievements of metaphysics, he still engaged in metaphysics sufficiently to serve as the foundation for Idealism. The later Idealists themselves pushed this line even further, pursuing metaphysics as though it was equivalent to knowledge. They believed the system itself served as a complete display of human understanding. Thus, knowledge and the system of understanding, which were important themes in the Enlightenment valuation of the autonomy of reason, were finally extolled as the highest pursuit of philosophy, indeed of all study.

A further theme of Idealism stemming from roots planted firmly within the Enlightenment is the emphasis on a theistic God as the ideal. Though Schelling's later philosophy pursued the notion of a personal God, Hegel, Fichte, and the early Schelling were more interested in defining the infinite in philosophical terms, such as the Absolute. Thus their interest in religion was largely a philosophical interest in defining

29. Hegel, *Lectures on the History of Philosophy*, 296.

the relationship of the finite to the infinite, and attempting to understand how knowledge of the infinite might be gained. The point of mentioning Idealism's focus on religion, as opposed to Christian theology, is to demonstrate the fact that their emphasis furthered the move away from a revealed religion to theism. Though certainly the Idealists were hardly alone in this move, they did serve to substantiate the direction in philosophy toward theism, if the philosopher was interested in religion at all.

Hegel's Influence

Any study of Hegel would be incomplete without some mention of his influence. One might expect his greatest influence to have been upon such political theorists as Marx and Engels. While it is true that they extended and developed many themes from Hegel's philosophy of history, they also so revolutionized his thought that they deserve attention in their own right.[30] Nevertheless, "Hegelianism, in a variety of manifestations, continues as the dominant motif in continental European intellectual life. Moreover, the transformation of Hegelianism through Marxism now shapes the dominant political and cultural ethos in many sectors of the modern world."[31] In the arena of politics, Hegel has maintained widespread influence, albeit through revised versions of his thought, but even his influence in politics cannot compare to his more intentional efforts to guide religious study.

It is in the area of theology and religious studies that Hegel could be said to have had his greatest influence. The first branch of Hegelian influence was felt in religion during and shortly after his lifetime. Many students of religion believed they had found in Hegel a supporter of the rational demonstration of historic Christianity, even a foundation for the rationality of Christianity. The relationship of theology and philosophy in Hegel follows the Enlightenment preference for autonomous reason, which meant that religion required justification by reason in order to be regarded as true knowledge. "Hegel agrees with G. E. Lessing that it is impossible to provide a historical foundation for eternal truths. Hegel believes that Christianity is not susceptible to a historical proof or justification. If Christianity is to be justified it will have to be justified by

30. For a good outline of the Hegel–Marx connection, see Taylor, *Hegel and Modern Society*, 140–54.

31. Lucas, "Hegel, Whitehead, and the Status of Systematic Philosophy," 3.

reason and philosophy; philosophy must show the rational element in religion and thus justify religion. However, philosophy for Hegel must be autonomous and self-justifying. Only because it is autonomous can philosophy provide justification for Christianity by generating it out of the concept."[32] Hegel was perceived as providing an *a priori* accounting of Christianity in his development of the Absolute, or Spirit. The progressive unfolding of the Absolute in the historical progress of Reason was interpreted, perhaps even at times by Hegel himself, as a justification for historical Christianity. What is of most interest in this regard is not the fact that Hegel, and others, believed a rational demonstration of Christianity was necessary, though that is obviously a useful subject. What is of most interest to this study is that Christianity, consequently for some of Hegel's interpreters, became a subset of theistic philosophy, further, of systematic philosophy. Philosophy of religion had successfully replaced any fundamental consideration of revelation. Hegel believed philosophy and theology dealt with the same subject: "[T]he eternal truth in its objectivity, God and nothing but God and the unfolding of God."[33] Therefore, "religion and philosophy come to the same thing."[34] Such a turn has obvious consequences for modern theology, not to mention the reaction of postmodern theology. Though perhaps not his intention, Hegel, and other Idealists, succeeded in encircling theology within the boundaries of autonomous systematic philosophy. Hegel especially furthered this move in religion away from revelation. "Where Rousseau had halted and Lessing had hesitated, and where Kant was ambiguous, Hegel pressed forward to subject religion to human reason definitively and thereby to secularize religion, religious history, and philosophy of religion with them."[35] Any subsequent appeal to revelation or even historical dogma in the generations to follow would necessarily have to justify their appeal in the court of metaphysics. Like Descartes' appeal to proofs for God's existence, the systematicization of Idealism had unforeseen consequences. In the end, "Hegel makes speculative philosophy the final arbiter of the inner meaning of Christian revelation."[36]

32. McGrath, *The Blackwell Encyclopedia of Modern Christian Thought*, 245.
33. Hegel, *Werke*, vol. XV, 37.
34. Ibid.
35. McCarthy, *Quest for a Philosophical Jesus*, 157.
36. Copleston, *History of Philosophy*, vol. vii, 241.

A more divergent branch of religious influence can be seen explicitly in the work of David Strauss (1808–1874), whose thought in his *Life of Jesus* (1835) is commonly regarded to be "under the spell of Hegelianism."[37] Specifically, Strauss relied on Hegel's theory of *Vorstellung* (representation) to demonstrate that the Gospel stories were myths. Strauss was keenly interested in demonstrating the implausibility of historic Christianity. Though this would not have been well received by Hegel, who believed his work to be in support of historic Christianity, Strauss believed his own work to be a true development of Hegel's thought. It is not difficult to see the line of influence when one observes the results of Hegel's Christology.

> Christian faith began in Jesus and in Christianity's sense of the spiritual presence of Christ, but the faith of philosophy purifies it to the sense of spirit as spirit. For Jesus' achievement gave rise to faith but was destined to issue in a faith that had spirit and not Jesus as its focus. Hegel's Christology thus points unmistakably beyond Jesus, even as doctrine had begun to. For doctrine, beginning with St. Paul, emphasized the spiritual meaning of Jesus. Philosophy completes the process. To the dismay of those fixated on the sensuous trappings of history, Jesus can now appear to be "in the way." The sensuous Jesus must go *and has gone.*[38]

Another more negative influence was reflected in the work of the anthropologist Feuerbach, who followed closely the path forged by Strauss.

> Initially, Feuerbach was strongly appreciative of Hegel's philosophy. He later broke with it and viewed it as a theological idealism that aimed to restore Christianity, and hence as a form of theology that cannot agree with the results of science. Any form of idealism that remains on the level of thought requires the supplementation of real objects through sensory perception. The new philosophy, which relies on sensation to think the concrete in a concrete manner, is therefore the truth of the Hegelian philosophy and modern philosophy in general. The new philosophy, emphasizing sensation over abstract thought, substitutes the real and whole being of man for the absolute, abstract mind. Hence,

---

37. McCarthy, *Quest for a Philosophical Jesus*, 222. For a brief discussion of Hegel's influence on David Strauss, see Hodgson, "Editor's Introduction," xviii–xxii.

38. McCarthy, *Quest for a Philosophical Jesus*, 158, emphasis his.

> Hegelian theology must be dissolved into anthropology, which,
> according to Feuerbach, becomes the universal science.[39]

Thus two very divergent branches of Hegelian influence developed directly from his thought: one using his work as supportive of religion and the other using his work as a replacement of religion. Both could easily be said to exist in one form or another to this day.[40]

Though the distance makes Hegel's influence somewhat remote for theological thought in the twenty-first century, the extent of his influence is still remarkable. One theologian's adoption of certain tenets of Hegel's thought should sufficiently demonstrate his influence is very much alive in contemporary theology.[41] Wolfhart Pannenberg's understanding of God's unfolding revelation in history bears obvious resemblance to Hegel's unfolding of the Absolute. In Pannenberg, what is at stake is not the coming to consciousness discovered in the dialectic between the finite and the infinite, though these still loom in the background in Pannenberg. Pannenberg's concern centers more on the historical issue of God's activity in history and yet His control over history. More specifically, how can we arrive at truth when any human construction of it is, by its nature, historically conditioned?

> In so far as Pannenberg has a solution to this problem, it is by
> following in the footsteps of Hegel and, indeed, he believes that
> Hegel's conception of truth as process, development and histori-
> cal coheres with a biblical account of the nature of truth . . . [F]or
> Hegel truth is historical, and until we arrive at the end of history
> we cannot absolutise any particular stage of human history as
> embodying the truth. It is only with Absolute Knowledge that we
> arrive at an encompassing sense of all truth, and this is possible
> only at the end of history. This fits, in Pannenberg's view, with a
> biblical view of truth: It does so firstly, by the fact that the truth
> as such is understood not as timelessly unchangeable, but as a

39. Rockmore, "Feuerbach," 245.

40. Another section of this study could be included on the influence of Hegel in America, especially amongst the "Hegelian School" at St. Louis. The contact between this school and the New England Transcendentalists like Alcott and Emerson deserves further study. It seems very little influence of one on the other was the result of their meetings; however, they did seem to share much in common. See Pochmann, *New England Transcendentalism and St. Louis Hegelianism.*

41. Though Alfred North Whitehead himself denied any dependence, Lucas ("Hegel, Whitehead, and the Status of Systematic Philosophy," 5) believes that Whitehead's later thought reflects a great deal of Hegelian influence.

process that runs its course and maintains itself through change. Secondly, it does so by asserting that the unity of the process, which is full of contradictions while it is underway, will become visible along with the true meaning of every individual moment in it, only from the standpoint of its end.[42]

Theologically, Panneberg posits the Lordship of Jesus as the truth that is always true independent of the finite; however, its realization is necessarily connected to its revelation within history.[43] Thus, Pannenberg arrives at a proleptic understanding of the affirmation of Jesus' Lordship from the end of history: the eschaton. This is the point at which the revelation of Jesus' Lordship will finally be seen by all in its fullest expression. Pannenberg believes, like Hegel, that such a final revelation is inevitable, since Jesus is already Lord. What remains is simply the revelation in its fullness in history. To accomplish this, Pannenberg himself adopts a dialectic of sorts between the Lordship of Jesus as it will be in the eschaton and His Lordship as it is in history today. Jesus' Lordship was already revealed in His Incarnation; however, it quite obviously was not a revelation that accomplished its claim. The interplay between the Incarnational Lordship and His eschatological Lordship is carried out on the stage of the practices of the church. As the church lives the Lordship of Jesus, she is dialectically demonstrating the historically conditioned reality that will finally culminate in the eschaton. In this way, the Lordship of Jesus, though a secure doctrine of the church revealed in history, is ever unfolding into a higher level of corporate consciousness. In essence, Pannenberg has simply adapted the Hegelian system to what he understands as the telos of history in Biblical revelation. As Raymond Plant makes clear,

> [Pannenberg] argues that, for the Christian, history can still be whole although its end has yet to come, in the sense that Jesus, against whom all events are meaningful, has already appeared in history. That which gives meaning to the historical process has already pre-occurred, and in the historical process, and thus within finitude, that which is still an open future for us, into which we are still entering, has already made its appearance in

42. Plant, *Politics, Theology, and History*, 82–83. Plant is here summarizing Pannenberg's understanding of truth from Pannenberg, "What is Truth?" 22.

43. For a complete depiction Pannenberg's understanding of Jesus' Lordship in relation to history, see Pannenberg, *Systematic Theology*, vol. 1, 327–36. Also cf. my *System and Story*, ch. 4.

him. The specific nature of the history of Jesus is to be ultimate in that way. Hence, this special event makes what is otherwise unconcluded history into a whole. History partakes of the nature of revelation only in terms of its end as it has appeared in Jesus Christ. Only from Jesus and towards him do the epochs and all the individual instances of history take part in divine revelation.[44]

Other similarities may exist between Hegel and Pannenberg, and certainly Pannenberg qualifies and nuances his use of Hegel. However, this one point of clear similarity demonstrates that Hegel's influence is still felt in significant ways today in theology, not to mention politics and the study of history.

Conclusion

Hegel's thought was an obvious extension of Kant's attempt at reaching final or absolute knowledge. Kant's epistemology remained restricted by the object in that rationality was the categorization of the perceived object. Kant made no attempt to move beyond the object by engaging in a metaphysics rooted in the process of synthesizing the perceptions. Hegel aimed his project at the abstraction of the perceptions, systematizing them into a coherent whole as they were abstracted from the objects themselves. Thus, Hegel believed his system could arrive at knowledge completely abstracted from the object, or universal. As such a method was applied to religion, it became necessary to divorce philosophy of religion from any knowledge rooted in tradition or revelation. Though Hegel may not have wished for his system to be used so, it was the impetus for further relocating the veracity of religious knowledge in rationality. Consequently, historic Christianity was subject to reducing its value and knowledge to universal statements of truth that were abstracted from the historical conditionedness of revelation and the faith of the historical community of the church. Theism and philosophy of religion seemed to rule the day in philosophical studies and were quickly overcoming the claims of theologians and Biblical scholars alike. However, a swift response would come in the philosophical/theological musings of Søren Kierkegaard. It is Kierkegaard's critique of Danish Hegelianism that links our study to the varied emphases of postmodern theology and contemporary narrative theological method. Having developed a brief

44. Plant, *Politics, Theology, and History*, 83–84.

synopsis of Hegel, we must now turn our attention to his further influence in Danish theology and the subsequent reaction by Kierkegaard that led to much of what is happening today.

9

Kierkegaard's Life of Faith
and the Rejection of System

Introduction

IN THE CONTEMPORARY THEOLOGICAL CULTURE OF POSTMODERNISM, system does not fare well as a strategy for constructing or considering Christian doctrine. Indeed, system has, since Hegel's application of system to the philosophy of religion, been subject to significant ridicule as a means for arriving at any conclusions regarding the truths of Christianity and has been roundly rejected as a suitable foundation for consideration of Christian practice, centered as it was on more academic pursuits. Most, if not all, theologians have to account for the postmodern rejection of system. Some may wish to attempt to do theology as non-systematic.[1] Others may attempt a more rigorous, but qualified, defense of system as a legitimate means for accomplishing more limited ends.[2] However, no one simply engages in an uncritical adoption of a systematic method after the fashion of Hegel's rigorous philosophical system.

The reason for system's negative reputation seems to stem from the claims made from the conclusions of systematic study. As discussed in regard to Hegel above, the systematic thinker believes he is afforded a transcendent perspective on knowledge. In other words, it seemed as though the philosopher was able to arrive at knowledge that was comprehensive as the systematic coordination of all areas of study provided a holistic

---

1. The work of narrative theologians like Stanley Hauerwas and James McClendon, among others, come to mind as representatives of this group.

2. E.g., Millard Erickson argues for the usefulness of a philosophical evaluation of the conclusions of theology, while at the same time recognizing that Scripture remains the primary authority in theology. See Erickson, *Christian Theology*, esp. 39–61.

view of nature and reality. Thus, one could supposedly inter-relate the various realms of knowledge into one final whole that depicted the patterns and themes of knowledge generally. The final product was absolute knowledge that was true regardless of circumstance, or "objective."

It has become rather commonplace for thinkers today to reject such knowledge as a mere chimera. Postmoderns and postliberals seem to be swelling their ranks by joining their voices in the rejection of such overstated epistemological claims. Indeed, even the title "postmodern" is indicative of the rejection of modernism, rather than a specific embrace of something positive. Presuppositionless thinking and conclusions that are stripped of all contextual baggage are simply an illusion of the academy. It is no longer possible to construct systems under the umbrella of Enlightenment rationality without being drenched by the deluge of pluralism. Though reason once shielded systematic thought from being subject to cultural contact, it has now become an anchor to any pretense to comprehensiveness. Reason is now no longer a means to universal claims, summarily connecting the truths of various fields of study. Instead, reason has become the handmaid of individual autonomy. Knowledge is now personalized to the extent that each individual claims truth as a private domain.

What should be clear from the reflections above is that Hegel's thought is a pivotal moment in the history of philosophy and theology. His influence was outlined above, but little was said of the growing vein of criticism that began in his own lifetime. Søren Kierkegaard (1813–1855) leveled several critiques at the far reaching claims of systematic knowledge. As will be seen below, Kierkegaard's influence on the rejection of system extends into contemporary theological history through thinkers such as Karl Barth (1886–1968) and Stanley Hauerwas (1940–present). However, to draw a solid line of influence from Hegel to Kierkegaard to Barth to Hauerwas is to miss several points of qualification in the historical connections amongst these thinkers. The connection of Barth to Hauerwas has been taken up elsewhere.[3] Further, the influence of Hauerwas on contemporary theology is hardly in need of documenta-

---

3. Heide, *System and Story*, esp. chs. 2, 4–6. Hauerwas is the primary subject of discussion in this work, but his connection to Barth is developed more fully throughout the chapters cited.

tion. What is needed is some discussion of the connection from Hegel to Barth through Kierkegaard.[4]

The goal of this study is to provide some careful qualification of the connection of Hegel to Kierkegaard. As will be discussed below, the commonly held position that Kierkegaard's rejection of system is a rejection of Hegel is in need of some reconsideration. It seems more plausible to see Kierkegaard's rejection as a rejection of Danish Hegelianism and specific proponents of Hegel in the Danish academy. Kierkegaard's rejection of system is based more plausibly on the application of Hegelianism on Christian theology by others than on the actual thought of Hegel himself. Hegel's thought seems directed toward philosophy and philosophy of religion specifically, rather than attempting to lay a foundation for Christian knowledge as faith.

Such qualifications of Hegel's system by no means disavow the critique of system offered by Kierkegaard. His comments still seem warranted on the basis that some Danish Hegelians were espousing a view of system coordinate to Kierkegaard's critique. However, to say that Kierkegaard was critical of Hegel specifically may be to caricaturize Hegel through the lens of Kierkegaard's polemic against other Danish theologians. The consequence of qualifying Kierkegaard's critique in such a way is that it may perhaps better be understood as a correction of exaggerated interpretations of Hegel than an outright rejection of Hegel. This places Kierkegaard in a more nuanced position with regard to the history of philosophy and theology. Instead of serving as a champion of the postmodern rejection of absolute knowledge, Kierkegaard may actually serve as a bridge between philosophical knowledge and theology. He rightly understood theological knowledge and the personal faith of the believer as a higher knowledge than the information and theistic perspective provided by philosophy. However, he did not reject philosophy and the use of Hegel's systematic knowledge outright. Kierkegaard simply wished to limit the overstated value being placed on philosophical knowledge by his Danish contemporaries. Our discussion best begins with a brief review of the extent of Hegel's claims regarding systematic knowledge.

4. It is entirely illegitimate to draw a single line from Hegel to Kierkegaard to Barth to Hauerwas. Such illegitimacy is seen specifically in the fact that Hauerwas acknowledges multiple influences on his thought, including the direct influence of Kierkegaard (see my discussion of this influence in ibid., 26–34).

Is Hegel's Absolute Really "Absolute"?

As seen in the chapter above, Hegel's thought was an extension and summarization of Kant's use of the categories. Whereas Kant still depended on the object, or phenomenal knowledge, in order to arrive at conclusions regarding knowledge of reality, Hegel desired to move beyond the phenomenal by examining the claims of knowledge in their relation to one another. Thus, Hegel's goal was as much organizational as it was epistemological. It was in the relationship of various areas of knowledge to other areas of knowledge that concluding remarks could be made about truth, since truth was not localized to any single branch of knowledge. Hegel believed in the unity of truth, which is to say that he believed there to be a holistic or comprehensive perspective on all areas of knowledge. However, it seems as though a distinction must be maintained between a comprehensive perspective on all that the categories present to the system and the implication that we can arrive at conclusions on knowledge that are absolute in the sense they defy all future historical consideration. The former distinction seems in line with Hegel's conclusions; the latter distinction seems to be a distortion of Hegel. Let us examine Hegel's own claims.

Hegel believed that "absolute knowledge" could be achieved by organizing the claims of various areas of knowledge into their organic whole. Hegel describes this ever evolving process of deepening understanding as the eventual arrival at the Absolute Concept: "The realm of spirits which is formed in this way in the outer world constitutes a succession in time in which one spirit relieved another of its charge and each took over the empire of the world from its predecessor. Their goal is the revelation of the depth of spirit, and this is the Absolute Concept."[5] The Absolute Concept is a way of abstracting all phenomenological concepts into an encompassing whole, allowing them to be understood as they relate to each other. This is not an attempt at abstracting knowledge of some particular area of knowledge. Instead, it is merely an attempt at organizing all forms of knowledge into a meaningful whole as they fit together into a unity. Hegel believes that the Absolute Concept is achieved by means of a dialectical movement between specific categorical knowledge (phenomenological knowledge) and the systematic organization of all categories of knowledge into the organic whole. In this sense, the

5. Hegel, *Hegel's Phenomenology of Spirit*, 492.

Absolute Concept says nothing about a specific area of knowledge, since the Absolute Concept is merely receptive of categorical perceptions in specific areas of knowledge, to use Kant's language. Thus, Hegel's system is not determinative of knowledge; instead, it is meant to be descriptive of the patterns of knowledge revealed by an overarching perspective of combined areas of knowledge. Jon Stewart rightly observes that identification of these patterns is the ultimate goal of the system.

> With absolute knowing, consciousness achieves the overview of the various spheres that allows it to recognize the unified patterns of world history, of religion, and so on as having a common structure, which is a pattern of its own thought. Consciousness ceases to see each concept individually in its particular phenomenological form but instead comes to recognize the unitary nature of all these forms since it sees that all of the concepts and forms of consciousness have in common the same categorical movement. Now the individual concepts are not seen in abstraction or taken individually but rather are taken in "their organic self-grounded movement." This overview and grasping of the systematic interconnection of the concepts is the Absolute Concept.[6]

Of course, the systematic organization of the various areas of knowledge seems to presuppose that those areas of knowing have arrived at forms of knowledge that are in some sense accurate in their relation to reality and to each other. In other words, each area of study must present the system with reliable knowledge in order for the system to be an accurate reflection of the organization of knowledge. As Hegel makes clear, "Only when the objective presentation is complete is it at the same time reflection of substance or the process in which substance becomes self. Consequently, until spirit has completed itself *in itself*, until it has completed itself as world spirit, it cannot reach its consummation as *self-conscious* spirit."[7] Systematic knowledge, then, depends on the presentation of accurate knowledge from the various categories of knowledge. As such, it is an abstraction of patterns of knowing revealed by the categories of knowledge. One might even say these patterns are pre-existent in nature and are simply being recognized by the abstraction of the system into a unified whole.

---

6. Jon Stewart, *Kierkegaard's Relations to Hegel Reconsidered*, 252. Stewart is here quoting Hegel, *Phenomenology of Spirit*, 491.

7. Hegel, *Phenomenology of Spirit*, 488, emphasis Hegel's.

From this depiction of Hegel's system, one might assume that knowledge is able to arrive at a completed state finally, given the dependence of the system on accurate knowledge. In other words, since the system must have accurate knowledge in order to organize knowledge rightly into a coherent whole, then the system will finally arrive at completed, or universal, knowledge. The implications of such a notion are obvious: history is at an end in systematic knowledge.[8] However, this seems to draw a conclusion that is beyond the scope of Hegel's intentions. As Stewart points out, "Hegel does not claim that history itself is actually at an end with absolute knowing. His point is that one can only understand and interpret philosophically or in the terms of the categories those events that have already taken place."[9]

Hegel's system does not make any claims toward predictive knowledge; indeed, it cannot make such claims on the basis that it only organizes what has been revealed. Certainly the patterns of what has been may lead one to conclude that the future is thereby predictable, but Hegel is not attempting to predict the future, only to systematize the categorical knowledge of what is past. Thus, Hegel's claims toward absolute and comprehensive knowledge are limited by what is available in the categories of knowledge. He is not attempting to explicate all of reality for all of time. Instead, his system is limited by the knowledge that is historically available at any given time.

Kierkegaard's Critique of Hegel

In the history of philosophy, a tradition seems to loom large over the subject of this section in our study. So strong is this traditional interpretation of Kierkegaard's critique of Hegel that it has held sway for well over a century and a half. This traditional interpretation pits the work of Kierkegaard against Hegel at every turn. Hegel is thereby understood to be the bastion of Cartesian logic, in which theology is ultimately and only a matter of rigorous rationale. In response, Kierkegaard is depicted as the existential champion of individual faith and ethics.

---

8. This has been an accusation that has followed Hegel since his lifetime. It may stem from one statement made by Hegel in his *Lectures on the Philosophy of History* (see Hegel, *Philosophy of History*, 103): "The history of the world travels from east to west, for Europe is absolutely the end of history."

9. Stewart, *Kierkegaard's Relations to Hegel*, 253.

The traditional interpretation of Kierkegaard as opposed to Hegel reaches even to the level of a seeming personal rejection of the lifestyle of Hegel. As Stewart describes it, "He is conceived as having criticized not just Hegel's thought on its own terms but also the way in which that thought led Hegel himself to a misguided life. Kierkegaard is thus said to have waged a rabid campaign against both Hegel's philosophy and his person."[10] Though one may expect a certain amount of critical effort to be associated with objections to Hegel's philosophy, Kierkegaard is regularly depicted as having something akin to a vendetta against the thought of Hegel. In one of the more known collections of Kierkegaard's writings, Robert Bretall's *A Kierkegaard Anthology* (1938), passages are selected and organized in such a fashion as to illustrate Kierkegaard's critical posture toward Hegelianism, which Bretall says Kierkegaard "hated above all else."[11] In all of Kierkegaard's critical comments against notions even resembling Hegel's thought, Kierkegaard is understood to be rejecting the whole of Hegel's project, which is conceived as being the climax of objective knowledge, devising instead a totally new vein of thought along the lines of subjectivity. In the end, Kierkegaard is presented as the father of existentialism—a claim based primarily on his response to Hegel.

While the traditional interpretation of Kierkegaard's rejection of Hegel has been entrenched in academia for over a century, some of the more detailed efforts at chronicling the rejection have come in the last 50–60 years, specifically in the work of the theologian Niels Thulstrup. Thulstrup attempts to chronologically account for the rise of Hegelianism in Denmark during Kierkegaard's career and detail Kierkegaard's response through the various references to Hegel and Hegelianism in Kierkegaard's writings. Unfortunately, Thulstrup only addresses the philosophical interaction in a more cursory fashion as he presupposes Kierkegaard's rejection of Hegel and sets out to prove it. His central thesis is to demonstrate that "Hegel and Kierkegaard have in the main nothing in common as thinkers, neither as regards object, purpose, or method, nor as regards what each considered to be indisputable principles."[12] Thulstrup attempts to address Kierkegaard's rejection of Hegel by detailing each textual reference to Hegel in Kierkegaard's work. However, Thulstrup does not take into consideration sufficiently

10. Stewart, *Kierkegaard's Relations to Hegel*, 4.
11. Bretall, editor, *A Kierkegaard Anthology*, 340.
12. Thulstrup, *Kierkegaard's Relation to Hegel*, 12.

Kierkegaard's aim to counter the Danish Hegelianism of his contemporaries, which seems more the scope of Kierkegaard's rejections than an outright rejection of Hegel.[13]

While it is far beyond the scope of this study to demonstrate the misinterpretation of Kierkegaard's relations to Hegel in the traditional interpretation, let us illustrate it by briefly encountering Kierkegaard's interaction with the concept of Hegel's system and the reach of systematic knowledge in religion, specifically in Christianity. Kierkegaard was, rightly, dissatisfied with the direction of speculative philosophy and its incorporation of Christian theology into its purview. If left at the level of attempting to understand epistemology, speculative philosophy exercises its tools to conclusions well within its scope. However, when philosophy attempts to tell the Christian how to believe, it oversteps its bounds. Kierkegaard was opposed to the way in which systematics (i.e., speculative philosophy) made claims of knowing beyond the reach of faith, or better, commended its own claims of knowledge as more sure due to their being rooted in a coherent system that incorporated the entirety of Christian knowledge. Kierkegaard finally saw systematics as a rejection of the very nature of Christianity. The "further" reaches of system in inter-relating phenomena into a whole he saw as destructive of the character of Christian faith. "Therefore, my precious human being, most honorable Mr. Speculative Thinker, you at least I value to approach in subjective address: O my friend! How do you view Christianity, that is, are you a Christian or are you not? The question is not whether you are *going further* but whether you are a Christian, unless *going further* in a speculative thinker's relation to Christianity means ceasing to be what one was."[14] Two issues should be noted from this passage. First, it is quite obvious that Kierkegaard regards *being* a Christian as something distinct from speculative knowledge about Christianity. Kierkegaard regards this as a critical point of concern as the Christian and the philosopher are concerned with two very different realms of knowledge, and the knowledge of one's self as a Christian is, for Kierkegaard, a higher realm of knowledge. The difference between the philosopher and the Christian

13. Jon Stewart has admirably demonstrated that Thulstrup's claims seem exaggerated when it comes to Kierkegaard's actual interaction with Hegel's texts and Hegelianism. See Stewart, *Kierkegaard's Relations to Hegel*, 14–27. Stewart here outlines Thulstrup's enterprise and introduces the ways in which he will demonstrate Thulstrup's claims to be overstated throughout the rest of his study of Kierkegaard's primary works.

14. Kierkegaard, *Concluding Unscientific Postscript*, vol. 1, 52, italics mine.

is that the philosopher is concerned with objectively knowing information about something, while the Christian is subjectively committed to
knowing with a view to belief and happiness, something objectivity cannot provide. "[I]f Christianity is essentially subjectivity, it is a mistake if
the observer is objective. In all knowing in which it holds true that the
object of cognition is the inwardness of the subjective individual himself,
it holds true that the knower must be in that state. But the expression for
the utmost exertion of subjectivity is the infinitely passionate interest in
its eternal happiness."[15] Kierkegaard regards Christianity as a realm separate from speculative philosophy. Further, he sees the goal of each realm
as completely distinct as well. Whereas speculative philosophy may have
as its goal an attempt to grasp knowledge in an abstract or overarching
manner, i.e., objectively, Christianity serves the goal of "eternal happiness" and draws its subject by means of "infinitely passionate interest."
Thus, the subjective nature of Christianity is readily apparent as each
individual must lay claim for him/herself to the faith requisite of a true
believer. Kierkegaard is making a clear distinction between knowledge
and faith in the sense that faith is more than mere information about
or knowledge of some object. Instead, faith is a higher form of knowledge, requiring the participant to engage at a more encompassing level
than abstraction or objectivity can muster. This does not mean that
scholarship or speculative philosophy is useless or unfruitful. Instead,
Kierkegaard means simply to demonstrate the limits of philosophy when
it comes to Christianity.

> Is scientific scholarship thereby abolished or made impossible?
> No. But the judgment about Christian scholarship has become
> something else. Instead of the inflated conceitedness about *going
> further* than faith, faith is established in its manorial right, and
> scholarship, or the scholar's life, is to be regarded as an enjoy-
> ment, a pleasure, etc. that he may wish for—which can also be
> granted him if he, please note, declares for the faith, receives and
> acknowledges his order to remain courteously within its bound-
> ary and recognizes scholarship not as higher but as lower.[16]

15. Ibid., 53.

16. Kierkegaard, *Concluding Unscientific Postscript*, vol. 2, Supplement, 156–57, italics mine. Here, Kierkegaard is commenting in a later journal reflection on the conclusions of the *Concluding Unscientific Postscript*.

The second issue to be noticed in the two immediately preceding quotes is the use of the phrase "going further." One might expect the object of Kierkegaard's critique here to be Hegel himself with the references to speculative thought and philosophical conclusions that seem to reign over all realms of knowledge. However, Kierkegaard's use of the phrase "going further" seems instead to be a direct reference to one of his contemporaries, namely Hans Lassen Martensen (1808–84), who was a major proponent of Danish Hegelianism. Martensen, along with others like Johan Ludwig Heiberg (1791–1860), pursued a path of applying Hegel's thought, or at least their understanding of it, to Christian faith. However, in so doing, they believed they must lead their readers beyond the reaches of Hegel, since Hegel never extended his thought beyond speculative philosophy. As Martensen states, "I had to lead my listener *through* Hegel; we could not stop with him, but rather, as was said, we had to go beyond him."[17] It is on this point that Stewart has summarily argued that Kierkegaard had Martensen in mind in this criticism and was not focused on Hegel at all, since Hegel stopped short of applying his speculative reasoning to Christian belief. "Here it is clear from Kierkegaard's use of the slogan "going further" that what is at issue is not Hegel's thought or speculative philosophy itself but rather Martensen's claim to have gone beyond faith. The criticism is of those Hegelian theologians, like Martensen, who confuse the two spheres and who base their faith on speculative knowing."[18] Kierkegaard does not appear to have objected to Hegel's use of the system as a tool for organizing knowledge comprehended by the categories. As a point of fact, speculative philosophy as its own realm does not seem to be the subject of Kierkegaard's critique. Instead, Kierkegaard focuses more specifically on the application of a Hegelian interpretation to Christian faith. Here, he rightly sees that speculative knowledge is limited in its scope and should be retained as a qualified tool for providing assistance to faith. In Kierkegaard's estimation, faith is finally the highest knowledge for the Christian.

This may be a good point to mention Kierkegaard's "leap of faith" repeated often in his works and for which he is probably best known. The concept of a leap likely derives from various sources.[19] With Kierkegaard's

17. Martensen, *Af mit Levnet*, vol. 2, 4.

18. Stewart, *Kierkegaard's Relations to Hegel*, 469.

19. For some discussion on the sources and development of Kierkegaard's conception of the leap, see ibid., 405–11.

critique of speculative philosophy fresh in mind, the temptation would be to see faith as its polar opposite in the sense that the leap is into nothingness or simply an escape from reason. However, though Kierkegaard does see the leap as a commitment to the absurdity of an "Absolute Paradox," it is hardly a vacuous notion. Kierkegaard sees the leap as a commitment to the God who defies humanity's rational constructions. "What then is the absurd? The absurd is that the eternal truth has come into existence in time, that God has come into existence, has been born, has grown up etc., has come into existence exactly as an individual human being, indistinguishable from any other human being."[20] The mysterious nature of God is thus contacted through a type of "knowledge" unavailable to reason. Faith is the only way in which humans can have any contact with the infinite God of the universe. Thus, the leap of faith is the ultimate realization of what it means to be human as one reaches, or "leaps," beyond the limitations of what is merely reasonable, which is finally keeping the self from being fully realized. The leap seems best understood as qualitatively distinct from the conclusions of speculative reason. Rather than being the culmination of knowledge in speculative philosophy, arriving at a quantitative compilation of evidence and systematic coherence, faith is a knowledge of a different, and better, sort for Kierkegaard.[21]

In the final analysis, it appears as though Kierkegaard may have been arguing primarily against Hegelian interpreters, rather than taking issue with Hegel himself. For the purposes of this study, it seems the question then may be moved over a space or two from focusing specifically on Hegel and his development of system to the interpreters of Hegel and the Hegelian system as it was applied by others to Christian faith. We will not take up this subject, since the end will likely be the same: the critique of Hegel in the traditional interpretation, though more precisely aimed at his interpreters, still fuels an existential turn away from "system" and "systematics" in theology. Though the critique of Hegel, as depicted by some interpreters of Kierkegaard, may be somewhat of a caricature of Hegel, Kierkegaard's critique still takes a life of its own in

20. Kierkegaard, *Concluding Unscientific Postscript to the Philosophical Fragments*, taken from *The Essential Kierkegaard*, 176.

21. The quantitative–qualitative distinction is one of the ways in which Kierkegaard's leap seems to owe some allegiance to Hegel's conception of a leap, though Hegel's thought seems limited to discussions of philosophy and makes no claims regarding how it might apply to theology. See Stewart, *Kierkegaard's Relations to Hegel*, 407–8.

succeeding generations of theology. It is to one of these critics of system we must now give brief attention.

Barth's Rejection of System

Over a century and a half have passed since Kierkegaard first began writing in response to the thought of his day. The overwhelming influence of Enlightenment rationality since then has led to as strong a reception for his critique today as in his own time, if not even stronger. Kierkegaard's thought is not only discussed in college and seminary classrooms, he is behind much of the popular thinking seen in the postmodern theological critiques of modern rationality. He was one of the first to critique the systematic endeavor in theology. His critique is as fresh and alive today as ever. His influence is as clear in the church as it is in the academy. Many narrative thinkers attribute their newfound epistemology to his leading through his rejection of system and primacy of ethics. So widespread is his influence that some have called him the greatest thinker of the nineteenth century.[22]

Kierkegaard seems to have signaled a rallying cry amongst philosophers and theologians alike. In contrast to the "rigid" or "cold" systems presented for all to admire and ponder, Kierkegaard presented a philosophy that had more to do with living life. More specifically, he wrote about the appropriate value of the Christian life and the foundational nature of ethics (sanctification?). Though primarily presented as a critique of Danish Hegelianism and their systematic rigor, Kierkegaard has since become an alternative to system and the rational orientation of theology. His spirit, if not his texts themselves, live on in the anti-foundationalist sentiments of the neo-orthodox and their post-liberal offspring. A simple illustration of his influence should sufficiently evidence the enduring nature of his thought.

Barth and the Post-liberal Turn

Karl Barth's early education provided him with all the tools needed to construct a socially aware and historically sound theology. He found he loved history and drama, though math and the sciences left him rather cold. Certainly this helps explain why he subsequently placed an

---

22. Watts, *Kierkegaard*, 3. Watts attributes this claim to Wittgenstein, but with no reference.

"emphasis upon the Word of God as action, as event. He never became interested in pure research abstracted from life, even in the fields of exegesis and theology."[23] However, it is more likely his passion for people and preaching the word of God that led him to leave behind his liberal theological training. Though no one event can be said to have signaled his re-orientation toward a more orthodox theology, certainly his *Epistle to the Romans* signals a sure and clear break from liberalism. Here he explains his intentions in the work. "Paul, as a child of his age, addressed his contemporaries. It is, however, far more important that, as Prophet and Apostle of the Kingdom of God, he veritably speaks to all men of every age. The differences between then and now, there and here, no doubt require careful investigation and consideration. But the purpose of such investigation can only be to demonstrate that these differences are, in fact, trivial."[24] Thus it is that Barth is able to set the historical-critical method of Biblical interpretation into what he sees as its appropriate place. The scientific and philosophical study of the Bible does, at times, have an appropriate place in the discussion for Barth, but he sees other issues as more critical. These issues seem to include many of the same as concerned Kierkegaard.

Barth's turn from liberalism toward a more orthodox/evangelical theology is well known. What is perhaps less known, and likely somewhat immeasurable, is his reliance on Kierkegaard for this turn. In the Preface to Barth's Second Edition of his *Epistle to the Romans*, he makes clear that Kierkegaard played a significant role. "I have also paid more attention to what may be culled from the writings of Kierkegaard and Dostoevsky that is of importance for the interpretation of the New Testament."[25] This culling process seems to have been a reliance on certain themes found in Kierkegaard, rather than a direct development of a specific stream of thought. First, Barth recognized that Kierkegaard's rejection of rationalism, and its incumbent reduction of faith to knowledge, was necessary to meet the demands of Christian existence. The "paradox of faith" developed at length in Kierkegaard was picked up by Barth as an important realization for the Christian in his/her understanding of being Christian. The mystery of God is destroyed if faith is reduced to mere knowledge from its primary state in revelation as absurdity or paradox. Christians

23. Come, *Introduction to Barth's "Dogmatics" for Preachers*, 25.

24. Barth, *Epistle to the Romans*, 1.

25. Ibid., 4.

must never attempt to "move beyond" the paradox of the divine revealed in the human Jesus.

> The truth, in fact, can never be self-evident, because it is a matter neither of historical nor of psychological experience, and because it is neither a cosmic happening within the natural order, nor even the most supreme event of our imaginings. Therefore it is not accessible to our perception: It can neither be dug out of what is unconsciously within us, nor apprehended by devout contemplation, nor made known by the manipulation of occult psychic powers. These exercises, indeed, render it the more inaccessible. It can neither be taught nor handed down by tradition, nor is it a subject of research. Were it capable of such treatment, it would not be universally significant, it would not be the righteousness of God for the whole world, salvation for all men. Faith is conversion: it is the radically new disposition of the man who stands naked before God and has been wholly impoverished that he may procure the one pearl of great price; it is the attitude of the man who for the sake of Jesus has lost his own soul. Faith is the faithfulness of God, ever secreted in and beyond all human ideas and affirmations about Him, and beyond every positive religious achievement. There is no such thing as mature and assured possession of faith: regarded psychologically, it is always a leap into the darkness of the unknown, a flight into empty air. Faith is not revealed to us by *flesh and blood* (Matt. xvi. 17) . . . The revelation which is in Jesus, because it is the revelation of the righteousness of God, must be the most complete veiling of His incomprehensibility. In Jesus, God becomes veritably a secret: He is made known as the Unknown, speaking in eternal silence; He protects Himself from every intimate companionship and from all the impertinence of religion. He becomes a scandal to the Jews and to the Greeks foolishness. In Jesus the communication of God begins with a rebuff, with the exposure of a vast chasm, with the clear revelation of a great stumbling block.[26]

The clear references to the "leap" and the rejection of a rationalistic faith in favor of a mystery are clearly the result of Kierkegaard's shadow being cast across Barth's reflections.[27]

The second influence of Kierkegaard observed in this early, yet formative, work of Barth is specifically seen in Barth's rejection of the more

26. Ibid., 98, Barth's italics.

27. Ibid., 98–99. Barth quotes Kierkegaard in support of his thoughts here immediately following the quote above.

liberal understanding of existentialism as psychology. The faith which humans receive is not something that can then be transformed or translated into a tradition or doctrine that can thereby easily be understood or somehow quantified. Instead, it is in the emptiness of the paradox or absurdity that the existential experience of faith resides. This emptiness is not meant to be an eternal emptiness, but an emptiness that is filled only by what we receive from the Lord. Barth believes everything must ultimately trace back to the revelation of God in history through the God-man, Jesus.[28]

This leads to one final conclusion of Barth that he attributes to Kierkegaard. Barth believes that human love is a supernatural activity. Loving one's neighbor is the result of having been loved and having experienced the emptiness filled only by God's own in-breaking into our own individual human life through Jesus. One could possibly attribute such a notion to a simple development of the Biblical text, e.g., "We love because He first loved us" (1 John 4:19). However, Barth built his conception of the notion on Kierkegaard's discussion of love for the individual.[29] Barth's love for neighbor stems from a love for the God who is unknown. "Do we, in the unknowable *neighbor*, apprehend and love the Unknown God?"[30] What he seems to mean by this is that the uncertainty of loving someone who is unpredictable and of uncertain action in response to our love can only be answered by the certainty of the Unknown God. The Unknown God is the One who is known in the paradox, or absurdity, of God's revelation of His eternal self in the person of Jesus. Thus, love requires a reliance on the paradox of faith, which is, for Barth, a pointer to the primacy of revelation, or more specifically the revelation of God in Jesus Christ.

Aside from Barth's own recognition of his allegiance to and dependence on specific themes discovered in Kierkegaard, one can also notice that Barth's affinity for a dialectic methodology stems from perhaps both Kierkegaard and Hegel. Hans Urs von Balthasar comments specifically on Barth's methodological heritage: "All those familiar with Kierkegaard or with Hegelian Idealism will recognize the family resemblances in Barth's own way of thinking. How could it be otherwise, since Barth studied at Marburg and had Hermann for his teacher—who took a rather strange

28. Ibid., 438–41.
29. Ibid., 494–97.
30. Ibid., 494, italics Barth's.

middle position between the famous German Idealist and Kierkegaard's existentialism. So why should Barth's theological style not be closer to that of the nineteenth century: after all, he never encountered the Greeks or the Scholastics until much later."[31]

Of course, Hegel and Kierkegaard are usually understood as opposite ends of the spectrum when it comes to method. However, as is well known, both used variations of the dialectical method in developing their thought and communicating ideas by stressing different aspects of the dialectic.

> The word dialectic (*dia-lektikē*) refers to a form of speaking that sets one work against another (*dia* in the sense of "against") and, in this necessary and unavoidable clash, finding a way or pointing to a direction (*dia* in the sense of "through") past the immediate confrontation. If we put the stress more on the first moment, the clash of opposites, we will be speaking of a predominantly static and dualistic dialectic, in the manner of Kierkegaard. But, if our stress is on the second moment, on finding a way through the clash, we will be speaking of a dynamic and triadic dialectic, in the manner of Hegel.[32]

Barth finds such a method especially attractive because it maintains an openness toward the mystery of God; God is never exhaustively understood or explained. At the same time, dialectic allows for us to say something, even if, at times, only through the negation of the dialectic.

> Dialectical thinking is a process of saying one thing and then countering it with another. It moves from question to answer and back again so that the conversation never breaks off . . . Essentially, there is no final word . . . Both sides of the dialectic must be incorporated in thought—irreconcilable but also inseparable, a word and its counterword: faith and obedience, heteronomy and autonomy, authority and freedom; the presence of the Holy Spirit addressing us from without and within; Incarnation of the Word and outpouring of the Holy Spirit; reconciliation and sin; history in Adam and history in Christ; history of origins and history of revelation; the Word of God in Bible and pulpit and the word of man in the same text and sermon. The prototype from which all this derives and that finally makes all of dogmatics nec-

31. Von Balthasar, *Theology of Karl Barth*, 34.
32. Ibid., 73.

> essarily dialectical is none other than the reality of God and man
> in the one person of the Redeemer Jesus Christ.[33]

Though dialectics is only a method, and implies nothing substantively, Barth finds such a method helpful as it allows him to move through examination of Biblical and theological thought without breaching what he sees as the limits of human knowledge of the divine. The divine-human paradox remains paramount for Barth. Thus, human reflection on revelation is a sort of dialectic in that it is a movement between the two worlds.

Barth followed much of Kierkegaard's lead early in his flight from liberalism and the rationalistic influences of historical criticism. However, later in Barth's more developed thought, he qualified his allegiance to Kierkegaard. [34] In the *Church Dogmatics*, Barth made clear where he objected to Kierkegaard and his influence over theology. His first objection drew an anthropological line from Schleiermacher through Kierkegaard to the liberal theology of Barth's day. Barth believed that Kierkegaard's existentialism, whether intentional or not, influenced an emphasis upon the human element in faith to such an extent that it opened the door for liberal existentialists to understand faith as merely a psychological experience.[35] Barth's second objection to Kierkegaard centered on another implication of Kierkegaard's existential emphasis. Kierkegaard's existential embrace of a personal faith necessitated that faith be a personal commitment, or "leap" as Kierkegaard would phrase it. As such, faith is highly individualistic. "[W]ithout having comprehended Christianity . . . I have at least understood this much, that it wants to make the single individual eternally happy and that precisely within this single individual it presupposes this infinite interest in his own happiness as *conditio sine qua non*."[36] Barth sees such individualism as destructive of the necessary Biblical doctrine of the church. The church is God's revealed and designed community for the formation of believers in God's Kingdom.

> What we can say of the community is only this, though we can
> say it in all seriousness: *extra ecclesiam nulla revelation, nulla fi-*

33. Karl Barth, *Die Lehre vom Worte Gottes*, 456–57.

34. See Clark, *Karl Barth's Theological Method*, 109–10. Clark demonstrates the progression in Barth away from tendencies earlier in his career that were clearly due to Kierkegaard's influence.

35. Barth, *Church Dogmatics*, I.1, 20.

36. Kierkegaard, *Concluding Unscientific Postscript*, vol. 1, 16.

des, nulla cognition salutis—and in so far as the knowledge and revelation of Jesus Christ and faith in Him and the ministry of the proclamation of His name constitutes the holiness of the Church: *extra ecclesiam nulla sanctitas*. What is true is that the typical and ministerial separation of an individual, in virtue of which he is distinguished and marked off from other men as one who believes and knows, is as such his separation to life and ministry in and with the community. If he does not have it as such, he does not have it at all. And if he withdraws from the fellowship of the Church, in so doing he denies himself as *sanctus*, as one who believes and knows. What is true is that there is no legitimate private Christianity. The question which in this light we have to address not only to all forms of mysticism and pietism but also to Kierkegaard is plain to see. As Calvin puts it (*Instit.* IV, I, 10), to try to be a Christian in and for oneself is to be a *transfuga et desertor religionis* and therefore not a Christian.[37]

Here Barth separates himself from the more typical exclusive individualism of existentialism. While Barth does not deny the necessity of individual faith, he places it in the larger context of the Biblical doctrine of the church.

In the end, Barth never seems to leave behind Kierkegaard's own critique of system as extra-Biblical and the heralding cry to return to the faith which Scripture commends to those who would truly know the Lord as He has revealed Himself.

[I]f I have a system, it is limited to a recognition of what Kierkegaard called the "infinite qualitative distinction" between time and eternity, and to my regarding this as possessing negative as well as positive significance: "God is in heaven, and thou art on earth." The relation between such a God and such a man, and the relation between such a man and such a God, is for me the theme of the Bible and the essence of philosophy. Philosophers name this KRISIS of human perception—the Prime Cause: the Bible beholds at the same crossroads—the figure of Jesus Christ.[38]

Barth seems to have been led to his conclusion that revelation and the supernatural reception of knowledge (faith!) is something at least begun by Kierkegaard. Barth is not attracted to philosophy's methods or conclusions, since they cannot treat revelation in its appropriate context.

37. Barth, *Church Dogmatics*, IV.1, 688–89; cf. 741.
38. Barth, *Epistle to the Romans*, 10.

Instead, Barth adopts "the mind-set of the prophets and apostles. It is not the attitude of observers . . . nor of philosophers, but that of witnesses, of people who, whatever else they may be, speak as those who are grounded in the reality of the 'and God spake' as an absolute presupposition."[39] Barth does not see the method of philosophy providing conclusions that aid in the faith of the believer or the commitment of the church to her Lord. Indeed, David Mueller even goes so far as to say that, for Barth, "[T]he Biblical attitude is the antithesis of the apologetic approach which presumes that somehow God may be known without beginning with God."[40]

Barth's own break with theological liberalism, in many ways, paralleled Kierkegaard's break with philosophical apologetics. Though obviously encountering different concerns and taking different approaches in solving the problems presented by the Christianity of their day, both called for a similar return to the faith commended by Scripture and the knowledge of revelation. Too close a parallel or dependence would do an injustice to the context and concerns of each author. However, Barth's sympathies toward Kierkegaard's driving concerns should not be underestimated.

Postmodernism/Post-liberalism

The connection of Kierkegaard, through Barth (and others), to the postmodern/post-liberal influences in contemporary theology seem obvious. Nevertheless some points of contact should at least be mentioned here. No development of the themes will be offered, though certainly such studies are needed. A more detailed analysis is taken up elsewhere.[41] Here, we will simply observe some connections that bring our study into the current trends in theological studies.

---

39. Karl Barth, *Die christliche Dogmatik im Entwurf*, vol. I *Die Lehre vom Worte Gottes*, 436.

40. Mueller, *Karl Barth*, 36.

41. A primary goal in my earlier work, *System and Story*, was to provide a detailed discussion of certain post-liberal/postmodern themes in relation to theological method. The focus of that study, Stanley Hauerwas, provides a clear link from Kierkegaard to Barth to today. Further, Hauerwas articulates the critique of Enlightenment thought and the embrace of postmodern epistemology with such clarity that he has become one of the leading figures of narrative/post-liberal thought. His influence is only continuing to grow.

First, the critique and rejection of system is repeated with regularity amongst postmodernists, post-liberals, and/or narrative theologians. The association of system with foundationalism and an epistemology that makes claims of knowledge that are comprehensive or "absolute" make system appear to be the climax of Enlightenment rationalism. Though, as we have shown above, this does not seem to be the system of Hegel's thought, nor is Hegel the object of Kierkegaard's critique of system, some theologians (e.g., some Danish Hegelians) did seem to take systematic method to a rather extreme end. Thus, Kierkegaard's critique and the postmodern rejection of system has some warrant, though at times may require further articulation, rather than simple dismissal. The epistemological arrogance often associated with a systematic approach is rightly rejected, but the development of a systematic school of thought associated with Enlightenment thinkers may be an overstatement. Many of the fathers of the Enlightenment, and Hegel himself in his development of system, seem more careful and limited in their scope. Nevertheless, how their thought has been used is another matter altogether. It is perhaps to their heritage we must turn for evidence of the caricatures sometimes associated with some of the original thinkers.[42]

It seems that just as postmodern theology has turned away from systematic thought, it has made a clear turn toward a form of existentialism stemming from Kierkegaard. Though Kierkegaard can hardly be blamed for the leanings of postmodern thinkers, he certainly initiated a revolution toward establishing the primacy of ethics and the living of the Christian life over and above any rational treatment of Christianity. Though perhaps Kierkegaard did not see the two as quite the opposites they are considered to be today, he does begin the mindset of favoring the ethical/practical over the rational. Many contemporary theologians have followed closely in this path, tracing it to Aristotle through Aquinas.[43] Such an emphasis on ethics provides fertile ground for theological engagement of contemporary issues, such as caring for the needy or the environment. Issues have always been an implication of theology. The difference in today's approach is that the issues and the ethical seem to be driving a pragmatic epistemology similar to that of Liberation

---

42. See my discussion of Hauerwas's rejection of system in *System and Story*, chs. 2–4.

43. See my *System and Story*, ch. 4.

Theology. The existential has come to full bloom in contemporary political theology.

A decided difference between Kierkegaard and postmodernism can be seen in the contemporary emphasis on community. Kierkegaard's existentialism, as was seen above, was necessarily individualistic. Though not necessarily stemming from the Enlightenment's emphasis on the autonomous rational individual, Kierkegaard's conception of the individual certainly complemented such a notion. In our contemporary global environment, such individualism simply will not do, at least not epistemologically. Narrative thinkers continue to assert that theology as practice can only be known in a community that forms every individual into a specific likeness. Thus, every individual is understood to be a product of community, rather than an isolated or *a priori* member of it. The irony in such an epistemology is that narrative epistemology does not seem capable of overcoming the same individualism entrenched in Kierkegaard's existentialism. In other words, on the one hand is the postmodern/postliberal attraction to Kierkegaard seen in the way he finally climaxes the realization of the self in the individual commitment of faith in the leap. On the other hand, the church would be seen by Kierkegaard as a dogmatic encumbrance if community was given priority over the individual. Kierkegaard's commitment to the self fits well with the postmodern pluralistic culture, but hardly values the priority of the community. The propensity in contemporary thought toward individual autonomy appears stronger than any appeal to communal commitment. Barth and Hauerwas have made great strides toward overcoming this propensity by appealing to the priority of the community of church for Christians. The larger goal of shaping a cultural shift is obviously beyond the scope of their study. What remains is to see if such an emphasis will overcome individual rationality as it is epistemologically foundational, even in the church and in much of contemporary theological study.[44]

Conclusion: System through the Ages

Our discussion of system and the use of system within theological methodology in the last few chapters is rather far removed from what we saw in the early centuries of the church. We have seen that theol-

44. The individual and anthropological nature of much of contemporary theology was certainly bemoaned by Barth and is, interestingly, critiqued by thinkers such as John Piper, who may only cursorily attribute any reliance upon Barth.

ogy has always been concerned with organization. Irenaeus harmonized various Scriptural ideas using what he called the "rule of faith." He was not attempting to be philosophical, though certainly philosophical considerations came into play in his theology. His primary concerns were apologetic and pastoral, centering on the use of theology to provide some sense of orthodoxy. Likewise, Origen organized his theology according to what he believed to be a systematic method, though he too still envisioned system as simply a tool to provide order and summarization. Philosophy was at work, but theology was still centered on interpreting and organizing revelation, and subsequent implications for speculation. His concerns were also apologetic and explanatory. Theology had not yet become metaphysics and would not for over a millennia. With Constantine and the Nicene Council, theology again maintained its function as apologetic and pastoral in nature, helping to establish and maintain orthodoxy. However, a political element now emerged as Constantine used the occasion of the Nicene Council to unify theological rivals who could incite a political schism. Here, theology became a tool of the state, in that orthodoxy was now an enforced unity. The systematic relationship of doctrines, such as the deity of the Father and the Son, served both as a harmonization of what could be understood as contradicting Scriptures and as a measure of orthodoxy. The distinct turn in post-Constantinian theology was that the theological community became unified by force, rather than voluntarily.

Centuries later, Thomas Aquinas was again concerned with developing a synthesis of theological truths with an order he found consistent with the nature of these truths. The order was derived from Aristotle's science, which reversed the typical path for knowledge. The more typical path for Thomas' contemporaries was from effects to cause. Thomas wished to know the cause in itself. One could perhaps see in Thomas a pre-cursor to a focus on metaphysics in the Enlightenment. Justification for such an insight could further be established by means of the historical influence of Scholastic humanism on Descartes, amongst others. However, in Thomas' defense, such a move to metaphysics seems hardly his intention, nor do his immediate successors take such a route. Wycliffe, though sometimes accused of not completing his philosophical understanding of the Eucharist, also does not seem inclined to couch his theology in a philosophical system that requires a metaphysical justification for his understanding of the elements in the Eucharist. Instead, his own theology was an attempt to provide a Biblical accounting of the doctrine in contrast to what he believed a mistaken philosophical approach. Philosophy has never been absent from theological reflection; however, Wycliffe serves to demonstrate that theology was not always driven or guided by philosophy. Biblical and creedal concerns were also the primary elements guiding and directing the theology of the Reformers. Calvin used the Apostle's creed to organize his theology, but even here, he still had pastoral and pedagogical concerns at the forefront of his method. He was not attempting to provide a metaphysics. He was only attempting to explain and summarize the doctrinal truth he observed in Scripture and the creeds.

It was during the Enlightenment that the relationship of theology and philosophy took a distinct turn. Theological truth claims now must be justified on philosophical grounds. Descartes believed philosophy could rescue theology from its critics. In the end, his philosophical defense of theology subsumed theology into philosophy. Further, it limited theology primarily to a form of theism. Kant furthered much of Descartes' program by demonstrating and defending the autonomy of human reason. Individual reason became the primary authority for all subsequent generations of theologians and philosophers, furthering the principle that reasonable demonstration precedes verification of theological truth. Hegel took up the task of illustrating the pinnacle of such a principle. In Hegel, metaphysics eclipsed theology to such an extent that theology was no longer necessary. Though Hegel, and others, believed he had provided a rational demonstration of the truth of Christianity, as a point of fact, Christianity was finally replaced by metaphysics. All truth claims became internalized as the system's veracity was measured according to the coherence of the inter-related parts. No longer was an appeal to the objective world necessary, or even plausible. System itself was the totalization of knowledge. Thus, for Hegel, system was not simply a methodological tool; it was finally an end in itself. In such a context, the revealed theology of the creeds and pre-modern theologians became uninformative and unnecessary.

Kierkegaard rightly objected to the overreaching claims of systematic metaphysics. Though it may be more likely that Kierkegaard's critique was leveled at Danish followers of Hegel, rather than Hegel himself, the stage was certainly set for a more wholesale rejection of systematic thought in general. Kierkegaard's critique did nothing to slow the development of more rationalistic tendencies in German idealism; however, he did strike a chord for many later theologians who wished to do theology for the church. As the influence of liberalism waned, and its incumbent rational development of moral and social implications, others, like Barth, took up the mantle of engaging theology from an epistemology rooted in ethics and the primacy of the community, rather than a theology rooted in the autonomous rationality of the individual. Kierkegaard forged a path for theological epistemology rooted in the faith of the believer rather than metaphysics. Though still entrenched in individualism, his appeal to faith opened the door to a recovery of theology specific to the church instead of the academy.

Today's theologians are, to a greater or lesser degree, striving in the shadow of theology's turn to metaphysics. For those enchanted with the metaphysical turn, philosophy still retains a foundational role. For those reacting against the priority of metaphysics, pre-modern theology and appeals to revelation, the creeds, and tradition, though sounding rather naïve or antiquated, have become the measure of orthodoxy. I have no illusion of predicting the future; nor am I proposing any sort of a synthesis. I am encouraged that the conversation continues and the church as a community has once again taken a prominent position in the discussion. Time may or may not be a friend to the debates, but at least the debates seem rightly aimed and Jesus is becoming ever more significant to the discussion. I'm certain all the theologians studied in this volume would be pleased, to a greater or lesser degree, with this turn, as it raises the discussion beyond its historical conditioned-ness into the realm of what is universally important, or better, it combines what is historically conditioned *with* what is universally important. In such a journey, we may certainly find great joy, and hopefully, the Lord Jesus may find great glory!

Bibliography

Introduction

Berner, Ulrich. *Origenes.* Erträge der Forschung 147. Darmstadt: Wissenschaftliche Buchgesellschaft, 1981.

Bowsma, William. *John Calvin: A Sixteenth Century Portrait.* New York: Oxford University Press, 1988.

Calvin, John. *Institutes of the Christian Religion.* 2 vols. Edited by John T. McNeill. Library of Christian Classics 20–21. Philadelphia: Westminster, 1960.

Childs, Brevard S. *The New Testament as Canon: An Introduction.* Philadelphia: Fortress, 1984.

Guthrie, Donald. *New Testament Introduction.* Downers Grove, IL: InterVarsity, 1970.

Dowey, Edward A. "Book Review, 'John Calvin: A Sixteenth Century Portrait.'" *Journal of the American Academy of Religion* 57 (1989) 845–48.

Heide, Gale. *System and Story: Narrative Critique and Construction in Theology.* Princeton Theological Monograph Series 87. Eugene, OR: Pickwick, 2007.

Henry, Carl F. H. *God, Revelation and Authority.* Waco, TX: Word, 1979.

Hodge, Charles. *Systematic Theology.* Grand Rapids: Eerdmans, 1977.

Leith, John H. "Calvin's Theological Method and the Ambiguity in His Theology." In *Reformation Studies: Essays in Honor of Roland H. Bainton*, edited by Franklin H. Littell, 106–14. Richmond: John Knox, 1962.

Origen. *On First Principles.* From Koetschau's text of *De Principiis.* Translated by G. W. Butterworth. Introduction to the Torchbook edition by Henri de Lubac. Gloucester: Peter Smith, 1973.

Pannenberg, Wolfhart. "God of the Philosophers." *First Things* (June/July, 2007) 31–34.

Runia, David T. *Philo in Early Christian Literature: A Survey.* Compendia rerum Iudaicarum ad Novum Testamentum, sec. 3: Jewish Traditions in Early Christian Literature 3. Minneapolis: Fortress, 1993.

Wendel, Francois. *Calvin: Origins and Development of His Religious Thought.* Translated by Philip Mairet. Durham, UK: Labyrinth, 1987.

Chapter 1

Barr, James. *Holy Scripture: Canon, Authority, Criticism.* Oxford: Oxford University Press, 1983.

Brox, N. *Offenbarung, Gnosis und gnostischer Mythos bei Irenäus von Lyon.* Salzburg, 1966.

Childs, Brevard S. *Biblical Theology of the Old and New Testaments.* Minneapolis: Fortress, 1992.

————. *The New Testament as Canon: An Introduction*. Philadelphia: Fortress, 1984.

Gager, John G. *Kingdom and Community*. Englewood Cliffs, NJ: Prentice-Hall, 1975.

Hägglund, B. "Die Bedeutung der 'regula fidei' als Grundlage theologischer Aussagen." *Studia Theologica* 12 (1958) 1–44.

Hefner, P. "Theological Methodology and St. Irenaeus" *Journal of Religion* 44 (1964) 294–309.

Irenaeus. *Against Heresies*. In *The Ante-Nicene Fathers*. Edited by Alexander Roberts and James Donaldson. Vol. 1. Grand Rapids: Eerdmans, reprinted 1996.

Lienhard, Joseph T. *The Bible, the Church, and Authority: The Canon of the Christian Bible in History and Theology*. Collegeville, MN: Liturgical, 1995.

Lindbeck, George *The Nature of Doctrine*. Philadelphia: Westminster, 1984.

Reynders, D. B. "La polémique de saint Irénée. Méthode et principes." *Recherches de théologie ancienne et médiévale* 7 (1935) 5–27.

Scalise, Charles J. *From Scripture to Theology: A Canonical Journey into Hermeneutics*. Downers Grove, IL: InterVarsity, 1996.

van Unnik, W. C. "De la regle Mhte prosqeinai mhte afelein dans l'histoire du canon." *Vigiliae Christianae* 3 (1949) 1–36.

Vallée, Gérard "Theological and Non-Theological Motives in Irenaeus's Refutation of the Gnostics." In *Jewish and Christian Self-Definition*, 1:174–85. Edited by E. P. Sanders. Philadelphia: Fortress, 1980.

Wisse, Frederick. "The Nag Hammadi Library and the Heresiologists." *Vigiliae Christianae* 25 (1971) 205–23.

Young, Frances. *The Making of the Creeds*. Philadelphia: Trinity, 1991.

Chapter 2

Berchman, Robert M. *From Philo to Origen: Middle Platonism in Transition*. Brown Judaic Studies 69. Chico, CA: Scholars, 1984.

Berner, Ulrich. *Origenes*. Erträge der Forschung 147. Darmstadt: Wissenschaftliche Buchgesellschaft, 1981.

Chadwick, Henry. *Early Christian Thought and the Classical Tradition: Studies in Justin, Clement, and Origen*. New York: Oxford University Press, 1966.

Crouzel, Henri. *Origen*. Translated by A. S. Warrall. San Francisco: Harper & Row, 1985.

————. *Origène et la Philosophie*. Collection Théologie 52. Paris, 1962.

Daniélou, Jean. *Origen*. Translated by Walter Mitchell. New York: Sheed & Ward, 1955.

Dorival, Gilles. "Remarques sur la forme du *Peri Archon*." *Origeniana*. Universita' di Bari: Institutio di Letteratura Cristiana Antica (1975) 33–45.

Harl, Marguerite. "Structure et cohérence de *Peri Archon*." *Origeniana*. Universita' di Bari: Institutio di Letteratura Cristiana Antica (1975) 11–32.

Harnack, Adolf von. *Dogmengeschichte*. 1909 edition. Reprinted in Darmstadt, 1964.

Kannengiesser, Charles. "Divine Trinity and the Structure of *Peri Archon*." In *Origen of Alexandria*, 231–49. Edited by Charles Kannengiesser and William L. Petersen. Notre Dame: University of Notre Dame Press, 1988.

————. "Origen, Systematician in *De Principiis*." In *Origeniana Quinta*, 395–405. Papers of the 5th International Origen Congress. Edited by Robert Daly. Leuven, 1992.

Kettler, F. H. *Der ursprüngliche Sinn der Dogmatik des Origenes*. Berlin: Töpelmann, 1966.

O'Cleirigh, P. M. "The Meaning of Dogma in Origen." In *Jewish and Christian Self-Definition*, 1:201–16. Edited by E. P. Sanders. Philadelphia: Fortress, 1980.

Origen, *Commentary on St. John*. Text revised by A. E. Brooke, with a critical Introduction and Indices. Cambridge: Cambridge University Press, 1896.

―――. *On First Principles*. From Koetschau's text of *De Principiis*. Translated by G. W. Butterworth. Introduction to the Torchbook edition by Henri de Lubac. Gloucester: Peter Smith, 1973.

―――. *Origène: Traité des Principes*. In the series Sources Chrétiennes. 4 volumes. Edited by Henri Crouzel and Manlio Simonetti. Paris, 1978.

Rius-Camps, Josep. *El Peri Archon d'Origenes: Radiographia del primer Tractat de Theologia dogmàtico-sapiencial*. Facultat de Teologia de Barcelon 1985.

Runia, David T. *Philo in Early Christian Literature: A Survey*. Compendia rerum Iudaicarum ad Novum Testamentum, sec. 3: Jewish Traditions in Early Christian Literature 3. Minneapolis: Fortress, 1993.

Steidle, Basilius. "Neue Untersuchungen zu Origenes." *Zeitschrift für die neutestamentliche Wissenschaft* 40 (1941) 236–43.

Chapter 3

Alföldi, Andrew. *The Conversion of Constantine and Pagan Rome*. Translated by Harold Mattingly. Oxford: Clarendon, 1948.

Athanasius. *Defence against the Arians*. In *The Nicene and Post-Nicene Fathers*. Volume IV. Second series. Grand Rapids: Eerdmans, repr. 1991.

―――. *Epistola Eusebii*. In *The Nicene and Post-Nicene Fathers*. Volume IV. Second series. Grand Rapids: Eerdmans, repr. 1991.

Baker, G. P. *Constantine the Great*. New York: Barnes & Noble, Inc., 1967.

Cochrane, Charles Norris. *Christianity and Classical Culture*. New York: Oxford University Press, 1957.

Cyril of Jerusalem. *Catechetical Lectures*. In *The Nicene and Post-Nicene Fathers*. Volume VII. Second series. Grand Rapids: Eerdmans, repr. 1996.

Dörries, Hermann. *Constantine the Great*. Translated by Roland H. Bainton. New York: Harper & Row, 1972.

Eusebius. *Ecclesiastical History*. In *Nicene and Post-Nicene Fathers*. Volume I. Second series. Grand Rapids: Eerdmans, repr. 1991.

―――. *Life of Constantine*. In *Nicene and Post-Nicene Fathers*. Volume I. Second series. Grand Rapids: Eerdmans, repr. 1991.

―――. *The Oration of Eusebius*. In *Nicene and Post-Nicene Fathers*. Volume I. Second series. Grand Rapids: Eerdmans, repr. 1991.

Grant, Robert M. *Augustus to Constantine*. San Francisco: Harper & Row, 1970.

Greenslade, S. L. *Church and State from Constantine to Theodosius*. Westport, CT: Greenwood, 1954.

Herrin, Judith. *The Formation of Christendom*. Princeton: Princeton University Press, 1987.

Jones, A. H. M. *Constantine and the Conversion of Europe*. New York: Collier, 1962.

Keresztes, Paul. *Constantine A Great Christian Monarch and Apostle*. Amsterdam: Gieben, 1981.

Lactantius. *De Mortibus Persecutorum*. In *The Ante-Nicene Fathers*. Volume VII. Grand Rapids: Eerdmans, repr. 1994.

Olster, David M. *Roman Defeat, Christian Response, and the Literary Construction of the Jew*. Philadelphia: University of Pennsylvania Press, 1994.

Smith, John Holland. *Constantine the Great*. London: Hamilton, 1971.

Socrates. *Ecclesiastical History*. In *The Nicene and Post-Nicene Fathers*. Volume II. Second series. Grand Rapids: Eerdmans, repr. 1989.

Sordi, Marta. *The Christians and the Roman Empire*. Norman: University of Oklahoma Press, 1986.

Sozomen. *The Ecclesiastical History of Sozomen*. In *The Nicene and Post-Nicene Fathers*. Volume II. Second series. Grand Rapids: Eerdmans, repr. 1989.

Chapter 4

Alexander of Hales. *Glossa in Quatuor Libros Sententiarum Petri Lombardi*. Quaracchi, Florence: Collegium S. Bonaventurae, 1951.

Aristotle. *Aristotle's Posterior Analytics*. Translated by H. Apostle. Oxford: Clarendon, 1963.

Augustine. *On Christian Doctrine*. In *Nicene and Post-Nicene Fathers*. Volume II. Edited by Philip Schaff. Grand Rapids: Eerdmans, 1993.

Bacon, Roger. *Opus Minus* (1267). In *Opera quaedam hactenus inedita*. Edited by J. S. Brewer. Rolls Series I, 15. London: Longman, Green, Longman and Roberts, 1859.

Burrell, David. *Aquinas: God and Action*. London: Routledge & Kegan Paul, 1979.

————. *Knowing the Unknowable God*. Notre Dame: University of Notre Dame Press, 1986.

Chenu, M. D. *Introduction a l'etude de S. Thomas d'Aquino*. Paris: Vrin, 1950.

————. "Le plan de la Somme theologique de S. Thomas." *Revue Thomiste* XLV (1939) 93–107.

Duhem, Pierre. *Le Système du monde. Histoire des doctrines cosmologiques de Platon à Copernic*. Volume V. Paris: Librarie scientifique A. Hermann et Fils, 1917.

Harak, G. Simon, S.J. *Virtuous Passions: The Formation of Christian Character*. New York: Paulist, 1993.

Lamadrid, Lucas. "Is There a System in the Theology of Nicholas Lash?" *Heythrop Journal* 33 (1992) 399–414.

Lash, Nicholas. *Easter in Ordinary*. Notre Dame: University of Notre Dame Press, 1988.

————. "Considering the Trinity." *Modern Theology* 2 (1986) 183–96.

————. "Ideology, Metaphor and Analogy." In *Theology on the Way to Emmaus*, 95–119. London: SCM, 1986.

Lindbeck, George. *The Nature of Doctrine: Religion and Theology in a Postliberal Age*. Philadelphia: Westminster, 1984.

Lombard, Peter. *Sentences*. http://www.franciscan-archive.org/lombardus/I-Sent.html.

Mascall, E. L. *He Who Is*. Rev. ed. Longmans Green, 1966.

Melchior Cano. *De Locis Theologicus*. Volume III. Rome, 1900.

Pegis, Anton C. *St. Thomas and Philosophy*. Milwaukee: Marquette University Press, 1964.

Pesch, Otto H. "Um den Plan der *Summa Theologiae* des hl. Thomas von Aquin." *Münchener Theologische Zeitschrift* 16 (1965) 128–37.

Principe, W. *The Theology of the Hypostatic Union in the Early Thirteenth Century*. II. Toronto: PIMS, 1967.

Rahner, Karl. *Theological Investigations*. Translated by Edward Quinn. London: Darton, Longman & Todd, 1984.

Seckler, Max. *Das Heil in der Geschichte*. München: Kösel Verlag, 1964.

Smith, Timothy L. "Thomas Aquinas' *De Deo*: Setting the Record Straight on His Theological Method." *Sapientia* 53:203 (1998) 119–54.

———. *Thomas Aquinas' Trinitarian Theology: A Study in Theological Method*. Washington, DC: The Catholic University of America Press, 2003.

Thomas Aquinas. *Summa Theologica*. Five volumes. Translated by Fathers of the English Dominican Province. Allen, TX: Christian Classics, 1981.

Weisheipl, James A., O.P. *Friar Thomas D'Aquino*. Washington: Catholic University Press of America, 1974.

Chapter 5

Augustine. *Homilies on the Gospel according to John, and His First Epistle*. In *The Nicene and Post-Nicene Fathers of the Christian Church*. Edited by Philip Schaff. Volume VII, XXVI.11.Grand Rapids: Eerdmans, 1996.

———. *Sermons on New Testament Lessons*. In *The Nicene and Post-Nicene Fathers of the Christian Church*. Edited by Philip Schaff. Volume VI, IV.7. Grand Rapids: Eerdmans, 1996.

Crockett, William R. *Eucharist: Symbol of Transformation*. New York: Pueblo, 1989.

Dugmore, C. W. *The Mass and the English Reformers*. New York: St. Martin's, 1958.

Genet, Jean-Philippe. "The Dissemination of Manuscripts Relating to English Political Thought in the Fourteenth Century." In *England and Her Neighbours*, 217–37. Edited by Michael Jones and Malcolm Vale. London: Hambledon, 1989.

Hudson, Anne. *The Premature Reformation: Wycliffite texts and Lollard History*. Oxford: Clarendon, 1988.

———. "Wycliffism in Oxford 1381–1411." In *Wyclif in His Times*, 67–84. Edited by Anthony Kenny. Oxford: Clarendon, 1986.

Keen, Maurice. "Wyclif, the Bible, and Transubstantiation." In *Wyclif in His Times*, 1–16. Edited by Anthony Kenny. Oxford: Clarendon, 1986.

Kenny, Anthony. "The Realism of *De Universalibus*." In *Wyclif in His Times*, 17–29. Edited by Anthony Kenny. Oxford: Clarendon, 1986.

———. *Wyclif*. Oxford: Oxford University Press, 1985.

Leff, Gordon. *Heresy in the Later Middle Ages*. Two volumes. New York: Barnes & Noble, 1967.

———. *John Wyclif: The Path to Dissent*. Raleigh Lecture on History Series of the British Academy. London: Oxford University Press, 1966.

———. "The Place of Metaphysics in Wyclif's Theology." In *From Ockham to Wyclif*, 217–32. Studies in Church History series. Edited by Anne Hudson and Michael Wilks. New York: Blackwell, 1987.

———. "Wycliff and Hus: A Doctrinal Comparison." In *Wyclif in His Times*, 105–25. Edited by Anthony Kenny. Oxford: Clarendon, 1986.

Matthew, F. D. "Letter to Michael Henry Dziewicki" In John Wycliffe, *De Apostasia*. Edited by M. H. Dziewicki. London: Trubner, 1889.

McFarlane, K. B. *John Wycliffe and the Beginnings of English Nonconformity*. London: The English Universities Press, 1952.

Robson, J. A. *Wyclif and the Oxford Schools*. Cambridge: Cambridge University Press, 1961.

Sergeant, Lewis. *John Wyclif: Last of the Schoolmen and First of the English Reformers*. New York: Putnam, 1893.

Smalley, Beryl. "John Wyclif's Postilla super totam Bibliam." *Bodleian Library Quarterly*, 4 (1953) 186–205.

Smith, III, L. Murdock. "The Influence of the Eucharistic Theology of Augustine of Hippo on the Eucharistic Theology of Thomas Cranmer." In *Church Divinity*. Edited by John H. Morgan, 1981.

Spinka, Matthew. *Advocates of Reform: From Wyclif to Erasmus*. In The Library of Christian Classics Series. Volume XIV. Edited by Matthew Spinka. Philadelphia: Westminster, 1953.

Stacey, John. *John Wyclif and Reform*. Philadelphia: Westminster, 1964.

Workman, Herbert B. *John Wyclif: A Study of the English Medieval Church*. Volume II. Oxford: Clarendon, 1926.

Wycliffe, John. *De Apostasia*. Edited by M. H. Dziewicki. London: Trubner, 1889.

———. *De Eucharistia*. Edited by Johann Loserth. London: Trubner, 1892.

———. *De Universalibus*. Edited by I. Meuller. Translated by Anthony Kenny. Oxford: Oxford University Press, 1985.

———. *Fasciculi Zizaniorum*. Edited by W. W. Shirley. London: Rolls Series, 1858.

———. *The English Works of Wyclif*. Edited by F. D. Matthew. London: Kegan, Paul, Trench, Trubner, 1880.

———. *Tracts and Treatises of John de Wycliffe*. Edited by Robert Vaughan. London: Blackburn & Pardon, 1845.

Chapter 6

Bouwsma, William J. *Calvinism as Theologia Rhetorica: The Fifty-Fourth Colloquy at the Center for Hermeneutical Studies in Hellenistic and Modern Culture*. Berkeley: Center for Hermeneutical Studies, 1986.

———. *John Calvin: A Sixteenth-Century Portrait*. New York: Oxford University Press, 1988.

Buckley, Michael J. *At the Origins of Modern Atheism*. New Haven: Yale University Press, 1987.

Calvin, John. *Institutes of the Christian Religion*. Edited by John T. McNeill. Library of Christian Classics 20–21. Philadelphia: Westminster, 1960.

Dowey, Edward A. "Book Review, 'John Calvin: A Sixteenth Century Portrait.'" *Journal of the American Academy of Religion* 57 (1989) 845–48.

Erasmus, *Paracelsis, id est adhortatio ad Christianae philosophiae studium* (*Opera* [Leyden, 1704]).

Holtrop, Philip C. "Between the 'Labyrinth' and the 'Abyss'—A Review Article." *The Reformed Journal* 39 (April, 1989) 21–28.

———. "Reply." *The Reformed Journal* 39 (July, 1989) 9–10.

Leith, John H. "Calvin's Theological Method and the Ambiguity in His Theology." In *Reformation Studies: Essays in Honor of Roland H. Bainton*, 106–14. Edited by Franklin H. Littell. Richmond: John Knox, 1962) .

Muehlen, Karl-Heinz, zur. Response to Bouwsma's "Calvinism as Theologia Rhetorica." In *Calvinism as Theologia Rhetorica*. Translated by W. Wuellner. Berkeley: Center for Hermeneutical Studies, 1986.

Wendel, Francois. *Calvin: Origins and Development of His Religious Thought*. Translated by Philip Mairet. Durham: Labyrinth, 1987.

Willis, E. David. "Rhetoric and Responsibility in Calvin's Theology." In *The Context of Contemporary Theology: Essays in Honor of Paul Lehmann*, 43–63. Atlanta: John Knox, 1974.

Chapter 7

Aristotle. *Parts of Animals*. Cambridge: Harvard University Press, 1937.

Boyer, Carl B., and Uta C. Merzbach. *A History of Mathematics*. New York: Wiley, 1989.

Bunt, Lucas N. H., et al. *The Historical Roots of Elementary Mathematics*. New York: Dover, 1976.

Descartes, Renè. *Correspondence*. Edited by C. Adam and G. Milhaud. Paris: Alcan, 1936.

————. *Discourse on Method* (1637). From *The Philosophical Works of Descartes*. Translated by E. S. Haldane and G. R. T. Ross. Cambridge, I, 1931; II, 1934.

————. *Meditations on First Philosophy*. Translated by Donald Cress. 3rd ed. Indianapolis: Hackett, 1993.

————. *Regulae ad directionem ingenii* (1628). Amsterdam: Rodopi, 1998.

Friedman, Michael. "Regulative and Constitutive." *The Southern Journal of Philosophy* XXX Supplement (1991) 73–102.

Guyer, Paul. "Reason and Reflective Judgment: Kant on the Significance of Systematicity." *Nous* 24 (1990) 17–43.

————. "The Unity of Reason: Pure Reason as Practical Reason in Kant's early Conception of the Transcendental Dialectic." *Monist* 72 (April, 1989) 139–67.

Hegel, G. W. F. *Enzyklopädie der philosophischen Wissenschaften* (1830) TI2. Suhrkamp, 2001.

Heide, Gale. *System and Story: Narrative Critique and Construction in Theology*. Princeton Theological Monograph Series 87. Eugene, OR: Pickwick Publications, 2009.

Heidegger, Martin. *Schellings Abhandlung über das Wesen der menschlichen Freiheit* (1809). Tübingen: Niemeyer, 1971.

Kant, Immanuel. *Critique of Judgment*. Translated by Werner S. Pluhar. Indianapolis: Hackett, 1987.

————. *Critique of Pure Reason*. Translated by Norman Kemp Smith. New York: St. Martin's, 1929.

————. *Foundations of the Metaphysics of Morals*. Translated by Lewis White Beck. New York: Macmillan, 1959.

————. *Metaphysische Anfangsgründe der Naturwissenschaft*. F. Meiner Verlag, 1997.

————. *Religion within the Limits of Reason Alone*. New York: Harper Torchbooks, 1960.

Leibniz, Gottfried W. *New Essays Concerning Human Understanding* (1704). IV. Translated by A. G. Langley. La Salle, IL: Open Court, 1949.

———. *On Wisdom* (ca. 1693). From *Leibniz, Selections*. Edited by P. P. Wiener. New York, 1951.

Makkreel, Rudolf A. "Regulative and Reflective Uses of Purposiveness in Kant." *The Southern Journal of Philosophy* 30 Supplement (1991) 49–63.

McRae, Robert. *The Problem of the Unity of the Sciences: Bacon to Kant.* Toronto: University of Toronto Press, 1961.

O'Farrell, "System and Reason for Kant." *Gregorianum* 62 (1981) 5–49.

Rockmore, Tom. *Before and After Hegel: A Historical Introduction to Hegel's Thought.* Berkeley: University of California Press, 1993.

Schöndörffer, Otto. *Immanuel Kant: Briefwechsel.* Selection and notes by Otto Schöndörffer. 3rd ed. Edited by Rudolf Malter. Hamburg: Meiner.

Chapter 8

Avineri, Shlomo. *Hegel's Theory of the Modern State.* London: Cambridge University Press, 1972.

Copleston, Frederick. *A History of Philosophy: Fichte to Nietzsche.* Volume VII. New York: Image, 1985.

Hegel, G. W. F. *Lectures on the History of Philosophy.* Translated by E. S. Haldane and F. H. Simon. Volume 1. New York: Humanities, 1974.

———. *Philosophy of History.* Translated by J. Sibtree. London, 1861.

———. *Hegel's Philosophy of Right.* Translated by T. M. Knox. Oxford: Clarendon, 1942.

———. *Science of Logic.* From *Hegel's Science of Logic.* Translated by A. V. Miller. London: Allen & Unwin, 1969. Original first published in 1812, 1813, 1816.

———. *Werke.* Jubiläumsausgabe. Edited by H. G. Glockner. Vol.1. Stuttgart, 1927–39.

Heide, Gale. *System and Story: Narrative Critique and Construction in Theology.* Princeton Theological Monographs 87. Eugene, OR: Pickwick Publications, 2009.

Hodgson, Peter C. "Editor's Introduction." In David Friedrich Strauss, *The Life of Jesus Critically Examined*, xv–l. Philadelphia: Fortress, 1972.

Jacobi, F. H. *Werke.* Volume 2. Edited by F. H. Jacobi and F. Köppen. Leipzig: Fleischer, 1812.

Kant, Immanuel. *Critique of Pure Reason.* Translated by N. K. Smith. New York: St. Martin's, 1962.

———. "What is Enlightenment?" In *Foundations of the Metaphysics of Morals*, 85–92. Translated and Introduction by Lewis White Beck. New York: Macmillan, 1959.

Lucas, Jr., George R. "Hegel, Whitehead, and the Status of Systematic Philosophy." In *Hegel and Whitehead: Contemporary Perspectives on Systematic Philosophy*, 3–13. Albany: State University of New York Press, 1986.

McCarthy, Vincent A. *Quest for a Philosophical Jesus: Christianity and Philosophy in Rousseau, Kant, Hegel, and Schelling.* Macon, GA: Mercer University Press, 1986.

McGrath, Alister. *The Blackwell Encyclopedia of Modern Christian Thought.* Cambridge, MA: Blackwell, 1999.

Pannenberg, Wolfhart. *Systematic Theology.* Volume 1. Translated by Geoffrey W. Bromiley. Grand Rapids: Eerdmans, 1991.

———. "What is Truth?" In *Basic Questions in Theology*, 1–27. Volume 2. Translated by George Kehm. Philadelphia: Fortress, 1971.

Plant, Raymond. *Politics, Theology, and History*. New York: Cambridge University Press, 2001.

Pochmann, Henry A. *New England Transcendentalism and St. Louis Hegelianism: Phases in the history of American Idealism*. New York: Haskell, 1970.

Ritter, Joachim. *Hegel and the French Revolution: Essays on the Philosophy of Right*. Translated and Introduction by Richard Dien Winfield. Cambridge, MA: MIT Press, 1982.

Rockmore, Tom. *Before and After Hegel: A Historical Introduction to Hegel's Thought*. Berkeley: University of California Press, 1993.

———. "Feuerbach." In *A Companion to the Philosophers*, 244–46. Edited by Robert L. Arrington. Oxford: Blackwell, 1999.

———. "Hegel." In *A Companion to the Philosophers*, 279–88. Edited by Robert L. Arrington. Oxford: Blackwell, 1999.

———. *On Hegel's Epistemology and Contemporary Philosophy*. New Jersey: Humanities, 1996.

Strauss, David Friedrich. *The Life of Jesus Critically Examined*. Philadelphia: Fortress, 1972.

Taylor, Charles. *Hegel and Modern Society*. London: Cambridge University Press, 1979.

Chapter 9

Balthasar, Hans Urs von. *The Theology of Karl Barth*. San Francisco: Ignatius, 1992.

Barth, Karl. *Church Dogmatics*. Edited by G. W. Bromiley and T. F. Torrance. Edinburgh: T. & T. Clark, 1936.

———. *Die christliche Dogmatik im Entwurf*. Vol. I. *Die Lehre vom Worte Gottes, Prolegomena zur christlichen Dogmatik*. Munich: Kaiser, 1927.

———. *Die Lehre vom Worte Gottes: Prolegomena zur christlichen Dogmatik*. Munich: Kaiser, 1928.

———. *The Epistle to the Romans*. Translated by Edwin C. Hoskyns from the 6th ed. London: Oxford University Press, 1933.

Bretall, Robert, editor. *A Kierkegaard Anthology*. Princeton: Princeton University Press, 1946.

Clark, Gordon H. *Karl Barth's Theological Method*. Philadelphia: Presbyterian & Reformed, 1963.

Come, Arnold. *An Introduction to Barth's "Dogmatics" for Preachers*. Philadelphia: Westminster, 1963.

Erickson, Millard. *Christian Theology*. 2nd ed. Grand Rapids: Baker Academic, 2005.

Hegel, G. W. F. *Hegel's Phenomenology of Spirit*. Translated by A. V. Miller. Oxford: Clarendon, 1977.

———. *Philosophy of History*. Translated by J. Sibree. New York: Wiley, 1944.

Heide, Gale. *System and Story: Narrative Critique and Construction in Theology*. Princeton Theological Monographs 87. Eugene, OR: Pickwick Publications, 2009.

Kierkegaard, Søren. *Concluding Unscientific Postscript*. Volume 1. Translated by Howard V. and Edna H. Hong from *Kierkegaard's Writings* series. Volume 12.1. Princeton: Princeton University Press, 1992.

———. *Concluding Unscientific Postscript*, Volume 2. Translated by Howard V. and Edna H. Hong from *Kierkegaard's Writings* series. Volume 12.2. Princeton: Princeton University Press, 1992.

Martensen, Hans Lassen. *Af mit Levnet*. Volumes 1–3. Copenhagen: Gyldendal, 1882–83.

Mueller, David L. *Karl Barth*. Makers of the Modern Theological Mind. Edited by Bob E. Patterson. Peabody, MA: Hendrickson, 1972.

Stewart, Jon. *Kierkegaard's Relations to Hegel Reconsidered*. Cambridge: Cambridge University Press, 2003.

Thulstrup, Niels. *Kierkegaard's Relation to Hegel*. Translated by George Stengren. Princeton: Princeton University Press, 1980.

Watts, Michael. *Kierkegaard*. Oxford: Oneworld, 2003.